SZYMANOWSKI ON MUSIC

Selected Writings
of Karol Szymanowski

SZYMANOWSKI ON MUSIC

Selected Writings of Karol Szymanowski

Translated and Edited
by Alistair Wightman

Musicians on Music
No. 6

TOCCATA
PRESS

First published in 1999 by Toccata Press
© Alistair Wightman, 1999

British Library Cataloguing in Publication Data
Szymanowski, Karol 1882–1937
  Szymanowski on Music: selected writings of Karol
  Szymanowski
  1. Polish Music. Szymanowski, Karol, 1882–1937
  I. Title
  780.92

  ISBN 0-907689-38-8
  ISBN 0-907689-39-6 (pbk)
  ISSN 0264-6889

This publication has been supported by the
Anne Felicya Cierpik Fund
of
THE KOSCIUSZKO FOUNDATION
An American Center for Polish Culture
New York City
Established 1925

Typeset in 11/12 Baskerville
by York House Typographic Ltd., London
Printed and bound by SRP Ltd., Exeter

Contents

List of Illustrations

PREFACE

Szymanowski's reputation as Poland's leading composer since the time of Chopin is now more or less secure. His music is becoming better known outside Poland thanks to the appearance of a scholarly collected edition and the increasing availability of recordings of his main works. But outside the company of Polish musicologists little is known of his activities as a writer. Throughout his career Szymanowski frequently devoted himself to literature, from the aphoristic *Sketch for my Cain* (an extra-musical programme probably dating from 1903–4 which may have provided the underlying 'idea' for the *Fantasy for Piano*, Op. 14) to an introduction to his memoirs, drafted in 1936, only a few months before his death (the memoirs themselves were never committed to paper). In between came several pieces of verse, theatrical sketches (*Benvenuto Cellini* and the draft libretto to the opera *King Roger*), the novel *Efebos*, two shorter novels, neither of which was completed (*Tomek, or the Adventures of a Young Pole on Land and Sea* and *The Story of the Wandering Juggler and the Seven Stars*), political articles written in the wake of the Bolshevik Revolution, and a large number of essays devoted to musical matters, all of which date from the years 1920–36.

This book contains approximately two-thirds of Szymanowski's total output of writings on music. He frequently repeated himself, and so, to avoid excessive over-lapping, a number of the less important articles have not been included. But no element of Szymanowski's ideology has been omitted: where the inclusion of a complete article would have led to an unacceptable degree of duplication, relevant portions have been introduced in editorial notes. A number of Szymanowski's foreign-language texts – chiefly his remarks on Beethoven, Schreker and Chopin – are also quoted in the notes, but with the exception of an obituary for Paul Dukas and a contribution to a conference dealing with the future of culture, the basic text consists entirely of translations from the composer's Polish articles.

This selection presents, in effect, Szymanowski's blueprint for the musical culture he was attempting to create for the Poland which regained her independence in 1918. The non-Polish reader will learn much about the difficulties which beset progressive musicians working in this newly emergent nation, but the enduring value of these writings stems from the author's ability to transcend local concerns. Szymanowski always looked outwards, offering a wide-ranging, penetrating and enlightened view of European art and music over the centuries. Here there is none of the prejudice and chauvinism which mars the outpourings of some of his contemporaries in other countries (not least Schoenberg and Vaughan Williams). Instead we find abundant evidence of the breadth and depth of Szymanowski's personal culture, and at the same time a telling demonstration of his search for an all-embracing humanistic synthesis.

Although Szymanowski's ideology and music were concerned with the quest for a new song for liberated Poland, his literary style was characterised by an incurably pre-war mode of expression, and his ornate style and grandiose Latinate syntax present formidable problems to the translator. Modifications have sometimes proved to be unavoidable, but I have made a determined attempt to preserve the fluency and richness of Szymanowski's style, and at the same time to render the translations both readable and faithful to the spirit of the composer's texts.

The articles have been arranged in subject category rather than chronological order, and a complete list of Szymanowski's writings, with details of first publication where applicable, is provided in the Appendix on pp. 359–69.

I am indebted to Katharine Tylko-Hill for her selfless work in checking my original versions from the Polish. That I have confidence in the quality of the final version of the text is largely due to her invaluable, painstaking labours. I also wish to express my gratitude to Teresa Chylińska, formerly of Polskie Wydawnictwo Muzyczne, Kraków. It was she who first urged me to undertake this project, and over the years she has given me much valuable support and advice, generously making available the fruits of her own researches. Finally, I wish to thank Martin Anderson, not only for having the courage to undertake the publication of this anthology but also for his considerable help and advice in the selection and editing of the texts.

ALISTAIR WIGHTMAN

Karol Szymanowski in the late 1920s

Introduction
SZYMANOWSKI'S
LIFE AND THOUGHT

A recurring theme in both Szymanowski's polemical writings and his correspondence is his sense of estrangement from Polish musical circles and, at times, Polish society in general. In a very real sense, he was an outsider. He came to live permanently in Poland in 1919, in his 38th year, and then only because he had been compelled to leave the family's Ukrainian estates and properties in the wake of the Bolshevik Revolution. There can be little doubt that his birth and upbringing, several hundred miles beyond Poland's ethnic frontiers, permitted him to view the music and culture of the Polish homeland from a more detached perspective, and this sense of detachment was further reinforced by his extensive foreign travels in the years preceding the First World War.

Some contemporary music critics in Poland regarded him as a disruptive, cosmopolitan intruder, but he possessed impeccable credentials as a Polish nobleman. The family name was taken from the village of Szymany, situated in the central Polish region of Mazovia, and the earliest records of the existence of the line date from the beginning of the sixteenth century. Several members of the family served in the Sejm, the Polish parliament, and others held such important offices as bishop, king's emissary and castellan (or castle governor). In 1778, during the reign of Stanisław Augustus, the last king of Poland, Dominik Szymanowski married Franciszka Rościszewska, daughter of Kajetan, the starosta (or 'foreman') of the Rożów province in the Ukraine. The Rościszewskis were well established in the Kiev district, territory which was subject to the Polish crown from the fifteenth century until the second partition

A view of the grounds at Tymoszówka

of Poland in 1793. Franciszka's dowry consisted of property in this region, and it was from this marriage settlement that the Ukrainian branch of the Szymanowskis originated.

The composer's father, Stanisław (1842–1905), married Anna von Taube (1853–1943) in 1874. The Taubes were Swedish in origin, but had long been associated with the province of Courland in Polish Lithuania, and in 1572 were endowed with the rights and privileges of the Polish nobility. For the first few years of their marriage, Stanisław and Anna lived at Orłówka, near Znamionka, on the Kiev-Jekaterynosławska railway line, and four of their five children – Anna, Feliks, Stanisława and Zofia – were born there. The third, Karol Maciej Korwin-Szymanowski, was born at Tymoszówka – the family estate then owned by Feliks Szymanowski, the composer's grandfather – on 3 October (21 September, old style), 1882.[1]

---

[1] Teresa Chylińska has established that this, rather than 6 October, was the composer's true date of birth: *cf.* 'Kiedy urodził się Karol Szymanowski?' ('When was Karol Szymanowski born?'), *Ruch Muzyczny*, Year XXIV, No. 9, 4 May 1980. Korwin was part of the full family surname. Its origin is obscure, and later generations usually employed it to enhance the noble aura surrounding their name.

The estate at Tymoszówka passed to Stanisław in 1889 on the death of his father, and it was there that Karol Szymanowski spent his formative years. Tymoszówka itself was situated in the Chehryn district authority of the Kiev province, and, according to the official government description of 1900, was a village with 1,739 inhabitants. Within its boundaries there were two large manor houses, one of which belonged to the Szymanowskis. In addition there were 363 farm-holdings, twenty mills, three blacksmiths' forges, a brickyard, a licensed retailer of liquor, and a fire-brigade with four appliances. The nearest railway station was Kamionka, seven versts away,[2] and the nearest landing-stage was Czerkasy on the Dnieper, some fifty versts distant.

The grounds of the Szymanowskis' estate included a lake and an orchard, while inside the single-storey manor-house there was abundant evidence of the family's service to the nation. Mementoes included a dagger, ivory horn and aigrette and brooch belonging to King Jan Sobieski (d. 1696), autographs and the goose quill-pen of the early nineteenth-century writer, Klementyna Hoffmanowa, collections of snuff-boxes and signet rings, and parchment scrolls conferring public offices on various Korwin-Szymanowskis. Other relics included pistols, swords, a staff of office with a large topaz set in its head which had belonged to a hetman (a commander-in-chief), a cuirassier's suit of armour and prints dating from the sixteenth and seventeenth centuries. On the walls were portraits of many of the ancestors, the earliest being Marcin Korwin-Szymanowski, an envoy to Rome on behalf of Władysław IV (1632–48).

At this stage of their history, the Szymanowskis were evidently prosperous, and, in economic and social standing, not much different from other land-owning gentry, both Polish and Russian, residing in the region. But they were exceptional in their nurturing of music and the arts in general, and for Bronisław Gromadzki, a friend of the

---

[2] A verst is 3,500 feet.

composer and a frequent visitor, the Szymanowski's home was

an oasis of culture, so elevated, so subtle, in plain words so enthralling, that not only in the Ukraine, but in the most cultured parts of the world, it would form an island, different from and superior to the general environment.[3]

Gromadzki described Karol's father as a man of 'deep musical culture and traditions, inherited from the home of his parents, where Tausig and Liszt had been guests, and where he had heard their masterly playing'.[4] Stanisław played both cello and piano, and was the first, and for many years, the only member of the immediate family circle to comprehend the extent of Karol's genius. He was able to watch over and guide his son's development all the more solicitously, as poor health prevented Karol from attending school in his early years. By all accounts he received a sketchy formal education from visiting tutors, but his solitary existence allowed him to cultivate his artistic gifts intensively. The foundations of his immensely broad personal culture were laid during these years. By his teens he was fluent in French, German and Russian, and already demonstrating intense interest in the fine arts and philosophy as well as music.

He received his first instruction at the piano from his father during his seventh year, and soon after took lessons from his uncle, Gustav Neuhaus, who ran a music school in Elizavetgrad. This town, now known as Kirowograd, had a population of approximately 75,000 before the First World War, and here the Szymanowskis had both property and numerous family connections. They were on closest terms with three of Stanisław Szymanowski's female cousins, nées Blumenfeld: Maria Przyszychowska, Joanna Zalewska and

[3] 'Wspomnienia o młodości Karola Szymanowskiego' ('Recollections of Karol Szymanowski's Youth'), in Jerzy Maria Smoter (ed.), *Karol Szymanowski we wspomnieniach* (*Karol Szymanowski Remembered*), Polskie Wydawnictwo Muzyczne, Kraków, 1974, p. 32.

[4] *Ibid.*, p. 35.

Marta Neuhaus, who was a pianist. Of these, it was the Neuhaus family, and in particular the German émigré, Gustav Neuhaus, who exerted the most profound influence on the young Szymanowski. Gustav was not only a fine musician, but a devoted exponent of German literature and philosophy. Among his favourite authors were Schopenhauer and Nietzsche, and he communicated this enthusiasm to Karol, who, with his father, was one of the few members of the family able to understand and appreciate the concepts of which Gustav spoke. Szymanowski's strong liking for German music and literature in the early stages of his career can undoubtedly be attributed in the first instance to his contact with Neuhaus, whom he counted as his one and only real teacher in all respects, both musical and non-musical.

Neuhaus introduced Szymanowski to the works of Bach, Mozart, Beethoven, Brahms and Chopin, and additional musical stimuli were provided by a touring opera company which visited Elizavetgrad periodically. Dargomizhsky's *Rusalka* was the first opera Karol saw, and later he attended performances of Glinka's *Russlan and Ludmilla* and Weber's *Oberon.* Another important formative experience came in 1894 when the family travelled to Switzerland to wind up the affairs of Oswald Szymanowski, a distant relative whose father had served under Napoleon. On the return journey, they stopped for a while in Vienna, and it was there that Karol saw a performance of *Lohengrin* at the opera house. It aroused an intense interest in Wagner, and from this time on he assiduously studied piano reductions of all the music dramas.

In spite of the importance of these isolated occurrences, it was the sustained musical and cultural atmosphere of the Szymanowskis' home which provided the necessary environment for the development of Karol's gifts. Gromadzki described the 'Florentine Evenings' which took place every Saturday when the Szymanowskis were residing in Elizavetgrad, one week at the Neuhauses and the next at the Szymanowskis. The first such evening he attended, probably

in 1896, took place at the Neuhauses. It started at seven
o'clock and went on to midnight, and opened with performances from Gustav's two children:

> Tala Neuhaus played Schumann's *Fantasia in C*, Harry [Hen-
> ryk] Neuhaus a Toccata by Bach and Beethoven's
> 'Hammerklavier' Sonata, Felcio [Feliks] Szymanowski per-
> formed Chopin's F major Ballade, the Impromptu in G flat
> major and three mazurkas, in F sharp minor, C minor and A
> minor, and it so happened that it was he who accompanied
> me in Grieg's F major Violin Sonata. After the performance
> of each work came criticisms of the work and its perform-
> ance. On that evening, most time was devoted to Chopin's
> F major Ballade and Felcio's performance.[5]

This programme in itself affords a good impression of the
range, depth and thoughtful nature of the domestic music-
making in the Szymanowski-Neuhaus circle. These evenings
sometimes included compositions by Karol. The next week
Gromadzki heard Karol's sister, Stanisława, sing works by
Schumann, Liszt and Brahms, as well as arias from an opera,
probably *The Golden Peak*, the words and music of which
were both written by Karol as early as his eighth or ninth
year. Nothing survives of the early works, of which the most
noteworthy were two piano sonatas and a sonata for violin
and piano. In Gromadzki's opinion, 'the piano sonatas in
G minor and F sharp minor were the most important and
significant documents of Karol's genius. The E major violin
sonata was in the unfamiliar, indeed the forgotten form of
the suite [...]'.[6] He also composed songs to words by
Nietzsche, Verlaine and the Polish poet, Kazimierz Tetmajer, but these too were lost in the destruction of
Tymoszówka by the Bolsheviks.

　According to Gromadzki, the earliest surviving works are
the seventh and eighth of the *Nine Preludes* for piano, Op. 1.
These were composed in 1896, although the rest of the cycle

---

[5] *Ibid.*, p. 33.

[6] *Ibid.*, p. 36.

The Szymanowskis' house in Elizavetgrad

was not finished until 1900. Some of the *Six Songs to words by Kazimierz Tetmajer,* Op. 2 and *Études* for piano, Op. 4, had also been completed by the time Szymanowski left for Warsaw in the autumn of 1901, at the age of 19, in order to continue his musical studies. By this time, Warsaw possessed an opera-house, the repertory of which was subject to the whims of the Russian censor, a musical conservatory (the Musical Institute), a Musical Society that co-ordinated various activities, ranging from the mounting of concerts to the promotion of musicological research, and from November 1901, the Philharmonia Orchestra. Given the effects of partition, it is remarkable that so many signs of musical life existed at all. The occupying powers – Russia, Austria and Prussia – had aimed at nothing less than the annihilation of Poland, and had agreed 'now that the annulment of this body politic has been effected [...] never to include in their titles the name or designation of the Kingdom of Poland, which shall remain suppressed as from the present and

Szymanowski, his sister Stanislawa, and his father (far right;
Gustav Neuhaus is second from the right

forever'.[7] Under the terms of the final treaty, signed on
15/26 January 1797, Russia had taken the whole of Lithuania, Courland and Black Russia, Austria the territory to
the North of Galicia, including Kraków, and Prussia the
lands up to the Vistula, originally including Warsaw. There
were subsequent territorial alterations. Warsaw was liberated during the Napoleonic Wars, but after the Congress of
Vienna in 1815 given to Russia, while under the terms of this
same treaty, Kraków was given the status of a free city, only to
revert to Austria after 1846.

These historical events had resulted in a cultural life of
considerable complexity since it was impossible for a single,

[7] Quoted in Norman Davies, *A History of Poland*, Vol. I, Oxford University
Press, London, 1981, p. 542.

organic national tradition to develop. Even after the reconstitution of Poland in 1918, a residual 'regional patriotism',[8] as Szymanowski described it, continued to militate against the creation of a uniform consciousness of national culture. It has to be said that early in his career Szymanowski himself was less concerned with nationalistic Polish culture than the quest for a compositional technique which would bear comparison with that of the most progressive composers in the rest of Europe. He distanced himself from Warsaw's official, and rather reactionary, musical circles, and instead of enrolling at the Musical Institute, took private lessons in harmony with Marek Zawirski and in counterpoint and composition with Zygmunt Noskowski.

Of the two teachers, Noskowski was by far the more influential. He apparently regarded Szymanowski as his spiritual son, and seems to have succeeded in giving his pupil helpful advice on theoretical matters without encroaching upon his individuality. He himself had been one of the first pupils of the Musical Institute when it opened in 1861, and had studied violin with Apolinary Kątski and composition with Stanisław Moniuszko. He was director of the Warsaw Musical Society from 1881 to 1902, professor in composition at the Institute from 1886 until his death in 1909, and conductor of the Warsaw Philharmonia from 1904 to 1907. His own compositions include two operas, a considerable number of songs – of which those contained in *Śpiewnik dla Dzieci* (*Songbook for Children*) are still popular in Poland – three symphonies, a string quartet, piano quartet and various orchestral pieces. Of these, the most significant is the symphonic poem *Step* (*The Steppe*), Op. 66 (1896–97), a well-composed, spacious work which demonstrates considerable technical ability if little appreciation of the most recent developments in European music.

[8] 'Uwagi w sprawie współczesnej opinii muzycznej w Polsce' ('On Contemporary Musical Opinion in Poland') in *Karol Szymanowski Pisma* (*Karol Szymanowski Writings*), Vol. I, ed. Kornel Michałowski, Polskie Wydawnictwo Muzyczne, Kraków, 1984, p. 36. *Cf.* pp. 73–94, below.

Like most late nineteenth-century Polish music, Noskowski's work has nothing of the uneasy, brooding expectancy
and frustration at the sense of inertia which prevailed
throughout society and which was so eloquently expressed
in other branches of Polish culture. In spite of the
undoubted value of Noskowski's tuition, the most important stimuli for Szymanowski came, on the one hand, from
his contact with foreign music, and particularly the works of
Strauss, and, on the other, from the literature of the period,
with which he had a deep and immediate sympathy. He
played Strauss' symphonic poems in reductions for piano
duet with Ludomir Różycki (1884–1953), another of
Noskowski's composition pupils:

> We were capable of repeating the close of *Death and Transfig-
> uration* in particular several times; the piano thundered and
> roared, giving us indescribable pleasure, and afterwards we
> would remain silent for a long time so as not to miss
> anything of the expression.[9]

Różycki eventually devoted himself chiefly to the composition of stage-works in which something of the styles and
techniques of Strauss and Puccini were merged uneasily.
Szymanowski privately regarded his work as 'cheap claptrap
and a "modernistic" joke',[10] and their relationship cooled
fairly rapidly. A more enduring friendship was forged with
another composer, the conductor Grzegorz Fitelberg
(1879–1953), to whom Szymanowski was introduced in May
or June 1905 in Berlin. Fitelberg's works, which include two
symphonies, symphonic poems, a violin sonata and a violin
concerto, reveal the impact of the late-Romantic German
tradition, and also an awareness of more recent developments in Russian music. His chief contribution to Polish
music was as conductor, and in this capacity he gave first

---

[9] Ludomir Różycki, 'Wspomnienie o Szymanowskim' ('Recollections of
Szymanowski'), in Smoter, *op. cit.*, p. 53.

[10] Letter to Grzegorz Fitelberg, dated 5 May 1908, in *Karol Szymanowski
Correspondence*, Vol. 1, ed. Teresa Chylińska, Polskie Wydawnictwo
Muzyczne, Kraków, 1982, p. 164.

performances of almost all of Szymanowski's orchestral works. After 1908 he all but ceased composition, and confined himself to transcription and orchestration. He advised Szymanowski on the scoring of some of his early works, and further aided the composer by encouraging him to associate himself with the Publishing Group of Young Polish Composers (Spółka Nakładowa Młodych Kompozytorów Polskich). An account of the aims of this organisation appeared in the course of an article by Feliks Starczewski, published under the pseudonym Jan Tetera in *Lutnista* (*The Lutenist*):

> The organisation came into being in autumn, last year [1905] on the initiative of Grzegorz Fitelberg with the financial support of Prince Wł. Lubomirski. The purpose of the organisation is the support of new Polish music through concerts and the publication of the musical works of its members, forging an artistic future for themselves on the basis of wide-ranging co-operation, and at the same time avoiding the often burdensome dependency on music publishers on the one hand, and all manner of impresarios on the other.[11]

As a preliminary announcement, published on 8 November 1905 in the Lwów periodical *Przegląd Muzyczny, Teatralny i Artystyczny* (*Musical, Theatrical and Artistic Review*) made clear, the group was established in Berlin as much to provide a way of penetrating foreign concert-life as to make names known in Poland:

> Berlin. Publishing Group of Young Polish Composers. Under this name, a publishing society has been created, the purpose of which is the publication of the works of young Polish composers in the centre of European musical life, namely Berlin.[12]

Besides Fitelberg, Władysław Lubomirski and Szymanowski, the group included Różycki, Apolinary Szeluto and, from 1907, Mieczysław Karłowicz. It remained in existence

[11] Quoted in Chylińska, *Karol Szymanowski Correspondence*, Vol. 1, p. 74.

[12] *Ibid.*, p. 68.

*The founding members of 'The Publishing Group of Young
Polish Composers': from the left, Apolinary Szeluto,
Szymanowski, their sponsor Prince Władysław Lubormirski,
Grzegorz Fitelberg and Ludomir Różycki*

only until 1911, but it mounted a number of performances
for Szymanowski and, before he signed a contract with
Universal Edition in March 1912, enabled him to publish
several of his early works. Many of these compositions were
deemed Chopinesque by Polish critics and so enjoyed
immediate success. But, as he once remarked to the musicologist Zdzisław Jachimecki, 'stones began to be thrown'[13]
when he attempted to break free of the Polish tradition. For

[13] *Ibid.*, p. 245. Letter dated 4 December 1910. Zdzisław Jachimecki was
born in Lwów in 1882 and died in Kraków in 1953. He studied music with
Stanisław Niewiadomski and Henryk Jarecki at Lwów Conservatory, and
musicology with Guido Adler in Vienna where he received a doctorate for
a dissertation on the Psalms of Gomółka (c. 1535–after 1591). He also
studied composition with Hermann Gradener and Arnold Schoenberg. He
was appointed lecturer in music history at the Jagiellonian University,
Kraków, in 1911, and subsequently became reader (1917) and professor
(1921). Later he became director of the University's Musicological Institute, a post he held until his death. His writings include studies of Haydn,
Mozart, Chopin, Moniuszko, Wagner, Wolf and Szymanowski.

the leading Polish music critic of the day, Aleksander Poliński, the pronounced Germanic influences which soon became apparent in the work of the 'Young Poland' composers could only be attributed to the operation of 'some evil spirit which depraves their work and tries to dispossess them of their individual, national originality and transforms them into parrots, clumsily imitating the voices of Wagner and Strauss'.[14]

[14] Quoted in Teresa Chylińska, *Szymanowski*, Polskie Wydawnictwo Muzyczne, Kraków, 1981, p. 34. In response to this attack, Szymanowski and Fitelberg published a reply in *Kurier Warszawski* (pp. 7–8) on 22 April 1907.

Their letter, the full text of which is given below, reveals that the most wounding of Poliński's remarks was the assertion that, unlike Chopin and Moniuszko, Young Poland composers failed to serve the nation and instead 'slavishly followed Viennese fashions and propagated the ideas of musical Bundists', this last gibe referring to the Allgemeiner Judischer Arbeiterbund, a Jewish, socialist workers' organisation of markedly cosmopolitan tendencies, active in Poland and Russia from 1897. The Hakata, to which Szymanowski and Fitelberg referred, was a German chauvinist organisation, formed in 1894, having as its chief aim the removal of the Polish population from the Poznań province, then controlled by Germany.
Respected Sir,
    In *Kurier Warszawski* (No. 110), your music reporter, Mr. A. Poliński, writing about our concert at the Philharmonic Hall, digressed from the field of critical considerations to the wilderness of personal conjecture, and in so doing was disparaging to us, both as grown men and good Poles.
    It now matters little that Mr. Poliński insulted us with such expressions as 'parrots', 'slavish' and 'sudden mental confusion' etc. That merely raises the question of the need to improve Mr. Poliński's social airs·and graces, and that is something which is quite beyond our capabilities.
    Mr. Poliński however accuses us of failing to serve our fatherland, as Chopin and Moniuszko served it.
    We cannot pass over such an accusation in silence.
    In founding the Publishing Group of Young Polish Composers in Berlin, we were aiming at the propagation of Polish Music abroad. It was precisely because of this that our concerts in Berlin met with a vicious response from a certain section of the German press, representing the Hakata.
    We maintain our previous position; and so one can only attribute all sallies in the nature of declarations that we are incomprehensible and inspired with the poison of malice, that we propagate the ideas

*Szymanowski with the violinist Paweł Kochański (centre)
and Grzegorz Fitelberg around the time of 'Young Poland'*

Szymanowski never had time for 'commonplace patriotism', as he described it, and soon realised that he would
always find between himself and the rest of Polish society 'an
impenetrable wall of differing ideas and artistic conven-
tions'.[15] The young Szymanowski never was a 'nationalist'
composer in any conventional sense of the word, yet for all
the criticism his apparently unpatriotic music attracted, his
solitary quest for purely artistic values proved to be in tune
with the new spirit of the age. The preceding generation
had come to accept that the occupying powers could not be

---

of musical bundists (?), to a desire to diminish the standing of our
activities in public opinion.
    We protest against this, referring the matter to the judgment of
society.
                    Karol Szymanowski and Grzegorz Fitelberg

[15] Letter to Zdzisław Jachimecki, dated 4 December 1910, in *Correspondence*,
Vol. 1, p. 244.

moved without outside help. The far-sighted prayed for a world war for the freedom of the peoples, and in the meantime, revolutionary zeal gave way to a form of social and intellectual positivism based on Auguste Comte's optimistic philosophy of perpetual progress through the application of scientific method and rejection of outmoded religious beliefs. The climate of 'induced stability', as it has been called,[16] led to a rapid expansion of the economy, especially in the Russian sector, and, as in most 'young' industrial societies, wages were low and conditions poor. Basic amenities for the maintenance of public health were almost non-existent, and in Warsaw itself, small-pox, cholera, tuberculosis and venereal diseases were widespread, while the suicide rate and percentage proportion of deaths from criminal violence were both comparatively high.

It is not surprising then to find that, by the end of the century, a reaction against the perceived Philistinism and materialism of the age had set in. It was led by a literary movement known as 'Młoda Polska' ('Young Poland') – not to be confused with Fitelberg's publishing group – and although the expression 'Young Poland' was only used for the first time in 1899, parts of its ideology had been current throughout the 1890s, in the writings of Artur Górski, among others:

> As disillusionment with the life of society and with its typical product, a modern philistine, grew, ties between the individual and that society loosened; disgust and protest against the banality and soulless existence of the organised mass increased. [...] More sensitive and profound minds, after having lost their respect for the philistine and their sympathy with social movements, began to withdraw from life, and look for its other, more durable values.[17]

[16] R. F. Leslie, *The History of Poland since 1863*, Cambridge University Press, Cambridge and London, 1980, p. 61.

[17] Czesław Miłosz, *The History of Polish Literature*, The Macmillan Company, Collier-Macmillan Canada, Toronto, 1969, p. 327. All translations quoted from this work are by Czesław Miłosz.

The definitive anti-positivist manifesto was published under the title 'Confiteor' on 1 January 1899, in a Kraków journal, *Życie* (*Life*). It was the work of the editor, Stanisław Przybyszewski, who had become closely involved with writers from the Young Germany and Scandinavia movements while studying architecture and psychiatry in Berlin. Here Przybyszewski declared art to be something absolute which, by its very nature, should not be made to serve any additional purpose:

> Art has no aim; it is aim itself; it is the absolute because it is a reflection of the Absolute – the Soul. And since it is absolute, it cannot serve any idea, it is dominant, it is the source from which all life comes.
>
> Art stands above life; penetrates the essence of the universe; reads to the ordinary man a secret, runic writing; interprets all that exists from one eternity to another; it knows neither limits nor laws; it knows only the duration and power of the soul; it binds men's souls to the soul of the universal nature and considers the soul of the individual as a phenomenon of that other soul.[18]

Because Art stood above life, it could not be used for moral or social purposes:

> To foster patriotism or social instincts through art means to humiliate art, to throw it down from the summits of the Absolute into the miserable accidentality of life, and the artist who proceeds that way does not deserve the name of artist. A democratic art, an art for the people, is even lower. An art for the people is a hideous and platitudinous banalising of the means used by the artist; it is a plebeian art of making accessible what, by the nature of things, is not easily accessible. The people need bread, not art; when they get bread they will find their path by themselves [...].[19]

Viewed in this light, Art becomes the highest religion and

[18] *Ibid.*, p. 330.

[19] *Ibid.*, p. 330.

the Artist its highest priest, a cosmic, metaphysical force through which the absolute and eternity are expressed:

> He is holy and pure, regardless of whether he presents the most terrible crimes, uncovers the most hideous dirt, or raises his eyes toward heaven and penetrates the light of God.[20]

Przybyszewski also advanced the proposition that man's freedom of action was in reality only an illusion. Man's actions arose from the operation of instinct and blind forces, and it was in the subconscious layers binding man to his animal ancestors that the naked soul beneath the persona was hidden away.

> What can we know of a power eternally begetting unhappiness, of a demon in ourselves who, like a medieval prince of darkness, lives in the eternal night of ourselves, in whose hands we are helpless, somnambulic tools?
>
> There is no free will at all, and, consequently, there is no responsibility; our acts of will are willed, yet not by us, but by a carnal man in ourselves over whom we have no power. There is no good and no evil because we ascribe these qualities, strictly speaking, to nature only, which rules over man; yet to praise it or blame it is nonsense.[21]

In his early works, Szymanowski drew on poetry by four writers associated with 'Young Poland' – Wacław Berent, Jan Kasprowicz, Tadeusz Miciński and Kazimierz Tetmajer – and in later life, he strongly denied ever falling under Przybyszewski's influence. Yet Przybyszewski's ideology undoubtedly suggested fundamental notions which he was to elaborate in his own work, most notably the opera *King Roger*, and, more superficially, his early acquaintance with 'Young Poland' authors led him to develop a grandiose, Latinate writing style which he retained in his later polemical works. Meantime, a combination of force of circumstance and 'Young Poland' thinking provided the

---

[20] *Ibid.*, p. 330.

[21] *Ibid.*, p. 331.

justification for artistic withdrawal into the self, while, paradoxically, the search for technical perfection in his music
took Szymanowski out into the world at large. From 1911,
he effectively abandoned Poland, and divided his time
between Tymoszówka and the main musical centres of
Germany and Austria. He also travelled widely, and became
increasingly sensitive to the cultures of Southern Europe
and the Mediterranean, especially those of Italy, Sicily and
North Africa. In 1910, he wrote to Zdzisław Jachimecki that
had Italy not existed, then he too would have been unable to
exist, because it was only the contemplation of those elevated works, 'for ever smiling down serenely and
indulgently on all that was base, stupid and soulless', that
persuaded him that life and work were worthwhile.[22]

In 1911 he journeyed to Sicily and wrote of the powerful
impression the scenery and the ancient ruins made upon
him. He returned to the island in 1914, and on this occasion
went on to North Africa, visiting Algiers, Constantine, the
'utterly divine' Biskra and Tunis. *Métopes*, *Mythes* and *King
Roger*, an opera based on the twelfth-century ruler of Sicily,
all draw directly on first-hand experience of Mediterranean
cultures, and it is perhaps significant that the vehicle for the
transition to Szymanowski's mature idiom should be the
lyric verses of the Persian poet, Hafiz of Shiraz (d. 1390). In
the second set of the *Love Songs of Hafiz*, completed in
August 1914, it is possible to hear for the first time Szymanowski's unique and utterly individual blend of an already
mastered Germanic method of thematic development with
an extreme sensitivity to high-tension harmony and the
possibilities inherent in the use of timbre as a means of
articulating musical structure. Undoubtedly, Szymanowski
was strongly affected by Stravinsky's music, and it is clear
from his later writings that he regarded Stravinsky as the
single most important composer of his generation. But on
the internal evidence of the works composed around the
time of the First World War, it seems that Stravinsky's

---

[22] Letter dated 4 December 1910 (*Correspondence*, Vol. 1, p. 245).

Zdzisław Jachimecki

influence was not so much direct as catalytic. Szymanowski's own form of 'impressionism', for want of a better word, has none of the primitivism of *Petrushka* or *The Rite of Spring*. Its refinement suggests rather an affinity with the music of Debussy, Ravel and Skryabin, although it is impossible to state with certainty that the similarities which exist between Szymanowski's work and the music of these composers, especially in matters of harmony and timbre, can be attributed to the absorption of outside influences.

The years of the First World War proved to be the most prolific period of the composer's life. He was excused military service because of the long-lasting effects of a leg injury he had sustained in early childhood and spent most of his time at Tymoszówka, alongside his mother, brother and eldest sister. He embarked on a series of works in which

he seems deliberately to have attempted to fulfil Nietzsche's
celebrated wish: 'Il faut méditerraniser la musique'.[23]
Métopes, Mythes, Masques, the Third Symphony and First
Violin Concerto are all magnificent examples of that type of
supra-European music of which Nietzsche dreamed, a
music 'that does not fade away at the voluptuous blue sea
and the brightness of the Mediterranean sky, nor [...] turn
yellow and then pale as all German music does, [...] a music
whose rarest magic would consist in its no longer knowing
anything of good and evil [...] '.[24]

The Szymanowski family were jolted out of their splendid
isolation in the Ukraine only by the threat of revolution. In
July 1917 a meeting of local land-owners was convened at
Tymoszówka to discuss what action was to be taken in the
face of impending anarchy. A considerable number of
'interested parties' attended, ranging from 'country bump-
kins and social activists to distinguished farmers'.[25] No firm
conclusions were drawn, and for a few months more Szymanowski managed to compose without interruption. But by
October, it became apparent that revolution was inevitable,
and shortly before the destruction of the manor-house at
Tymoszówka during the first disturbances, the Szymanowskis transferred as much property as possible to one of their
houses on Bezpopowska Street in Elizavetgrad.

Initially Szymanowski seems not to have been opposed to
the revolution, but on losing his family home he abandoned
his previous attitude, describing it subsequently as a
'revolutionary intermezzo' and a 'spring-time revolutionary

---

[23] Nietzsche, *Der Fall Wagner* (*The Case of Wagner*), 1888, Section 3; translated by Walter Kaufmann, Vintage Books, New York, 1967, p. 159.

[24] Nietzsche, *Jenseits von Gut und Böse* (*Beyond Good and Evil*); translated by
Walter Kaufmann, Vintage Books, New York, 1966: Aphorism 255,
p. 195.

[25] Władysław Burkath, 'Moje Wspomnienia o Szymanowskim' ('My Recollections of Szymanowski'), in Smoter, *op. cit.*, p. 73.

prostration' which had made of him a 'different, almost sick man'.[26] In the short term he contrived to remain philosophical:

> I have undergone an interesting development in relation to surrounding events. I have arrived at a state of total harmony within myself, and this accounts for my relatively good humour and internal peace. It appears that in my historical plan the total bankruptcy of the present movement was not only historically inevitable, but a desideratum, and it has cleared away all my doubts concerning the evolution of mankind. There is a terrible and horrifying satisfaction in this, but I cannot deny its very real existence. [...] I have thrown over all social sentimentalism, and seem to have come a little closer to understanding the mechanism of history.[27]

Szymanowski's professed good humour proved to be short-lived, and he responded to the increasingly grim post-revolutionary life of Elizavetgrad by retreating from reality as much as possible. He rarely left the family's town-house and, as Jarosław Iwaszkiewicz recalled, lived in another

---

[26] Letter to Jarosław Iwaszkiewicz, dated 16 November 1917, in *Correspondence*, Vol. I, p. 514. Iwaszkiewicz (1894–1980), to whom we are indebted for much background information concerning the composer's life and family, was strongly influenced by Szymanowski, his cousin, in his youth. After contemplating a musical career, he decided instead to devote himself to literature, and established a considerable reputation as a novelist, dramatist and poet. In addition to the libretto of *King Roger*, he provided texts for other works by Szymanowski, namely *Songs of the Infatuated Muezzin*, Op. 42, and *Three Lullabies*, Op. 48.

[27] Letter to Stefan Spiess, dated 25 October 1917, in *Correspondence*, Vol. 1, p. 512. Stefan Spiess (1879–1968) first met Szymanowski in 1904. He was the grandson of the painter Józef Simmler, and his mother, Jadwiga, was a talented pianist. The Spiess' home was regarded as one of the few important artistic salons in Warsaw in the early years of the century, and it was through the generosity of the Spiess family that Szymanowski was able to travel as widely as he did in the years before the First World War.

Jarosław Iwaszkiewicz

world, surrounded by books and music.[28] By the middle of
1918 he claimed to be in a state of extreme depression and
found himself unable to compose. Once before, he had
fought this state of mind by channelling his creative energies into literary work. The prose-poem *Ostatnie pożegnanie*
(*The Last Farewell*) describes his feelings and experiences
following the death of his father in 1905. In 1918, his
protracted musical 'sterilité', as he called it,[29] gave rise to

[28] Iwaszkiewicz, *Spotkania z Szymanowskim* (*Meetings with Szymanowski*),
Polskie Wydawnictwo Muzyczne, Kraków, 1947, p. 65.

[29] Letter to Paweł Kochański and his wife Zofia, dated 15 November 1918,
in *Correspondence*, Vol. 1, p. 568. Paweł Kochański, one of Szymanowski's
closest friends, was born in Odessa in 1887. He was taken to Warsaw to
continue his studies there by Emil Młynarski, and went on to complete his
training at the Brussels Conservatory with César Thomson, leaving after
only a few months with a first prize 'avec la plus grande distinction'. At the
age of fourteen, he was appointed concert master of the newly formed
Warsaw Philharmonia. He collaborated with Szymanowski many times,
aiding the composer in the creation of a highly distinctive violinistic idiom.
He died in New York in 1934. *Cf.* also pp. 353–57.

two much more substantial literary projects. One was the novel *Efebos* and the other, devised and written in collaboration with Iwaszkiewicz, the libretto to *King Roger*. Szymanowski started *Efebos* as no more than a pleasurable way of passing the time. In the end it became both an apologia which dealt with love in all its forms and an ardent assertion of the Omnipotent Beauty of Life. Alas, scarcely anything of Szymanowski's original text survives. Because of its frankly autobiographical nature (Szymanowski was homosexual), the composer did not attempt to publish it during the life-time of his mother. In the event, she outlived him, and the one complete copy, bequeathed to Iwaszkiewicz, was almost totally destroyed during the first raids on Warsaw in 1939.

In his description of the content of the novel, Iwaszkiewicz recalled that the book developed from a short story written by another of Szymanowski's cousins, Michał Kruszyński. Kruszyński drew on memories of boarding-school life, and depicted in near-pornographic detail the relationship between Prince Alo Łowicki and an older, rather gloomy friend, Mykita, who eventually committed suicide following the disclosure of the nature of his erotic predilections to the Jesuit fathers. Szymanowski took over the character of Alo, and described his career after leaving school. The early chapters were chiefly concerned with the evocation of pre-war high society, but as the novel progressed, superficial elegancies were stripped away and issues of profound moral and philosophical significance raised.

The novel deepened in tone when Alo was parted from his fiancée in dramatic circumstances, unspecified by Iwaszkiewicz, and obliged to leave the country in disgrace. He travels to Italy and encounters various characters who initiate him into the mysteries of Italian art and, at the same time, confront him with problems of a social, moral and political nature. Gradually he undergoes a transformation from naive Polish aristocrat to potentially mature artist. The Italian scenes were carefully written, and their considerable detail displayed both erudition and artistic sensibility.

Indeed, Szymanowski claimed in the still extant introduction that the book sprang from an intense, majestic vision of
Italy, in all her imperious beauty and seductive grace, but
admitted that with the passing of time

> she appeared like a distant mirage, already dimmed by the
> subtle mist of the intervening years, only half emerging from
> the eye's forgetfulness – and the inevitable and fatal con-
> sequence of this is that everything which forms the natural
> background of the story, the landscape against which its
> hero's inner experiences are seen, appears faded and lifeless,
> with the muted hues of a gobelin rather than the throbbing,
> vivid colours of immediate experience [...].[30]

In Iwaszkiewicz's opinion, one of the best sections was
devoted to Alo's Florentine experiences, and his conversations there with Count von Relow, a German nobleman
educated in the classical traditions of Goethe and the
German archaeologist and art historian, Johann Joachim
Winckelmann (1717–68). A substantial part of the action
was set in Rome and involved the Countess Łanskaya,
modelled on Natalie Dawydow, a member of a distinguished, cultured family whose estate had bordered on
Tymoszówka. Natalie was 'a beautiful person, truly a grande
dame [...], serious, intelligent, musical and full of goodness'[31] and, in her epiphany as the Countess Łanskaya,
revealed a profound understanding of Szymanowski's own
attitudes to art and life. Yet ultimately, the novel was concerned chiefly with the developing relationship between the
young Alo, anxiously searching for 'true' love, and Marek
Korab, a successful Polish composer who embodied everything which Szymanowski wished to be: great, handsome
and very, very famous.

The second volume of the novel contained two 'set-piece'
scenes, the first of which was entitled 'Symposium'. It was set
in a Roman tavern, and the principal characters discussed
thoroughly the nature of love and eroticism. There were

[30] Quoted in Chylińska, *Szymanowski*, p. 89.

[31] Iwaszkiewicz, *op. cit.*, p. 36.

obvious parallels with Plato's work of the same name, although it is clear from a recently discovered Russian translation of this section, completed by Szymanowski himself, that at times the discussion degenerated into the expression of an ill-disguised misogyny. Impressed by Korab's more spiritual contribution to the debate, Alo realised that he could only develop as a human being by associating himself with the composer.

The second set-piece was an elaborate account of a ball given by a Prince Primoli. In the course of these proceedings, the poet, Gleba Nieszczerow, treacherously revealed to Korab that in the past Alo's erotic experiences had resulted not from the impulses of true love but had been bought from prostitutes. Korab, disillusioned, abandoned Alo. In despair, the younger man departed for Sicily where his spiritual rebirth eventually took place. Iwaszkiewicz considered this to be the most beautiful part of the novel, and remarked on the psychological insight it revealed. It also contained material suggestive of the libretto of *King Roger*. One such section was 'The Tale of the Miracle of the Youth Enoch Porfiry – the Iconographer', which purported to be a sample of Alo's own mature work. In style it was derived partly from the English aesthetist and author, Walter Pater (1839–94), and partly from Iwaszkiewicz's own legends, but was 'richer, more magnificent – with its now seemingly classical description of the city of Palermo under King Roger or soon after'.[32] The parallels with the opera go beyond details of historical period and geographical location, for the legend is concerned with an underlying tension of physical and spiritual love and advances the proposition 'that only through physical love is it possible to approach the mystery of divine love and accomplish creative work'.[33] Furthermore, like the hero of the opera, Alo divested himself of all the trappings and props of his previous existence to experience a healing revelation at night amongst ancient

[32] *Ibid.*, p. 95.

[33] *Ibid.*, p. 95.

ruins, in this case, the temple at Segesta. Here he suddenly met Korab again, and his new-found maturity made it possible for both men to reach a more profound mutual understanding. Thus it was that 'Szymanowski's psyche, divided into the two figures of Korab and Łowicki, again became at one with itself, and in this unity found harmony and peace'.[34]

In the last analysis, both *Efebos* and *King Roger* were concerned with the quest for self-knowledge and the integration of apparent opposites. Although they were conceived within months of each other, composition of the opera extended over a period of six years, and it is clear from surviving source materials that, as work proceeded, Szymanowski himself deepened the philosophical and psychological significance of the libretto he had originally worked out in collaboration with Iwaszkiewicz. The earliest plans dated from June 1918, when after a Sicilian subject had been selected in preference to adaptations of either the memoirs of Benvenuto Cellini, Pater's *Denis l'Auxerrois* and *Apollo in Picardy* or Wyspiański's *Klątwa*, Iwaszkiewicz drew up a preliminary sketch with Frederick II and his black prince, the Arabian Sage, as the chief characters. In broad outline, the action corresponded to the first and third acts of the final version of *King Roger*, and concerned simply 'the initiation of the hero of the drama into the Dionysian mysteries, and the revelation of the eternally living Dionysus against the background of the ruins of the theatre at Syracuse or Segesta'.[35]

Szymanowski responded enthusiastically to Iwaszkiewicz's first thoughts:

> I like it terribly of course! And more than anything else, I should like you to begin to develop it seriously. [...] from the staging point of view, I would very much like Byzantine-Arabic palace interiors. Just imagine: the tarnished gold and

[34] *Ibid.*, p. 95.

[35] *Ibid.*, p. 76.

stiffness of mosaic figures, or arabic filigrees as a background – what barbarism and voluptuous opulence! Of
course all this would be difficult to get into one night.
Perhaps two? Something in the style I have described (as a
spectacle) – as a prologue to the drama itself (your idea),
which would then be experienced on a truly spiritual level.
Both connected by the central figures (Frederick and the
Arabian Sage) [...]. At any rate I am now terribly enthusiastic about this idea, and should like to instil some of my
enthusiasm into you![36]

Iwaszkiewicz provided Szymanowski with an additional
middle act, incorporating Arabic elements and a Dionysian
dance, and as late as 1921 Szymanowski himself altered the
third act so that the King became the true hero of the work.
Iwaszkiewicz had misgivings about the new conclusion, but
later admitted that he and Szymanowski had each wanted to
express something different in *King Roger*. His own version
had been much simpler:

Roger not only discovered Dionysus in the ruins of the old
theatre, but followed him and what is more, flung himself
into the chaos of the mysterious Dionysian cult [...]. It
was contrary to history, but dramatically more logical.
Roger not only recognised Dionysus in the shepherd,
but followed him into the darkness, abandoning everything
for him. Szymanowski changed this conclusion. Perhaps he
did not understand that ultimate repudiation of the world
which I had introduced, perhaps he considered my simple
conclusion to be a superfluous elucidation. Whatever the
reason, he cast aside my third act, and substituted the
almost completely different one which today appears in the
opera [...].[37]

It is, to say the least, arguable that Szymanowski's alterations really weakened the drama. Indeed, from an
ideological point of view, they confer a far deeper significance on the whole conception. Szymanowski's Roger,

[36] Letter dated 18 August 1918, in *Correspondence*, Vol. 1, pp. 542–43.

[37] Iwaszkiewicz, *op. cit.*, p. 80.

who has been stripped of his temporal and ecclesiastical authority in the earlier stages of the opera, journeys to the ancient theatre at Syracuse, where he at last understands the mystery of the shepherd's power. In spite of impassioned pleas from the shepherd and his followers, he refuses to abandon all for the cult of Dionysus, but remains alone with the sage, Edrisi, to greet the rising sun in an ecstatic hymn which reveals a new awareness of the vital forces within himself. Indeed, the opera provides a rich but concise expression of Szymanowski's faith and philosophy, and the component strands of its ideology can be detected in sources as various as Euripides, Goethe, Carlyle, Pater and Nietzsche, as well as Young Poland in Literature.

The general tone of both novel and opera is optimistic. Evidently Szymanowski enjoyed more success at controlling the destinies of his fictional characters than he did his own. Throughout the *Efebos* period, he attempted, not always very purposefully, to escape to Poland with the family. By the middle of 1918, Elizavetgrad was under the control of the Austrian army, and there was then a distinct chance of the Szymanowskis' leaving for Warsaw. Instead, the family postponed a final decision to leave the Ukraine and took a six-week holiday in Odessa. On his return to Elizavetgrad, Szymanowski found letters from his old friend, Stefan Spiess, informing him that the Warsaw Conservatory intended to offer him a post as a professor. In response to Spiess' hint that this offer in itself could facilitate his passage westwards, Szymanowski stated bluntly that he could not leave without his mother and sister.

> You will understand that for me this is quite impossible morally! Especially in view of the increasingly dark clouds on our horizons here! [...] A second important question is one of finance. We must sell one of our houses here, and this always takes some time. I have recently become a bit irritable because the hugely inflated prices of houses here have started to decline, and I am afraid we have lost out by staying too long in Odessa. [...] We are sitting around here at present, the three of us, awaiting customers, and when they

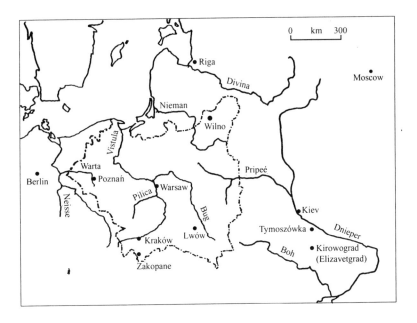

Poland at the time of the Second Republic (1921–39)

eventually do appear, they consider our price to be too high (and personally I do not find that very strange).[38]

By January 1919, all hope of an early departure had to be abandoned as the Austrians had retreated before the Red Army. In the short term, Szymanowski could only curse the family's 'idiotic naivety' during the preceding summer, and he eked out an existence by serving on the local music committee of the People's Education Commissariat:

> I get a reasonable stipend, and this protects us from much unpleasantness. Harik [Harry Neuhaus] and I and a few others have organised concerts, and we are supposed to be opening a school. They are pressing us to go to Odessa [. . .]

[38] Letter to Stefan Spiess, dated 27 October 1918, in *Correspondence*, Vol. 1, p. 559.

of his works given in the Conservatory Hall on 24 January 1920:

> In effect there weren't 600 people in Warsaw who were interested in hearing what I had been doing during the last five years. You must admit that this is not a very pleasing state of affairs. Imagine the response in Petersburg or Moscow were Skryabin or Rakhmaninov to return with something new [...].[40]

The letter from which this quotation is taken is of particular importance, for other reasons. It reveals why at first Szymanowski reacted as he had in the years before the Great War. It also contains pointed remarks about the state of Polish music criticism, and these are especially interesting in the light of a major article he was to publish six months later:

> I have again become convinced that the conditions which previously forced me to leave Warsaw seven years ago still prevail, namely that there is no real contact between the Polish public (or at least the Warsaw public) and myself, that for them I am alien, incomprehensible and perhaps even unnecessary within the overall structure of 'Polish Music' [...]. Their provincialism makes the European atmosphere of my art simply indigestible; [...] the criticisms are ample expression of this. I am not speaking of all of them, but only those I have already seen. In all these quasi-recommendations there is one dominating tone: that everything I do has already been done by Schoenberg, Debussy, Skryabin *e tutti quanti*! Of course I am not concerned with the particular opinions of the various idiots x, y or z, but these remarks are characteristic of the furtive, cunning campaign that is being mounted against my efforts to raise the standard of our art. With their artful suggestions, they attempt to avert understanding of my intentions by redirecting the healthy, instinctive consciousness of the

[40] Letter to Zdzisław Jachimecki, dated 29 January 1920, in Karol Szymanowski, *Z Listów* (*Selected Letters*), ed. Teresa Bronowicz-Chylińska, Polskie Wydawnictwo Muzyczne, Kraków, 1958, p. 185.

more sincere part of the general public, especially by way of that protecting 'all-knowing' tone. [...] Of course, that campaign has again been successful. I am too completely indifferent to want to fight all and sundry [...]. In other words, at the first opportunity I shall once again leave Warsaw [...].

I do not want you to accuse me of indifference and lack of sympathy at the present time in a Polish sense. Completely the reverse. I am more deeply and sincerely a patriot than many [...]. But in the present period of our history and culture, the type of artistic breed which I represent is not only superfluous, but almost injurious. So one thing remains: I must abandon my own personal life, and take my place alongside those lowly, devoted, honest workers who today are building the nation from its foundations. Poland has neither the time nor the need for such an artistic luxury as myself. I now understand this clearly, harshly and terribly. The honest policeman on the beat is worth far more from this point of view [...]. But I have an inner life which is too strongly developed to be able to make such an unparalleled abnegation, and in the face of this I am obliged to decide on a second, extreme alternative, namely on a ruthless self-enclosure that involves the cutting-off of myself from everything, and the devoting of myself only to those things that most immediately concern me in my own life and art.[41]

The outbreak of hostilities with Russia persuaded the composer to remain to help the war effort as best he could:

At present I am simply not in a state to leave Warsaw, even though I am not much use for anything here. I cannot of course join the army because of my leg, but I am doing what I can all the same! There is an artistic committee here which is organising various things for the soldiers, etc., etc. I have been suffering terribly, not from personal fear. You know that out there in Russia for two years I was afraid of nothing

---

[41] *Ibid.*, pp. 182–83.

and coped splendidly, but it is different here in the homeland [. . .]. I am occupying myself now writing marches and
soldiers' songs.[42]

One of his marches was given at a Warsaw Philharmonic
concert in August, and, as the composer said, 'the beast
sounded not bad'.[43] But in general, the year 1920 was
characterised by an unsuccessful quest for a new mode of
expression which would enable the composer to establish
himself as a useful member of Polish society. Completed
works from this period are all 'functional', and comprise
Mandragora (incidental music for a production of Molière's
Le Bourgeois Gentilhomme staged at the Teatr Polski in May),
and a number of patriotic songs and marches. The incomplete sketches reveal that the composer was experiencing
some difficulty in effecting a transition from the aesthetic of
the war-time works to that of the 'new song' for the new
Poland.

While in the throes of this creative crisis, Szymanowski
wrote his extended article 'On Contemporary Musical
Opinion in Poland'. Its underlying complaint – that Polish
critical opinion was incapable of adapting to the new situation in which it now found itself – was one which the
composer reiterated with increasing vehemence in subsequent articles. But the starting-point of Szymanowski's
argument lay in the aesthetic of an earlier generation with
the questioning of the assumptions underlying criticism. He
admitted that it was generally believed that artistic criticism
had an educational role to play in so far as it shaped public
taste, but he argued against immediate evaluations in favour
of an open-minded approach which set out positively to
reveal the beauties of the work in question. He cited Walter
Pater and Oscar Wilde as the sources for these theories, and
it is not difficult to discover abundant evidence of support

---

[42] Letter to the Kochańskis, dated 17 August 1920, in Teresa Chylińska
(ed.), *Dzieje Przyjaźni* (*Story of a Friendship*), Polskie Wydawnictwo Muzyczne,
Kraków, 1971, pp. 38–39.

[43] Letter to Iwaszkiewicz, dated 11 August 1920, in *Z Listów*, p. 191.

for 'positive' criticism in their writings. For example, in the preface to *The Renaissance*, first published in 1873, Pater shifts the burden of making the work of art comprehensible from the artist to the critic. While agreeing that the aim of all true criticism has always been to see the object as in itself it really is, the first step in aesthetic criticism is 'to know one's impression as it really is, to discriminate it, to realise it distinctly'.[44] Pater considered that the critic had to consider all the objects with which he had to do 'as powers and forces producing pleasurable sensations, each of a more or less peculiar or unique kind', and from this it followed that the critic required not so much 'a correct abstract definition of beauty for the intellect, but a certain kind of temperament, the power of being deeply moved by the presence of beautiful objects'.[45]

Wilde went further, arguing that criticism itself was an art, since artistic creation by its very nature implied the operation of the critical faculty. Like Pater, he emphasised the importance of active participation of the critic in the receiving and understanding of artistic experience: 'the meaning of any beautiful created thing is, at least, as much in the soul of him who looks at it as it was in the soul of him who wrought it'.[46] He also believed the critic had to be endowed with 'a temperament exquisitely susceptible to beauty, and to the various impressions that beauty gives us'.[47] In other respects, Wilde's point of view is not dissimilar from that of Przybyszewski, for example, in his statement that the successful critic had to recognise that 'the sphere of Art and the sphere of Ethics are absolutely distinct and separate'.[48] In reality, Art was concerned with things beautiful, immortal

[44] Walter Pater, *The Renaissance*, Collins, London, 1961, p. 27.

[45] *Ibid.*, p. 29.

[46] *Complete Works of Oscar Wilde*, ed. Vyvyan Holland, Collins, London, 1948, p. 1029.

[47] *Ibid.*, p. 1049.

[48] *Ibid.*, p. 1048.

and ever-changing, and so was beyond the reach of morals: 'all the arts are immoral, except those baser forms of sensual or didactic art that seek to excite to actions of evil or of good'.[49] Indeed, it becomes clear from a reading of the composer's first major essay that both he and Wilde shared the view that 'it is criticism that, recognising no position as final, and refusing to bind itself by the shallow shibboleths of any sect or school, creates that serene philosophic temper which loves truth for its own sake, and loves it not the less because it knows it to be unattainable'.[50]

'On Contemporary Musical Opinion' proved to be the first of a series of articles and interviews in which the composer tried to lay the theoretical foundations for a fitting culture for the newly independent Poland. He dealt with a wide range of subjects, including folk music, Romanticism, Chopin, contemporary music, education and the critics. This last topic was one to which Szymanowski returned in his next major publication, an interview with Jerzy Rytard, entitled 'Karol Szymanowski on Contemporary Music', which appeared in *Kurier Polski* on 12 November 1922.

Between the appearance of his first article and this interview, Szymanowski had travelled widely in Western Europe and the United States, and the interview drew extensively on recent experiences. It introduced several themes which were to be developed more fully in subsequent articles, namely the end of the German musical hegemony, the rise of nationalism, the necessity for new criteria in assessing new music, and the importance of the music of France and Russia in the undermining of German superiority. It also contained observations about some of the more peripheral musical cultures which were later to be of no concern to the composer. But it was his concluding remarks about Polish music critics, and in particular Stanisław Niewiadomski (1859–1936) and Piotr Rytel (1884–1970), which triggered

[49] *Ibid.*, p. 1042.

[50] *Ibid.*, p. 1057.

off a major polemical battle in the Polish press. Szymanowski objected particularly to Niewiadomski's description of 'the rather beautifully cultivated flowers' of the First Violin Concerto as 'simply garish', pointing out that there were many other flowers besides innocent little forget-me-nots.[51] To Rytel, who had complained that it was difficult to understand why Szymanowski perpetually 'zigzagged' from one work to another, he retorted that his goal was 'good music' and that, in spite of the hostile criticism to which his work was subjected, he took comfort in the Nietzschean concept of 'Pathos der Distanz'. Not surprisingly, it was this remark which caused particular offence. Reference to Nietzsche's text reveals that Szymanowski saw himself as an artistic aristocrat far superior to the lower order of music critic:

> Every enhancement of the type 'man' has so far been the work of an aristocratic society [. . .], a society that believes in the long ladder of order of rank and differences in value between man and man, and that needs slavery in some sense or other. Without that pathos of distance which grows out of the ingrained difference between strata – when the ruling caste constantly looks afar and looks down upon subjects and instruments and just as constantly practises obedience and command, keeping down and keeping at a distance – that other, more mysterious pathos could not have grown up either – the craving for an ever new widening of distances within the soul itself, the development of ever higher, rarer, more remote, further stretching, more comprehensive states – in brief, simply the enhancement of the type 'man', the continual 'self-overcoming' of man', to use a moral formula in a supra-moral sense.[52]

Rytel retaliated ten days later with an article in *Gazeta Warszawska* entitled 'P. K. Szymanowski o "swojskiej" krytyce i "dobrej" muzyce' ('Mr. K. Szymanowski on "Tame" Criticism and "Good" Music'), in which he stated that

---

[51] *Karol Szymanowski Pisma* (*Karol Szymanowski Writings*), Vol. 1, p. 62.

[52] Nietzsche, *Beyond Good and Evil*, p. 201.

Szymanowski's activities as a composer and polemicist reminded him of a 'much more beautiful' phrase from Goethe's *Faust*: 'Es irrt der Mensch, so lang er strebt' ('For man must strive, and striving he must err').[53] He also attacked Szymanowski for turning away from German music, condemned his work for an absence of distinguishing creative individuality and expressed distaste for the composer's enthusiasm for French and Russian music. Niewiadomski, by contrast, replied facetiously with 'Magdalena Samozwaniec o muzyce nowoczesnej. Wywiad telefoniczny' ('Magdalena Samozwaniec on Contemporary music. A Telephone Interview'), published on 19 November 1922 in *Rzeczpospolita (Republic)*. Because Szymanowski's attack had appeared in the course of a discussion with an eminent writer, Niewiadomski concocted a response in the form of a chat over the telephone with Magdalena Samozwaniec (1894–1972), the authoress of feuilletons of a viciously witty nature. Niewiadomski put his replies to Szymanowski's views into the mouth of Samozwaniec, to which he provided a malicious running commentary.

Szymanowski answered both critics in the article 'My Splendid Isolation', which appeared in *Kurier Polski* on 28 November. This provoked a further round of hostilities, Rytel's response in particular ('Mr. K. Szymanowski's "Splendid Isolation"', published in *Gazeta Warszawska* on 1 December) being markedly chauvinistic and anti-semitic in tone. One of his more ludicrous notions was the proposition that Ravel was Jewish 'like Milhaud and several other propagators of the newest directions in art'.[54] Indeed, his remarks about Stravinsky are indicative both of the quality of his thought and his manner of expression:

> It is possible to look on Stravinsky and his companions as savage, barbarous invaders who, without doubt, have spread to the West and so broadened the musical landscape [...].

[53] *Faust*, Part 1, translated by Philip Wayne, Penguin, Harmondsworth, 1949, p. 41.

[54] *Karol Szymanowski Pisma*, Vol. 1, p. 73.

Listen to *Petrushka*, a brutal piece, repellent to us. Every bit of it is alien, teeming as it does with traditional birch-tar, soldiery and vodka. This one work is enough to disgust us thoroughly with the attainments of the Russian soul, about which Mr Szymanowski spoke so beautifully.[55]

In the rather more sympathetic 'Karol Szymanowski "wspaniale osamotniony" ' ('Karol Szymanowski, the "Splendid Solitary" ') published in *Rzeczpospolita* on 5 December, Niewiadomski argued that Szymanowski was in danger of losing contact with the Polish public because of the growing complexity of his work:

> It is enough to compare the Sonata in C minor with the one in A major (let alone the 3rd Sonata!) or the newer songs with the earlier. A common feature of them is a characteristic refinement of expression, the earlier works being marked with the tenderness of an ephebe, today's being more masculine, more serious.[56]

The exchanges closed with Szymanowski's 'Opuszczę skalny mój szaniec [...]' ('I will leave my rocky entrenchment [...]'), published in *Rzeczpospolita* on 8 January 1923. Szymanowski was not entirely without support in the press, as is shown by Jarosław Iwaszkiewicz's remarks published in the December 1922 edition of *Skamander*, a periodical which represented the progressive views of the younger generation of writers and poets:

> The wide-ranging polemics between Szymanowski and Messrs Rytel and Niewiadomski are still not finished. One thing is clear now, as much as it was before they started, that these gentlemen are absolutely unable to come to an understanding with Szymanowski. [...] Niewiadomski does not understand Szymanowski, although he shows very great good will; he simply does not understand how anyone can be brought up to have different views. He belongs to another generation, and does not understand the efforts of the young. [...] On the other hand, the misunderstanding with

Rytel lies in a wrong-headed confusion of ideas, a confusion
which permits him first to treat the work of Debussy and
Ravel as 'café philosophy', then to predict a speedy end to all
such 'balderdash' and a return to the sacred groves of
German music, and finally to sniff out Bolshevism (Stravinsky) and Jews (Ravel). Following the example of his
editorial colleague, Mr Pieńkowski, he uses the word 'Jew' as
the final argument *ad hominem*, and even applies the epiphet
to the racially pure Frenchman, Ravel. Why so? Because he
wrote Jewish Songs [*Deux mélodies hébraïques*]? [...] One is
involuntarily reminded of the two black marketeers who,
finding themselves at a concert given by the celebrated
singer Stanisława Korwin-Szymanowska [the composer's
sister], walked out of the hall ostentatiously during a performance of precisely these songs by Ravel, performed in
French, complaining loudly that Szymanowska was singing
in Hebrew.[57]

The live-and-let-live attitude which pervades Szymanowski's own writings about music, and which underlies his
remarks concerning the importance of applying correct
criteria in evaluations of music, undoubtedly derived from
his own efforts to come to terms with music outside the
mainstream German tradition – his own hard struggle 'with
the obstinacy of convention, with the suffocating nightmare' which he eventually 'succeeded [...] in crushing'.[58]
At the same time it is symptomatic of that search for an all-
embracing humanistic synthesis which led Iwaszkiewicz to
liken him to Erasmus of Rotterdam and describe him as 'a
humanist in the oldest and best sense of the word [...] , that
sort of *homo universalis* who is encountered increasingly
rarely today'.[59] The quest for the new song for the new
Poland involved a further expansion of Szymanowski's cultural synthesis, and in particular the inclusion of elements
which for the most part he had previously avoided, namely
folk-music and an 'old-Polish' style which was often

[57] *Ibid.*, p. 88.
[58] *Ibid.*, p. 69.
[59] Karol Szymanowski, *Z Listów*, pp. 7–8.

employed in conjunction with relatively unambivalent religious content.

It will already have become apparent that Szymanowski had consciously distanced himself from the conventional nationalism of the preceding generation, and indeed only three of the early works show any trace of Polish folk influences. The Variations in B flat minor, Op. 3, and the last of the *Three Fragments on Poems by Jan Kasprowicz*, Op. 5, employ stylised mazurka rhythms in passing, and in the *Variations on a Polish Folk-tune* in B minor, Op. 10, a melody from the Polish highlands is used in the version given in a collection of Polish folk tunes edited by Jan Kleczyński (1837–95), published in 1888. Here the original melodies were 'corrected' to such an extent that essential ethnic characteristics were obliterated, and the use of such material in itself is indicative of the younger Szymanowski's fundamental lack of sympathy with genuine folk music. It was not until he had come to terms with recent developments in European music – an action requiring the renunciation of the academic nationalism underlying much nineteenth-century Polish music – that he felt able to resort to folk-music in his own work and so, incidentally, escape from the creative crisis which had befallen him since his return to Poland.

Szymanowski was introduced properly to the music of the Podhale district of southern Poland in March 1920 by Adolf Chybiński, professor of music at the University of Lwów:

> The increasingly topical matter of musical folk-lore in relation to musical creativity came up because it had to. And as I was occupied at that time with the musical culture of Podhale, I could not let slip the chance to bring up the primitivism and individuality of the music of the Tatra. One of the 'Sabała' motives, played with a primitive harmonic accompaniment of only two notes (bagpipe drones) caught Szymanowski's attention with its particular tonal individuality. He asked for it to be repeated. We went through other mountain melodies, but we came back to it. I repeated this so archaic, and, in its barbaric 'simplicity', so powerful

motive [. . .] with the thought that 'perhaps something will come of this', so stubbornly did Szymanowski dwell on it.[60]

Szymanowski eventually used this 'Sabała' motive three times, first in the song-cycle *Słopiewnie* (1921), and subsequently in the first of the Op. 50 Mazurkas and the ballet *Harnasie*, which is based on the legends of the Polish mountaineers. Szymanowski's nationalistic music was by no means a coldly calculated response to the motives which Chybiński had played outside their natural environment. When Szymanowski heard the genuine article on the spot, 'he could not keep quiet from rapture. These melodies and harmonies penetrated to the depths of his being, and from then until the end of his life he was unable to withstand them, although he tried to free himself [. . .] when finally "he had had enough of all this folk-lore"'.[61] He immersed himself in the life and customs of the region. From 1922, he began to spend more and more time in Zakopane, the health resort which is the capital of the southern Polish mountain district, and eventually made his home there. He became a close friend of those who were attempting to preserve the culture of the mountain folk, notably Juliusz Zborowski, curator of the Tatra Museum, and Karol Stryjeński, director of the School of Wood Crafts and the creator of a new Zakopane style of architecture and fine arts. He was especially friendly with Bartek Obrochta, 'one of the few surviving specimens of the old breed of Tatra highlander. He had a native quick wit and intelligence, but he intrigued Szymanowski mainly as a first-rate musician'.[62] Music and dance parties formed a regular feature of Zakopane life, and dance also played a vital part at folk-weddings, and it was at such events that Szymanowski heard this very distinctive music at first hand. It differs markedly from other Polish

[60] Adolf Chybiński, 'Karol Szymanowski a Podhale' ('Karol Szymanowski and Podhale'), in Smoter, *op. cit.*, pp. 134–35.

[61] Jarosław Iwaszkiewicz, *Spotkania z Szymanowskim*, pp. 121–22.

[62] Mieczysław Rytard, 'Wspomnienia o Karolu Szymanowskim' ('Recollections of Karol Szymanowski'), quoted in Chylińska, *Szymanowski*, p. 123.

Adolf Chybiński

folk-music in its tonal properties (akin to those of Carpath-
ian folk-cultures), its instrumentation (two fiddles and bass,
with the now rare addition of bagpipes) and its hard-driven
duple metres. This music depends to a considerable extent
on the improvisatory skills of the performers, as Szymanowski himself frequently discovered: 'When Bartek
sometimes repeated a refrain at Karol's request, Karol was
surprised by certain variations in the original tune [...]
which was never quite the same'.[63] Szymanowski regarded
this 'improvisation à 3' as a valuable means of regenerating
the anaemic music of post-war Poland, and undeniably it
contributed to the lechitic, or 'old-Polish' character of his
own 'nationalistic' music from *Słopiewnie*, which, as the
composer himself said, formed a 'turning-point, initiating a

---

[63] Rytard, quoted in *ibid.*, p. 124.

development which was continued in the Mazurkas, *Stabat* [*Mater*] and a new ballet [*Harnasie*] [. . .] the crystallisation of elements of racial inheritance'.[64]

Several of the articles in this collection deal with folk-music. One is specifically concerned with Szymanowski's direct quotations of Tatra folk-music in *Harnasie*, and another with the danger of the imminent destruction of the highland culture. The most substantial, written in response to an essay by Béla Bartók[65] which appeared in Polish translation in *Muzyka* in 1925, is about the application of folk-music to art-music and musical nationalism in general, and 'A Footnote to the Stabat Mater' throws light on the composer's use of religious material in the formation of a nationalist mode of expression.

Most of Szymanowski's remaining articles were written during the 1920s when he was dividing his time between Warsaw, where he took a flat on fashionable Nowy Świat between 1922 and 1926, Zakopane, and the major musical centres of Western Europe, mainly Paris, London and Vienna. Because Szymanowski believed that the struggle to change Polish attitudes to music and culture was one which involved the whole of Polish society, the articles are to be found not only in musical publications such as *Muzyka* and *Kwartalnik Muzyczny*, but in literary and artistic journals – *Nowy Przegląd Literatury i Sztuki* (*New Review of Literature and Art*), *Skamander*, *Wiadomósci Literackie* (*Literary News*), *Sztuka Piękna* (*Fine Art*) – as well as newspapers (*Kurier Polski*, *Rzeczpospolita*, *Kurier Warszawski*, *ABC*, *Kurier Czerwony*, *Kurier Poranny*, *Warszawianka*, *Gazeta Polska*) and even women's magazines – *Pani* (*Lady*).

Szymanowski left no single work, like Stravinsky's *Poetics of Music* or Vaughan Williams' *National Music*, which encapsulates his fundamental 'philosophy'. Indeed, many of the

---

[64] Letter to Jachimecki, dated 2 February 1927, in *Z Listów*, p. 263.

[65] Béla Bartók, 'The Relation of Folk Song to the Development of the Art Music of Our Time', included in *Béla Bartók Essays*, selected and edited by Benjamin Suchoff, Faber, London, 1976, pp. 320–36.

Bartuś Obrochta

articles were occasional pieces, written to provide the composer with additional income, but some of the writings on education provide a reasonably comprehensive summary of the main strands of his ideology. These articles were the direct result of Szymanowski's activities in Polish higher musical education between 1927 and 1932, first as Director of the Warsaw Conservatory until 1929, and then, from 1930, as Rector of the newly founded State Academy of Music. His health deteriorated markedly during these years, and he found little time to compose (the Second String Quartet is the only substantial work from the end of the decade). But he regarded his work in education as a necessary part of his efforts to revitalise post-war musical culture in Poland.

Like all other areas of Polish life, the development of educational institutions had been seriously impeded by

partition. All universities and music schools were closed by
the Russians after the failure of the 1830 uprising, and in
the middle years of the nineteenth century, attempts to re-
open the conservatory were discouraged lest it bring about
a resurgence of Polish national culture. In the meantime,
music tuition was provided only by private teachers, and to a
very limited extent, theatrical schools. Then in 1858, the
Russians permitted the establishment of a commission to
look into the possibility of setting up some sort of higher
musical school. From the outset, its meetings were stormy
and marked by the waging of personal feuds:

> Malicious people maintain that all the members of the
> committee aspired to the position of director, as a con-
> sequence of which deliberations would not have reached
> any positive conclusion and perhaps would have continued
> until Judgment Day had not the impatient Apolinary Kątski
> obtained a separate licence for himself, and in this way freed
> the committee from any further work.[66]

Kątski was a virtuoso violinist who had performed in public
from the age of six. In the course of a spectacular career he
had forged strong connections with the Tsarist court in St
Petersburg, and these he frequently exploited to his own
advantage, not least in acquiring the licence to establish his
Musical Institute in an old, dilapidated building:

> In the course of its long existence, the latest monument to
> the cult of Apollo had fulfilled many functions: it had been
> a fortress, a magnate's residence, a boarding-school for
> young noble-women, a refuge for a band of robbers so
> dangerous that the police authorities of the time were
> unable to clear the cellars and underground hiding places
> for several years [...]. It had also been a fever hospital, an
> army barracks, a gum factory, an institution devoted to the
> moral welfare of children, an alms-house for the flood-
> stricken citizens of Powisla, a hospital for those suffering

---

[66] Tadeusz Strumiłło, *Szkice z Polskiego Życia Muzycznego XIX w.* (*Sketches of
Polish Musical Life in the 19th century*), Polskie Wydawnictwo Muzyczne,
Kraków, 1954, p. 210.

from epidemic illnesses, a hall for botanical exhibitions and finally – the Musical Institute.[67]

The Institute opened on 26 January 1861, admitting 153 pupils in the first year. The course lasted six years, and the final diploma entitled the holder to work in theatres, orchestras, schools and in a private capacity, not only in occupied Poland but throughout the Russian Empire. The first examinations were held in 1867, and one of the successful candidates was Zygmunt Noskowski, the composer who later taught Szymanowski.

Szymanowski took up the post of Director of the Conservatory, as the Institute had come to be called, in March 1927 on the understanding that he could carry out all the reforms he considered necessary. In an interview – 'A New Spirit in the Warsaw Conservatory' – given to *Kurier Czerwony* and published on 24 February 1927, Szymanowski talked in general terms of his plans and aims:

> First of all, if anyone expects 'revolutionary' steps from me, whether in hope or fear, they will in great measure be disappointed. [...] I shall resolutely endeavour to effect what I consider to be reforms, but in an evolutionary rather than revolutionary way. [...] The Conservatory should become the advocate of the most deeply conceived musical culture. Of course, in keeping with my fundamental stance, with my recognition of the achievements of contemporary music as being of very great, real value, I shall take into account the latest developments in this field. [...] I acknowledge artistic traditionalism – what I call a 'good musical education' – as a point of departure, but after all our aim is not 'yesterday', but 'today' and 'tomorrow' – creativity is the word, and not a retreat to already exhausted achievements.[68]

A letter written to Zofia Kochańska one month after he took up his responsibilities reveals that Szymanowski's powers were indeed considerable:

[67] *Ibid.*, pp. 213–14.

[68] *Karol Szymanowski Pisma*, p. 202.

I can count on the absolute support of the Ministry of Education, and already, in the first month of my official duties, I have succeeded in making changes in the statutes which ensure me complete freedom of action [...]. I am faced with the huge task of reforming the Conservatory both educationally and financially, and that means continual struggles over new grants [...]. In the Conservatory they fear me like the plague [...], because they sense the backing I have behind me [...]. There are some professors who are delighted with me [...], while the rest, even Rytel, are unbelievably polite. Basically they hate me, but extraordinarily respectfully, because they sense that I can do what I want. [...] Before the vacation some terrible conflicts must occur, because I intend to get rid of the whole lot *ohne Weiteres*. You can imagine how they will like me then!![69]

Indeed, Szymanowski attempted to deal with members of the conservative faction not so much by rooting them out as by diluting their influence through the introduction of new staff sympathetic to his ideas. Not surprisingly, his reforms met with increasingly bitter opposition, and an article entitled 'The Generation War between Old and Young Musicians and the Conflict between their Respective Creative Outlooks', published on 12 January 1928, in response to an anonymous attack ('Protectionism in the Conservatory'), clearly indicates the nature and extent of the problems facing him. For a start, it transpires that the building itself was in a deplorable state: 'dirty, in disrepair, a veritable Augean Stables!'[70] Renovation had to be instigated immediately. Szymanowski's pedagogical reforms included the appointment of new professors to help in the compulsory piano classes and in the teaching of harmony and counterpoint, but it seems that the worst of his 'sins', and the one which triggered the accusation of protectionism, was the re-organisation of the orchestral class:

[69] Letter dated 7 April 1927, in *Dzieje Przyjaźni*, pp. 139–40.

[70] *Karol Szymanowski Pisma*, p. 208.

When I came to the Conservatory, the orchestral class was taken by a 'talented oboist'. He took the orchestral class since the conducting class only existed on paper in the official prospectus of the Conservatory. My 'sin' is that in place of this 'talented oboist' I have managed to appoint 'my friend' Grzegorz Fitelberg, who, incidentally, is Poland's leading symphonist and enjoys a commanding position among the world's conductors on account of his twenty years' hard work championing the cause of Polish music at home and abroad. Now, after so many years, the Conservatory's students really can learn the art of playing in an orchestra and, what is more important, the demanding skill of standing in front of one. *Mea culpa, mea culpa.*[71]

Szymanowski was soon able to claim with some justification that his reforms were beginning to show the desired results:

The improvement in the standard of the Conservatory after one year of my work is obvious, and my worst enemies are now unable to deny the fact. The display concert at the Philharmonia was one long ovation. The Orchestra (which after all is entirely composed of young 'uns), really is a proper symphony orchestra after being trained for a year by Ficio [Fitelberg]. It was a good concert [...] and there was un-alloyed enthusiasm, as if it were a concert given by great celebrities.[72]

In December 1928, Szymanowski was granted several months' sick leave to undergo a rest cure at Edlach, near Vienna. Although it later became clear that he was already suffering from pulmonary tuberculosis, the treatment at Edlach was primarily for alcoholism, exacerbated by the tensions of the previous eighteen months at the Conservatory. He returned to Warsaw in March 1929, and by the end of July the arrangements for his resignation, with effect from the following September, had been made. In August

[71] *Ibid.*, p. 209.

[72] Letter dated 21 June 1928 to Zofia Kochańska, in *Dzieje Przyjaźni*, pp. 181–82.

he again went to Edlach, but after becoming dissatisfied with the treatment, left for Vienna, where his doctor diagnosed tuberculosis of the right lung. At the end of August he was admitted to the Guardaval Sanatorium in Davos, Switzerland, and there he remained until May 1930.

During these months he wrote 'The Educational Role of Musical Culture in Society', his longest and finest piece of polemical writing. By March his health had improved sufficiently for him to accept the post of Rector of a new musical Academy in Warsaw, created through the elevation of the existing Conservatory to university status. He took up his responsibilities the following September, and for the formal opening of the Academy on 7 November 1930 he composed his inspirational *Veni Creator* (Op. 57) to Stanislaw Wyspiański's Polish translation of the Latin hymn. He also delivered an address in which he set out in succinct form many of his educational theories, acting, as he put it, as 'spokesman and representative of those Polish musicians who consciously combine their deep love for, and conviction of, the elevating nobility of true art with a sense of social responsibility for the well-being of the nation's culture'.[73] Here Szymanowski starts from the proposition that in contemporary society music is the most popular art and as such offers society elevated, ennobling artistic values and also, unfortunately, 'in its negative manifestations, exerts an almost depraving influence in the way in which it can maim and disfigure the inborn artistic instinct of the masses'.[74] The musical educationalist had to dam this free-flowing 'popular music' so that a music of indisputable creative value could permeate society.

A musical education should impart to the future generation of performers, composers and teachers not only basic technique but 'an objective knowledge about music, [...] knowledge about its history, and about those fundamental philosophical and aesthetic concepts which touch upon

[73] *Karol Szymanowski Pisma*, pp. 302–3.

[74] *Ibid.*, p. 303.

music, [...] in other words, a wide-ranging concept of the role of art in the life of society and the history of the nation'.[75] A sound, all-embracing musical education should supplement aesthetic considerations with that ethical element, 'that powerful, enduring thread which, in every area of work and human activity, binds the individual to society in general, and defines not only his rights but his obligations'.[76] In short, the new syllabus would include a wider range of subjects of a more general educational nature: 'Such subjects, in that they broaden and deepen a student's knowledge, would exert positive influences, developing initiative and independence of thought, heightening powers of perception and of passing critical judgments, and of preparing a conscious, rational outlook for the individual tasks which await our students in the future'.[77] Anyone who has had to train technically gifted students who, nonetheless, seem to be quite incapable of telling Bach and Tchaikovsky apart, will surely applaud Szymanowski's views on the teaching of the history of music, a subject which is frequently unpopular with the stylistically insensitive student because it has no immediate bearing on technical, motor activity and also requires intellectual effort. It forms, however,

> an organic part of a wider musical education. Above all, it develops an understanding and feeling for the style peculiar to the musical works of various historical epochs, and this in itself exerts a direct influence on the level of competence in stylistically appropriate performances of these works. In other words, it does have an immediate application in the professional or practical field. Moreover, and this is perhaps the most important aspect, the history of music is not a self-contained subject, a separate leaf torn from the great history of man's spiritual conquests. At every step of the way, there

[75] *Ibid.*, p. 304.

[76] *Ibid.*, p. 304.

[77] *Ibid.*, p. 304.

are mutual interactions, dependences, parallels and divergences not just in the closely related fields of literature,
theatre and the fine arts, but also in more general areas and
ideas that have a bearing on the spiritual evolution of
mankind.[78]

The similarities between the argument of the 'Rector's
Address' and that of 'The Educational Role of Musical
Culture in Society' soon become apparent. The latter again
takes as its starting-point the 'democratic' nature of music –
for good or ill – and eventually goes on to refute the idea
that those in a supposedly advantageous social position *ipso
facto* have more lively and appreciative perceptions ('one
has only to hear the conversation of the smart set, emerging
from the Teatr Wielki [Grand Theatre] or the Philharmonia, after the performance of some truly great work to be at
last persuaded of the strangeness of this notion'[79]). But this
essay goes considerably further in that it seeks to demonstrate the existence of constructive elements in music which
ought by their very nature to ensure state support. By way of
a brief historical survey, Szymanowski attempts first to show
that the history of man in reality proves to be the history of
his art. Much more to the point is the very nature of music's
immense, democratically operating power, capable of exerting influences both destructive and constructive more
widely than all the other arts:

> There is not, or rather there ought not to be, such a force
> which would not oblige the state to bring it within the orbit
> of its activities, directing along the appropriate track in
> general terms its works and resources [...].[80]

This is faintly redolent of Matthew Arnold's argument
against that which he described as the specifically British
form of quietism, prevailing during the middle years of the
nineteenth century. According to this 'quietist' theory,

[78] *Ibid.*, p. 305.

[79] *Ibid.*, p. 270.

[80] *Ibid.*, p. 273.

the common reason of society can check the aberrations of individual eccentricity only by acting on the individual reason, and it will do so in the main sufficiently, if left to this natural operation.[81]

Such an attitude, in Arnold's view, reflected an excessive reliance on an over-ruling Providence:

> Providence, as the moralists are careful to tell us, generally works in human affairs by human means; so when we want to make right reason act on individual inclination, our best self on our ordinary self, we seek to give it more power of doing so by giving it public recognition and authority, and embodying it, so far as we can, in the State. It seems too much to ask of Providence, that while we, on our part, leave our congenital taste for bathos to its natural operation and its infinite variety of experiments, Providence should mysteriously guide it into the true track, and compel it to relish the sublime.[82]

There are here the makings of a very doubtful argument. Setting aside the difficulties which would inevitably accompany the attempt to compel any citizen 'to relish the sublime', account has to be taken of the fact that if compulsion is involved at all, it is usually directed at artists rather than audiences. Arnold was so concerned with fighting the laissez-faire attitude of the age that the implications of his argument for the absolute freedom of the artist went unheeded. Szymanowski recognised the problem as it existed for literature, but somewhat naively believed that music was inviolate because of the purity of its aesthetic. In any case, he attributed a non-specific 'disinterested' role to the musical creator, and so expected state intervention to stop at extensive patronage and the organisation of an educational programme, expressly designed to channel the general and as yet ill-formed musicianship of the nation into a creatively valuable culture.

[81] *Matthew Arnold, Culture and Anarchy*, ed. J. Dover Wilson, Cambridge University Press, Cambridge and London, 1971, p. 124.

[82] *Ibid.*, p. 124.

He also believed that music could be regarded as an archetype for the social order, and in support of this argument, isolated three fundamental elements in music and its performance. The first was that very democratic quality which permitted it to penetrate with ease the depths of society, 'there where no line of the most idealistic and elevating poetry reaches'.[83] Appearing in a constant state of flux (unlike most of the other arts), creating by its enchanting power ever new forms, it frees the potential capacity for experiencing mysterious emotions in every human soul. Music seizes and unites listeners in the common experience of an almost unearthly, but real and tangible event, and it is this unifying effect which constitutes its second fundamental element, an element also recognised by Stravinsky when he quoted the Chinese sage, Seu-ma-Tsen: 'Music is what unifies'.[84] For both Stravinsky and Szymanowski, musical performance had a markedly ritualistic significance. For Stravinsky, it brought him into communion with his fellow man and the Supreme Being,[85] while, for Szymanowski, it united his listeners at the highest degree of contemporary experience, removing the petty divisions which result from our egoistic affairs and day-to day concerns.

This sense of unity arises from the third fundamental element of music: its organising power. Unlike its sister arts (drama excepted), music requires intermediary links between composer and audience, provided by a performer or groups of performers. This observation forms the basis for a theory of social organisation which is both original and far-reaching. The musical performance is conceived as an intricate complex of many various elements which only reveal a fundamental unity under the control of an individual, organising will. The excellence of the performance

[83] *Karol Szymanowski Pisma*, p. 281.

[84] Igor Stravinsky, *Poetics of Music in the Form of Six Lessons*, translated by Arthur Knodel and Ingolf Dahl, Harvard University Press, Cambridge (Mass.), 1947, p. 141.

[85] *Ibid.*, p. 142.

depends on the individual responsibility of each participant, and so the musical group is seen as an archetype, a cell
for all social organisation, 'with this categorical distinction,
however, that a fundamental disinterestedness is its guiding
principle'.[86] Szymanowski draws an analogy between the
microcosm of the music group and the macrocosm of the
all-embracing contemporary state on the one hand, and the
structure of the atom and that of a planetary system on the
other. His concept of the state also calls to mind Matthew
Arnold's notion of the state as the embodiment of our own
'best self' for, although the state stands in contrast to the
individual, it is in reality extracted from, and is the logical
fulfillment of, the best self of each member of the music
group. Furthermore, the immediate task of the state, as of
the musical director, is a blending or harmonisation of
particular elements 'with the aim of attaining that ideal of
unity [. . .] which is only expressed when the process of
crystallisation of the superindividual idea attains a sufficiently vigorous form within the framework of the
individually conceived state organisation'.[87] An overall historical view also emerges, for without the superindividual
idea of unity in the state, the history of man would appear
incomprehensible – a meaningless game, lacking in regula-
tion, just as music without a shaping creative will would be
nothing more than a cacophonous chaos.

Whatever the long-term value of Szymanowski's writings
on music (and not least of these is his plea for the broadening of the aims of modern education so that schooling is
not confined merely to the inculcating of a certain, limited
intellectual materialism), his attempts to apply his theories
met with very little immediate support or success. From the
beginning, the very existence of the Academy aroused bitter
opposition. Its formation had involved the division of the
old Conservatory into three main sections: the 'High
School' or Academy proper, with Symanowski at its head;

[86] *Karol Szymanowski Pisma*, p. 282.

[87] *Ibid.*, p. 283.

a middle school, directed by Eugeniusz Morawski;[88] and the
Seminarium Nauczycieli, a teacher-training college under
Stanisław Kazuro.[89] Morawski became the leader of an anti-
Academy faction, and it was to the attacks of this group that
Szymanowski responded in his article 'The Dispute over the
Academy of Music', published in November 1931. In the
succeeding months, Szymanowski's position was undermined and he found himself unable to retain the support of
the Ministry. Throughout the 1930s Polish governments
became increasingly authoritarian, and the ruling cabinets,
most of which contained a majority of army officers, avoided
contact with the Sejm, so dispensing with any form of
genuine parliamentary consultation. In March 1932, the
government, then led by Alexander Prystor, secured for
itself powers of legislation by decree, and the usual symptoms of military rule began to appear. Freedom of assembly
was restricted, press censorship increased and the right of
workers, and particularly of the railwaymen, to strike was
curtailed. Co-ordinated academic opposition was destroyed
with the removal of university autonomy and the dismissal
of fifty or so university professors. After representations
from the conservative factions of the various music school,
the decision to close the Academy was taken, without prior
consultation, on 29 January 1932. The closure became
public knowledge in February, when Kazimierz Sikorski,
Fitelberg and Różycki at the High School, and Władysław
Raczkowski at the Middle School, were informed that they
had been relieved of their posts. A substantial number of
students took strike action and were duly suspended. Szymanowski heard of these events in Zakopane through

---

[88] Eugeniusz Morawski (1876–1948) was a composer, painter and sculptor.
He trained at the Musical Institute with Noskowski, and subsequently
studied in Paris with Gédalge and Chevillard. He held the post of director
of the Warsaw Conservatory until 1939.

[89] Stanisław Kazuro (1881–1961) was a composer, teacher and conductor.
He specialised in performances of choral music (Szymanowski dedicated
the *Six Kurpian Songs for Chorus* to him). He was director of the Warsaw
Conservatory from 1945 to 1951.

newspaper accounts, and immediately sent in his resignation. He also wrote an open letter to the press explaining
the reasons for his action, and shortly afterwards, another
colleague, the distinguished musicologist and scholar, Hier-
onymous Feicht, resigned in sympathy. Szymanowski wrote
of his mixed feelings in a letter to Zofia Kochańska:

> Above all there is that awful contempt [...] – that slap in the
> face from those for whom I have worked for five loyal years.
> In short, it is a terrible, tragic story, involving distinguished
> people, about which one will read in biographies with a
> sense of resentment and bitterness. I understand this all too
> well from the total indecency of the haste with which they
> got rid of me, and of course I suffer on that count. But
> imagine, somewhere at the bottom of my soul [...] there is
> huge joy at my liberation [...]. And this feeling has been
> reflected, absolutely automatically, in the desire to com-
> pose.[90]

Within months Szymanowski completed his Fourth Symphony and had substantially completed the Second Violin
Concerto. It proved to be the final creative outburst of his
career. Subsequently he composed very little at all (only two
piano mazurkas and the exquisite but relatively small-scale
Litania survive from the last years), and his 'literary' output
was confined to obituaries for Paul Dukas, Paweł Kochański
and Emil Młynarski and occasional interviews with newspapers and magazines. His final project was an
autobiography, but by the time of his death at Lausanne, on
29 March 1937, he had sketched only an introduction – an
attempt to define the essence of a good biography.

[90] Letter dated 9 March 1932, in *Dzieje Przyjaźni*, pp. 314–15.

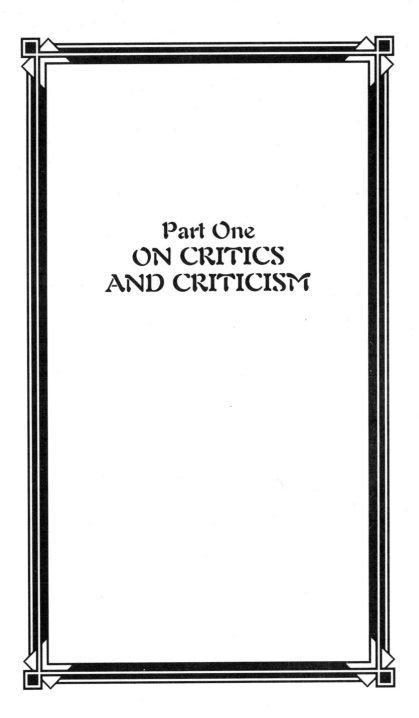

Part One
ON CRITICS
AND CRITICISM

On Contemporary Musical Opinion in Poland

First published in *Nowy Przegląd Literatury i Sztuki*
(*New Review of Literature and Art*) in July 1920.

It is generally accepted that the educational task of the artistic criticism that so abundantly fills the columns of the current daily, weekly, political, social and specialised artistic papers is the shaping of public taste by means of a *summary* judgment on a work of art, an authorative indication of its absolute worth.

Whether current artistic criticism in general, and *ours* in particular, performs this task – still more, whether it is fundamentally capable of so doing, is a disturbing problem which will of course remain unanswered. Such an important matter is far beyond the scope of the present article.

The present author, however, is convinced that artistic criticism of a completely different nature can exist. Oscar Wilde, thinking for a certainty of his distinguished mentor, Walter Pater, dreamt of this criticism. It does not sit in judgment, signing untimely death warrants. Instead, being essentially *amoral*, it is beyond 'right' and 'wrong'. It reveals with a gracious, but wise smile, new worlds of beauty which the short-sighted eye of the Philistine would perhaps be unable to perceive without its all powerful help.[1]

[1] To avoid dwelling on particular aspects of artistic criticism in the course of this article, it is essential to say at this stage that any 'writing' on art which in itself is not touched by the genius and exaltation of the original fails to arouse in the reading public any response, and *eo ipso* does not possess any educational significance. Objective 'expertise', bereft of personal style and taste, is in general exceedingly tedious, and simply impossible in artistic matters. In this respect, alas, musical articles in our papers, with some exceptions of course, are far from ideal. In most cases the long-suffering reader is submerged in a veritable ocean of 'expertise' and colourless jargon, and the more enlightened of these readers frequently declare regretfully that this 'expertise' is often of a highly suspect kind. –KS

It would of course be impossible to exact just such a criticism from the veritable crowd of artistic 'reporters' who occupy responsible positions in almost all the editorial offices of the newspaper world. But we can make other demands of them. Even if they frequently make mistakes in their factual evaluations of an artist and his works, they should at least reflect faithfully the 'taste' prevailing at a given time. In other words they should advocate artistic opinions holding sway at any given time in those strata of society interested in such matters. They should reveal the often deeply concealed and unconscious aesthetic currents stirring within society, and they should at least proclaim the *vox populi*, which, it must be said, has always in the last analysis proved itself to be correct, born as it is out of the deepest instincts of the people at large.

Undoubtedly this has been the role of day-to-day journalistic criticism in countries with a long-established, well-founded culture. A characteristic example is the great journalistic war declared on Richard Wagner and his followers by Hanslick[2] during the final decades of the last century. Naturally the composer of the *Nibelungenlied* triumphed because he was an artist of great genius. His opponent,

---

[2] Eduard Hanslick (1825–1904), the Austrian music critic, musicologist and aesthetician. He held the view that the beauty of music lay in its sheer sound and structure and not in any extra-musical content. Although he recognised the scale of Wagner's achievement, he opposed the notion of the synthesis of the arts and believed that Wagner forced music to exceed its expressive bounds. Later in his career he criticised the concept of the music drama so relentlessly and vehemently that even Brahms, a long-standing friend and sympathiser of Hanslick, found his views unbalanced. Wagner himself retaliated by using Hanslick as the model for the pusillanimous, carping Beckmesser in *Die Meistersinger von Nürnberg* (in an early draft, the Beckmesser character was named Veit Hanslich).

Further remarks about Hanslick ('Concerning Hanslick and his Aesthetic') are to be discovered among the rough and rather chaotic notes which Szymanowski made in preparation for a monograph on contemporary music that, in the end, he did not complete (*cf.* pp. 207–22):

At the end of the 19th c., the Viennese critic Hanslick, author of *Vom Musikalisch-Schönen*, instinctively, rather than rationally, sensed the danger of the direction being taken by German music during the Romantic epoch, the greatest expression of which is to be found in

mistaken once again, eventually fell in battle, but not before he had paved the way to fame for Johannes Brahms, the composer whom he had commandeered as his heaviest gun in the heroic attack on Wagner.

The Brahms-Wagner controversy has an almost symbolic significance in that it fully exposes the fundamental tendencies of the German artistic psyche, and the two courses along which their music was henceforth to flow. On the one hand, there is the deeply tragic pathos of Wagner, which in its absolute 'will to power' approaches brutality; on the other, there is the romantic 'academicism' of Brahms. This contrast recalls Nietzsche's mystical antithesis of *das Apollinische und das Dionische* in art, an antithesis which appears for the first time in *Die Geburt der Tragödie*,[3] a book which,

---

the works of R. Wagner. I say instinctively, because the whole logical construction pursuing that train of thought – in general the whole philosophical plane upon which his thinking worked – in the above-mentioned work – is marked by a complete lack of depth. In general that plane has been 'superseded' and a protest against romanticism must seek a deeper justification. The venerable critic would of course be amazed were he to be told that in spite of everything he was in a certain (elementary today) sense a spokesman of that which characterises today's tendencies – not only in music, but art in general!

If he were to hear one of Stravinsky's recent works, for example, he would tear his hair out at the thought that he was able to contribute ideologically, albeit in the tiniest measure, to its inception! In spite of the complete and utter dryness and intellectual basis of today's art – especially the fine arts – on the one hand, in spite of the totally committed acceptance (as the emotional atmosphere) of the only reality today: towns, the dynamism of contemporary life, machines, aeroplanes etc. – somewhere at the depths of the most distinguished of her exponent's beings, that same 'romantic' dreaming about the 'eternity' of one's own work lies concealed, and all theoretical debates about form are only a yearning for a solution to that eternal problem of finding a shape that will never erode, never rust.

Szymanowski, *Pisma Muzyczne*, p. 485.

[3] *The Birth of Tragedy out of the Spirit of Music* (*Die Geburt der Tragödie aus dem Geiste der Musik*), first published in Leipzig in 1872, was the earliest extended work by Friedrich Nietzsche (1844–1900). It exerted a powerful influence on Szymanowski from his early youth. He once told Iwaszkiewicz that this work and *Gespräche mit Goethe* (*Conversations with Goethe*) by Johann

quite apart from its own individual value, is in principle an ideological echo of the disputes provoked by the work of the Bayreuth master for whom it constitutes a profound, if perhaps over-enthusiastic, apologia.

In the declining years of the nineteenth century, the Brahms-Wagner conflict was the most important artistic question in Germany, where it excited a vigorous response among the general public. The many critical writings to be found in newspapers were simply the faithful echo of this conflict – the reasoned, highly characteristic response to that pathos by a society which took a lively part in everything concerning the fate of its art.

There was an analogous phenomenon in Russia, where, in the decades preceding the [1914–18] war, music developed to a remarkable extent, moving rapidly towards the creation of a rich and, in its characteristic features, peculiarly Russian nationalistic school. Here again the devotion and truly enormous interest on the part of the public, faithfully reflected in journalistic criticism, focussed on two schools differing in their fundamental aims and principles, the ideological centres of which were the conservatories of Moscow and St Petersburg. At the same time, by a strange irony of fate, the Petersburg school, which developed amidst the cosmopolitan buzz of the official Tsarist capital, was characterised by aspirations towards extreme nationalism based on the almost ideological application of folklore to art (Rimsky-Korsakov, Mussorgsky, Borodin *et al.*). In contrast, even though it was situated hard by the Kremlin, in the midst of a veritable forest of gaudy, bulbous cupolas, the Moscow group, under the leadership of the patriarch, Piotr Tchaikovsky, 'orientated' itself very much more towards 'European' styles, and ultimately gave rise to

---

Peter Eckermann were the two most beautiful books in the world, and the Nietzschean concept of Dionysus played an important part in the ideology of *King Roger*.

the almost total cosmopolitanism of the often eccentric, yet deeply artistic and magical art of Skryabin.[4]

Here was an opposition of two distinct 'schools', two tastes and two different conceptions of the fundamental nature of national art, and the most far-reaching consequences arose from this clash. At the same time we must acknowledge the appearance of mysterious, aesthetic currents which emanated from the soul of the nation, objectifying themselves in highly characteristic works of art. It is precisely the attrition of seemingly contradictory ideas which is a measure of the strength and vitality of the artistic instincts of the masses.

Could something similar happen in Polish music today? I think not, and for the following reasons. Our musical criticism certainly has the right to publish more or less right or wrong judgments about each work as it is performed on the concert platform or operatic stage. It possesses that right, but it cannot be said to be representative of public opinion in the way that we have attempted to define it. Polish musical criticism does not possess this ability because musical opinion on musical matters simply does not exist (and the present author would not dare to speak on matters beyond the sphere of music!), or else exists in such a primitive, nebulous state that any sort of untimely concept,

---

[4] During his one return visit to Russia after the revolution, for a concert of Polish music in the hall of the Moscow Conservatory given on 12 November 1933, Szymanowski gave an interview to the Moscow weekly *Sovietskoye Iskustvo*. In the course of the interview, published under the title 'The Co-operation of Nations', he spoke about the leading composers of the pre-revolutionary era. It seems that his admiration for Skryabin was not latterly as intense as once it had been:

> I must however admit that Tchaikovsky and the 'Mighty Five', and above all Mussorgsky, are much closer to my heart than Skryabin. In particular, I consider Mussorgsky's work to be first-rate; it is so national in character and so international, universal in its deepest musical ideas. With Skryabin one senses a sort of detachment, an indulging in day-dreams [...].

Pisma Muzyczne, p. 439.

authoratively propounded, albeit by a critic *minorum gentium*, could lead to its total disorientation.

We have observed that journalistic criticism in this country is more dangerous than anywhere else. It takes as its starting-point a position based on its own norms and definitions, and frequently stands between the creative artist and the healthy and essentially well-adjusted instinct of the masses. It is dangerous because it is not directed by a true compass, by a clear sense of the tastes and temperament of the listening public. It gropes among spectres and hallucinations of its own making. It fails to raise any essential questions organically linked with art; it makes no positive, unambiguous declarations, but clasps to its heart that rather problematic Polish music which it tries to conjure up from a state of non-existence – a vain attempt as it is incapable of revealing its true likeness. Certain conditions, which today are surely unacceptable, are imposed in advance. Our music criticism goes in fear and trembling of the sinister phantom of futurism (also known as Bolshevism). It roundly curses atonality, but although it builds walls to keep out both Eastern and Western influences, it smiles with a certain embarrassed sympathy on that good old German music. But in the end, it has to be said that our critics really only feel safe in the Teatr Wielki at a performance of *Halka*.[5]

In fact, the general public is not at all interested in what Mr X, the reviewer of one paper or another, thought of opera Y or artist Z, because our public regards music merely as a congenial evening pastime and is not much concerned about its fate. In such an atmosphere of general indifference, the deep devotion which does exist here and there has to remain a series of guttering flames. These flames cannot flare up into a white-hot national fanaticism for art, and so the conditions necessary for the fostering of art cannot be provided.

---

[5] *Halka* is the most celebrated of Moniuszko's operas. It was first staged in its revised four-act form in 1858. The Teatr Wielki (Grand Theatre) is Warsaw's opera house.

This undoubtedly explains to a certain extent the faults and short-comings of our critics, since even the best wills are powerless in the face of indifference and *je m'en fiche'isme*. It would, however, be interesting to examine the fundamental reasons for this situation.

There are pessimists who declare that the Poles are the least musical nation in the world. Personally I prefer to say nothing in response to this bitter reproach, save to remark · that all our cultural problems undoubtedly stem from historical catastrophe and the abnormal conditions which have prevailed here for the last century and a half.

Now that the forcefully imposed barriers of partition have at last been removed, we can see how difficult it is for the different regions of the country to come together again in one indissoluble whole. We can also begin to understand fully the immense damage caused by enforced provincial-ism in that it has retarded the creation of a uniform consciousness of the nation as a cultural entity. The fatal influence of this state of affairs, now a thing of the past, can be discovered in every area of our spiritual and intellectual life and also, without doubt, in the musicality of those parts of society which have attained some degree of culture. Let us approach the problem then from this standpoint, start-ing with an investigation of the local conditions prevailing in each of the three sectors of pre-war Poland.[6]

The Principality of Poznán is situated closest to those first-rate' centres of musical life, namely the major cities of Germany. But in the fanatical, boorish, obstinate struggle with the superior power of the enemy, a struggle waged over every inch of land, for the basic right to existence as a national entity, there simply was not time 'to mourn the rose while the forest burned'. Consequently, the cultural offer-ings from the 'other' side were spurned, and so the province

[6] In the years immediately preceding the First World War, Poland was divided between three occupying powers. Germany held the western lands, known as the Principality; the southern lands, including Kraków, formed part of the Austro-Hungarian Empire, and Russia held the Eastern territo-ries, including Warsaw. *Cf.* Introduction, p. 20.

became 'unmusical'. Even here in Poland it is generally
admitted to be *terre à terre* and uncultured. One would
prefer, however, to see in that rigorous self-denial and
prudent economy of the powers of self-preservation the
natural instinct of what may be the healthiest branch of the
nation. Perhaps in the not-too-distant future these battle-
trained forces, no longer fighting their terrible old
adversary, will turn their energy in new directions, and
begin to create new values in the spiritual sphere which
really will bring liberation from 'Eastern and Western
influences'.

Circumstances in Galicia were completely different.
Beautiful music was one of the countless 'graces and
favours' which emanated from Vienna, along with a friendly
pat on the back. It swept over Galicia, and the province
received visits from excellent orchestras, first-rate virtuosi
and singers who performed the truly marvellous works of
Wolf, Brahms and Reger. Consequently Małopolska is today
easily the most musical part of the land, and is endowed with
the most discerning public and the most cultured and
educated critics.[7]

But what of it, when the development and flowering of
this musicality was exclusively linked with German music!
Lulled by the subtly lapping Danube, Małopolska now
sleeps and dreams, and is unable to bring herself to make
the necessary gesture of protest. Such a protest may be

[7] The attention of the reader is drawn to one very characteristic symptom.
In recent decades, Viennese musical life, and to a significant extent, the
musical life of other major German cities in almost all its forms has become
the monopoly of the Jews. As is well known, the Jews are very musical, but
it has to be remarked that this musicality is rather superficial, being more
of a gesture than a deeply felt emotion. Their gifts, capabilities and
opinions have a facility indicative of gesture rather than a manifestation of
creative instinct. These truths are known and recognised. Yet it should not
be forgotten that wherever they play some sort of role, Jews introduce their
cosmopolitan (not to say international) disposition. For the present, this
short note can serve as an explanation of the nature of contemporary
'musicality' in central European states, and to a certain extent those
provinces which were formally Austrian, such as the area presently under
discussion. –KS

brutal, perhaps even boorish, but it is the only *creative* response to the sorceries flowing into the province from outside. The suggestive power of German music is mighty and intoxicates like an old dry wine. But under its influence it is impossible to consolidate and project a common consciousness which will ultimately become 'Polish Music'. Unfortunately the experiments of this kind that have been attempted in Galicia have usually been typified by an incurable dilettantism, for example Jan Wydżga's 'opera' *Pan Tadeusz*, a work that stirs unhappy memories.[8]

In the Russian sector a political state of affairs existed which at first recalls that prevailing in the Principality of Poznań, except that in this instance the national existence had to be stubbornly defended from attacks from the East. There was, however, one important difference: Warsaw, the nation's feverishly beating heart and highly active brain, lay at its centre. Furthermore, the Russians were not so uniformly restrictive, nor so ruthless as the Prussians in the Principality. Cunning poisons trickled through from the 'other' side, namely the two-edged influences of their widely disseminated literature. It revealed genius, but was hostile to us in that it smuggled in ideas which were fundamentally alien to our western national psyche.

To one thing we remained almost entirely unresponsive, and that was their music.[9] Admittedly it would have been impossible under the circumstances for the Teatr Wielki to have staged the beautiful operas of Mussorgsky, Rimsky-

[8] Jan Wydżga (1873–1936). The opera *Pan Tadeusz*, based on Mickiewicz's epic poem of the same name, was staged in Lwów (Lemberg) in 1908. The composer was an amateur musician, and his work enjoyed considerable notoriety.

[9] For only the most cosmopolitan of the Russians (Tchaikovsky, and to a lesser extent, Rakhmaninov and Skryabin) was there toleration, and perhaps even affection here. Other names appeared extremely rarely on our concert programmes. We are not, of course, concerned with the – *horribile dictu* – composers of the so-called 'cyganesque-romances' which were once exceedingly popular amongst Warsaw's less prepossessing social circles. –KS

Korsakov and Borodin, not to mention the exceedingly interesting ballets of the 'futurist' Stravinsky, with all the boyars' costumes, Moscow church bells, Russian Orthodox liturgical choirs and other such trappings. Theatrical management evidently took this into account, and bored us to death with the tender *Onegin*, the dashing guardsmen of the *Queen of Spades*, and worst of all, Rubinstein's unspeakably revolting *Demon*.

Yet when we take into consideration the fact that, quite apart from the 'patriotic' atmosphere of Russian opera, music was the healthiest and most fascinating form of Russian art, it is almost to be regretted that we are not better acquainted with it. There was no question of any specific influence, and in any case we were already partially on our guard against such a danger. But it is possible to learn much from the Russians. We have already observed that in recent years their music has moved decidedly in the direction of the creation of a national school whose music is on a par with the finest works of European music in general,[10] or, in other words, it has advanced far enough for us to make a careful and penetrating examination of its nature. And, of course, the most valuable skill in the waging of a war is the capture of the enemy's most accurately aimed weapon! I also believe that, at the present time, when our cultural relationship with contemporary Russia, or rather that already decomposing corpse, cannot in general be taken into account, and while the Russia of yesterday (our enemy, even though her art was of an incontestably high standard) belongs to the irretrievable past, we are able to rid ourselves of those earlier prejudices originating in the period of captivity, and examine objectively and carefully those perhaps few real values which Russia bequeathed to the treasury of humanity.

But we must return to our deliberations. In spite of everything, Warsaw, or the Kingdom, became in recent

[10] It is worth noting at this point the feverish interest shown in Russian art by the West, an interest which is by no means based merely on political calculation as is here so frequently, but wrongly, thought. –KS

times the most important centre in the gradual shaping of Polish culture. It was in her white-hot furnace that weapons for the defence of the nation's existence were obstinately forged. Ideas were born; thoughts were shaped. The Kingdom became acutely aware of the need for external demonstrations in its spiritual life since all other possibilities were forcibly cordoned off.[11]

Under this banner, literature developed even more rapidly than it had done previously. So did painting. The theatre, however, became bogged down in unreconcilable contradictions. It had to struggle not just with its own internal problems but also with external obstacles, and so it gradually strayed from the natural course of organic development. Only music remained an unwritten book, its pages blank apart from the heading: 'Polish National Music'.

Polish Music – Polish Art – National Art! Here reigns a veritable chaos of ideas, contradictions and unanswerable questions.

Was it really just a matter of the ideological 'building' of Polish culture in accordance with some masterplan, each part being entrusted to a suitable 'craftsman'?

'You will do this and that in the course of raising over the palace of Polish culture a cupola of art; in so doing you will take care not to go beyond our prescribed measurements, calculations and models.'

None of these plans and calculations worked. There was very little which did not count as National Art during the years of captivity, but it took the form of a hopeless plumbing of the depths of a once splendid past, the conjuring up of dead spectres, and with it a fearful escape from the hurly-burly of everyday life as it rushed by. National Art also involved 'going out among the people', and led to a hypnotic fascination with mazurka-carols and collections

[11] This is a reference to the collapse in 1863 of the final attempt to liberate Poland from Russian rule by force. The failure of this rebellion led to a change in Polish attitudes, reflected artistically in the rise of the Positivist movement.

of awful raspberry-coloured wycinankas[12] and green ribbons. Even the Teutonic, academic fugue on the theme 'Niedaleko Krakówa' or even 'Chmielu, chmielu zielony'[13] counted as National Art, and National Art could also on occasion become a treacherous poisoned rapier with which the heart of an 'ideological' opponent could be unexpectedly pierced.

The simplest, and indeed the only solution to this problem, is for an artist to work with a sense of absolute freedom. And here the still illustrious name of Fryderyk Chopin automatically comes to mind.

Chopin was the only musical genius in the history of our art, a mysterious visitant who retained no organic connection with our musical culture. He had no ancestors, just as he had no descendents. Like a lone star shining in the midst of the black night, his absolute 'uniqueness' was almost paradoxical. Chopin really was a Pole who composed Polish Music which at the same time is universal art of the highest standard. The six volumes of his collected works are to this day the only great Polish national music.

But what of this? He flung open the gates leading to that Kingdom, and, for a twinkling of an eye, a blinding light shone. It seemed that the problem was solved. For a while, the soul of the people, their unfathomable ethnic depths decked out in festal garments which glittered with the priceless jewels of a noble art, could be heard reverberating in the undeniably nationalistic rhythms of his mazurkas and polonaises. The great compositions ring out with the tragic, albeit heroic, pathos of a nation which, although on the verge of exhaustion, still defended passionately its fundamental right to existence.

The gates swung to again, and who of his successors managed to re-open them? A few dilettantes who were such lamentable parodies of their inspiration?

[12] Wycinankas are paper cut-outs used to produce silhouettes.

[13] These are titles of folk-songs, 'Not far from Kraków' and 'Hop-plant, green hop-plant'.

It has to be said that Chopin did not lay the foundations of Polish music. Unfortunately it moved in a different direction. Chopin was such an unexpected and dazzling phenomenon that at the time he seemed almost alien to us.[14]

It is now too late to follow the example of Chopin; in any case broken strings cannot be retied. He belongs to the past, to the period of captivity. He was one of the most profound and tragic artists to oppose the violation of the Polish soul, but today he is only a sacred relic, an eternally living and priceless monument to bygone days. We, the living and the free, should be seeking new paths and singing other songs.

It is, however, a particularly malicious and cynical twist of fate that while Chopin passed fleetingly amongst us like a ghost, in isolation and adversity, arousing no long-lasting echo in the art of the next period, the sparks from his music kindled the flames of what, in time, was to become a great fire in the camp of our most bitter enemies, namely in the art of the leading Russian composers of the age. Today there is not the slightest doubt that the deepest foundations of that Russian musical nationalism which subsequently became so vital were based on a boundless adoration of Chopin and also an understanding of his true genius and his original ethnic characteristics – also a distinguishing feature of the Russian musicians of the day.[15]

[14] I am not of course forgetting the atmosphere of 'Adoration' which surrounded him during his life-time, and which still today surrounds his name. But adoration can be a very complicated emotion, composed of many different psychological elements which have nothing to do with a truly worthwhile objective evaluation. –KS

[15] Genetic links with Chopin are constantly apparent in the works of Glinka, Balakirev, Serov (the composer and critic), their successors, Rimsky-Korsakov, Glazunov and Lyadov, and, in the music of our own time, Rakhmaninov and, above all, Skryabin (even in his final 'futurist' inspirations). Those interested are referred to Russian musical bibliographies, memoirs, correspondence, criticisms, etc., and among others, the exceedingly interesting memoirs of Rimsky-Korsakov: *My Musical Life* [translated by Judah A. Joffe, first published by Alfred A. Knopf (1923), and subsequently by Ernst Eulenburg Ltd (1974)]. –KS

He unconsciously taught them how a primitive song or folkdance could become a work of art of universal significance when transformed by the alchemy of genius with an instinctive musical knowledge (as opposed to an acquired 'technique' which blunders helplessly through a series of mathematical formulae). He showed them how to proceed from a narrow parochialism to a vast new world in which their music, liberated from the mighty aegis of Bach and Beethoven could still be both great and truly original, with its own yardsticks and scales of values. Finally Chopin's inexpressibly subtle harmony revealed the way the strange foundations of their unsettled and magical exoticism could be laid.

We, on the other hand, could only mount a jealous guard over the treasures he left us, even though we really had no idea what to do with them. We stubbornly made of him an inviolable national taboo, imprisoned on raised altars in cumbrous golden monstrances, and in so doing failed to realise that his works were like living flowers, capable of bearing fruit filled with mighty, fertile, life-giving strength.

The great period of Polish music began and ended with Chopin. The music of the second half of the nineteenth century lost all organic connection with him. Furthermore, music also lost contact with the living depths of the nation's soul. In this respect music trailed far behind the chariot of literature, which, although not so dazzling as that of the great Romantic period, at least accompanied the nation faithfully along her thorny path. Her inner life was stubbornly recorded in an ethnically distinctive literature until at last the undeniably great art of Wyspiański,[16] Kaspro-

[16] Stanisław Wyspiański (1869–1907) was born in Kraków and studied there at the Jagiellonian University and the School of Fine Arts. He is remembered both for his paintings (especially those of children) and his dramas, the most celebrated of which is *Wesele (The Wedding)*. Szymanowski drew on the drama *Achilles* for the words of *Penthesilea* (Op. 18), a song for voice and orchestra. He also used Wyspiański's translation of *Veni Creator* in his setting for solo voice, chorus and orchestra, composed in 1930.

wicz,[17] and Żeromski[18] blazed up at the dawn of the present century.

How can one explain the fact that when we think of contemporary poetry, and that of the very recent past, the name of the author of *Król Duch*[19] automatically springs to mind? Why, on the other hand, is there nothing in the music of the recent past to suggest that Fryderyk Chopin

[17] Jan Kasprowicz (1860–1925) was born in the Prussian sector of occupied Poland, and was educated in Germany. He eventually became professor of comparative religion at Lwów. He was responsible for numerous translations into Polish from English, although his reputation now rests upon his poetic works. Szymanowski drew on his free-verse hymns *To the Perishing World* and *Salve Regina* in *Three Fragments* (Op. 5).

[18] Stefan Żeromski (1864–1925), novelist and dramatist. He wished Szymanowski to write incidental music for his drama *Sułkowski* in 1910, but the composer withdrew from the project at an early stage. Żeromski's chief works are the novels *Ludzie Bezdomni* (*Homeless People*), *Popioły* (*Ashes*), *Wierna Rzeka* (*The Faithful River*) and *Przedwiośnie* (*Before the Spring*).

[19] Juliusz Słowacki. The son of a professor of literature, he was born in Krzemieniec, Volhynia, in 1809. He spent most of his youth in Wilno, and graduated in law from the university there. He worked in the Ministry of Finance in Warsaw during the years 1829–30, after which he served as a diplomatic courier to the Revolutionary Government. He settled in Paris in 1832 after the collapse of the 1830–31 rebellion, and subsequently travelled widely, visiting Germany, Switzerland, Greece, Egypt, the Holy Land and Lebanon. He returned briefly to the Prussian sector of Poland during the 1848 Revolution, and died of consumption in Paris the following year. He is recognised as one of the great Polish Romantics, although his works draw on the example of Shakespeare, Calderon, Lope de Vega and old, mainly Baroque, Polish poetry. His dramas include *Kordian* (1834), *Balladyna* (1834), *Mazeppa* (1839), *Lilla Veneda* (1839) and the unfinished *Samuel Zborowski*. His later poetic works, of which *Król Duch* (*King Spirit*) is the most celebrated, are symbolist in technique and mystical in tone. In *Król Duch*, Słowacki attempted to recreate Poland in his imagination through the operation of the King Spirit which had informed the hearts and minds of leaders, monarchs and saints in preceding ages. Because of the relatively inaccessible nature of the poetic language, Słowacki's work was misunderstood and in the middle years of the nineteenth century, he was partially eclipsed by Mickiewicz (*cf.* note 16, pp. 171–72). During the 'Young Poland' era, however, the prophetic elements in his work led to a revaluation which considerably enhanced his reputation. He exerted a strong influence on writers working at the turn of the century, most notably Tadeusz Miciński, Szymanowski's own favourite 'Young Poland' poet.

ever existed? And by this, I do not refer to 'influences' in the
ordinary plagiaristic sense of the word, although it would be
pleasing to discover in the highly typical musical epigonism
that has prevailed since his time just a shadow of his original
greatness, just a distant echo of his mighty wings beating in
the vastness of infinity.

In the second half of the nineteenth century there certainly seemed to be new hope for our music on the horizon,
resulting mainly from the emergence of the talent of Stanisław Moniuszko.[20] It once again seemed that firm
foundations were being laid in the quicksands of our
musical creativity. Incidentally this composer undoubtedly
deserves a large-scale, exhaustive monograph, although it
looks as though we are going to have to wait a long time for
this to appear.[21]

The task of the author of such a biography would be not
only the critical examination of the peculiarities and traits
of the internal structure of his music and the accurate
sketching of a spiritual portrait. He would also eventually
have to establish his position in the history of our music,
demonstrating the links which bound him to the past and

[20] Stanisław Moniuszko was born on 5 May 1819, in Ubiel, near Minsk. He
was the son of a landowner, Czesław Moniuszko, and received his earliest
musical training at home. When the family moved to Warsaw in 1827, he
continued his studies with the organist, August Freyer (1803–83). The
family returned to Minsk before the outbreak of the 1830 revolution, and
Moniusko continued his studies there and, from 1837–40, in Berlin. He
moved to Wilno (Vilnius) in 1840, where he worked as an organist and
teacher of piano and theory. His correspondence from these years provides
valuable insights into the state of musical life in the provinces. He moved to
Warsaw in 1858 after the success of the opera *Halka*, and died there on
4 June 1872. His chief works include the operas *Straszny Dwór* (*The Haunted
Manor*), *Hrabina* (*The Countess*) and *Flis* (*The Raftsman*). He also composed
numerous songs which formed the backbone of the Polish domestic
repertory for decades, several religious works, including motets and a Mass,
and the concert overture *Bajka* (*Winter's Tale*).

[21] At the time Szymanowski wrote this article, there was indeed no extended
study of Moniuszko's life and work in existence. The first to appear, by
Zdzisław Jachimecki, was published in 1921, and another study, by Henryk
Opieński, came out in 1924.

describing the extent and nature of his influence on later composers.

For example, it now seems that Moniuszko was also something of an isolated phenomenon, like his great predecessor. There is almost no connection between him and Chopin, or at least there is no clear and unambiguous element of his work which permits us to define such a connection. Could this be attributed to his having an exuberant artistic personality? It seems not. Many of his admittedly tasteful folk-song harmonisations reveal a characteristically Germanic professorial manner, acquired during his brief studies in Berlin, while the stage works are marked by symptoms of an addiction to Italian opera which are at odds with a fundamentally Polish, and at times somewhat sickly, sentimentality. Nevertheless, the excessively gruff 'nobility' and the idyllic 'folkiness' of *Halka* may easily be forgiven when weighed against those lengthy sections which are marked by real dramatic tension or truly beautiful lyricism.

In the end he cannot be classed with Chopin, and it is not just because of that notorious lack of 'musical knowledge' to which all his artistic failures are usually attributed.

(That wretched 'musical knowledge' again, about which we hear so much that is so wrong-headed in this country! When will it be understood that it is not a ready-made 'apparatus' sold in conservatories and academies through the operation of which an infinite series of operas and symphonies can be produced? When will it be understood that the tools of a composer's creativity have to be forged through his own toil and endurance, and that any conservatory will only give elementary guidelines in matters of creativity? When will it be understood that 'musical knowledge' and artistic knowledge in particular is not an objective value divorced from a work of art? On the contrary, it is a highly subjective, unerring sense of form so conceived that it is organically connected with the work of art as a whole. A brief list of 'theoretical formulae' serves as a mere prop and is scarcely adequate as the basis for such knowledge, and it is possible that Moniuszko really did not possess such all-embracing musical knowledge.)

He also lacked that inner greatness, that creative fanaticism characteristic of Chopin and so necessary before a truly great, universal art can come into being.

The plots of most of his stage-works are arbitrary, not to say incoherent, in nature, and often operate at a very naive intellectual level. This, and the very poor texts of many of his often exquisite songs are symptomatic of a perpetually juvenile immaturity in his art, indicative of an insufficient awareness of his tasks and aims. As in the case of Chopin, but for different reasons, Moniuszko's huge, heaven-sent talent also remained an isolated fragment in the history of our culture. He remained our private property, making no impression on the history of art in general, as a consequence of which he failed to lay foundations for a national school of music as Glinka had done in Russia.

In spite of the undoubted value of his art, he did not widen our horizons or open up new ways forward, and for this reason he also became no more than another relic of the past. This became apparent in the next generation when Żeleński[22] and Noskowski[23] wielded the musical sceptre. Strictly speaking, neither composer was an heir of

[22] Władysław Żeleński was born on 6 July 1837, near Kraków. He was a composer, pianist, organist and teacher. He initially studied music in Kraków and Prague before going on to the Paris Conservatoire. On his return to Poland, he took up a teaching post at the Musical Institute in Warsaw. In 1881 he became director of the conservatory run by the Kraków Musical Society. He died on 23 January 1921. His works include the operas *Goplana, Janek, Konrad Wallenrod,* and *Stara baśń (The Old Fairy-tale),* the orchestral works *Trauerklänge* and *W Tatrach (In the Tatry),* and numerous songs and piano pieces.

[23] Zygmunt Noskowski was born on 2 May 1846 in Warsaw. He trained at the Musical Institute before going on to Berlin to complete his studies. From 1880 he was active in Warsaw as conductor of the Musical Society's concerts, and from 1888 he held a teaching post at the Musical Institute in which capacity he trained most of the composers of the next generation. Szymanowski himself received lessons in composition from him. His works include three symphonies, the symphonic poem *Step,* the opera *Livia Quintilla,* songs and choral works.

Moniuszko. Neither constituted a link in an evolutionary chain, and here again it cannot be said that this resulted from their possession of exuberant creative personalities. On the contrary, the artistic level of their work was markedly lower than that of Moniuszko's music, not merely in absolute artistic terms but also in their use of ethnic peculiarities. In other words, we have arrived at that period of our musical history in which National Art became a standard prerequisite, and its creation almost a patriotic obligation.

That national character, when it is not a consequence of some kind of gift or individual talent, must inevitably be alien, and only loosely connected with a work of art. From this point of view, the work of the aforementioned composers is very typical. They were both educated in the rigorous Germanic tradition, and throughout their lives this left an indelible mark on their compositions even though there were differences of approach. Żeleński was endowed with a more dramatic temperament, and early in his career turned to the stage, attempting to marry the Wagnerian operatic tradition with a somewhat forced Polish folk-style. He was more or less successful, depending on the greater or lesser value of each individual dramatic concept. In general, however, such a style will always be a rather unstable artistic alloy, and can hardly be considered a spontaneous organic unity. In contrast, Noskowski was primarily a symphonist who attempted in vain to conceal the strict, set features of the correct academic behind the mask of Polish folkloristic melodies and harmonies. That organic lack of style apparent in the works of both composers, but especially those of Noskowski, resulted in their seeming to be out of sympathy with the instinctive musical feeling of the nation. Apart from a few works (e.g., *Step* [*The Steppe*], *Spiewnik dla dzieci* [*Songbook for Children*], and some of his other songs), Noskowski's music was never popular in the best sense of the word, in spite of its undeniable artistic value. It floated on and off our stages and concert platforms like a sleepy dream, fading gradually in the mists of time.

That was 'yesterday'. It is still too soon to speak of the music of today, and also too difficult to take our bearings amidst the welter of conflicting ideas, contradictions, squabbles and animosity. In any case, we are concerned not with a critique of contemporary music so much as an examination of the general, social background behind the history of Polish music, and behind the formation of those musical opinions which circulate amongst the general public in the field of criticism. It was with this aim that some of the most important factors which have a bearing on the history of Polish music during the most recent period of our national life – the period of captivity – have been mentioned in this rough sketch. They were intentionally presented so as to demonstrate clearly the tenuous and arbitrary nature of the connections existing between Polish music and Polish culture in general.

It is my conviction that Polish music has been typified by intermittent manifestations of genius, ranging from the blazing genius of Chopin, to the bright talent of Moniuszko, and latterly to the craft of a number of markedly lesser lights. These creative manifestations have not formed a single sustained process of development, as in the case of Germany, and indeed as has been the case in Polish literature. Because of this, our music is incapable of inspiring either a genuine following among the public, genuine opinion, or a sound artistic criticism which reacts warmly, faithfully and with subtlety to music's inner vicissitudes, be they failures or undeniable successes. Professional music criticism, as well as the public opinion it has done much to confuse, is clearly moving in the wrong direction. It makes demands which cannot be met, and also refuses to acknowledge anything of value that by chance falls outside its own range of tenets. Such a state of affairs undoubtedly has an inhibiting effect upon the free, independent development of artistic creativity within our society, and in view of this, a sense of responsibility for the fate of art should constantly govern the pens of our appointed judges.

In many areas of our cultural life, and consequently in

our opinions concerning music, we must effect a fundamental reconstruction of certain intellectual and emotional
habits which still linger from the pre-war era of captivity.
This is extremely important in the present critical time,
when the whole nation is intoxicated with the feeling of
freedom. That is a feeling which should be permitted to
penetrate to the depths of our self-awareness, and in so
doing, all the sinister ghosts of the past should be laid to rest
without remorse. At such a time, we must all become active
and creative; we must all contribute to the formation of that
imperative, driving force which will decide the route we
should now take. Whatever happens, all of us today are
more or less consciously building the foundations of the
future.

Our music must recover its age-old rights: absolute freedom, and complete liberation from the yoke of 'yesterday's'
norms and precepts of creativity. Let us be nationalistic in
the cultivation of our ethnic peculiarities, but let this
nationalism aspire without fear to that state in which its
elevated values become all-embracing. Let us be 'nationalistic', but not 'provincial'. Let us sweep aside 'yesterday's
dams', stubbornly erected to keep us isolated from influences which were alien to us. We should not fear 'today';
after all, we have iron constitutions and hard knuckles.[24]

Let all streams springing from universal art mingle freely
with ours: may they impregnate, differentiate and transform
it in accordance with its particular attributes.

We ought not to lose organic connection with universal
culture, because it is only on such a plane that a truly great,
living art, including nationalistic music, can flourish.

We once possessed precisely this type of music in the work
of Chopin.

I know that these observations will meet with a sharp
rejoinder not only from our critics, but also the majority of
our musicians. *N'importe!* I shall always assert stubbornly that

---

[24] This refers to the defeat inflicted on the Russian army by the Poles in the
summer months of 1920.

Polish national music is not the grim phantom of a polonaise or mazurka, nor a fugue on 'Chmielu zielony', nor a blunt instrument for belabouring the heads of 'ideological' enemies. It is rather the lonely song, joyous and free, of a nightingale singing spontaneously in the fragrant Polish May nights.[25]

---

[25] This is perhaps a reference both to Szymanowski's own nightingale in the second of the *Songs of a Fairy Princess* (Op. 31) and to his evocation of a May night in the First Violin Concerto (Op. 35).

'My Splendid Isolation'

First published in *Kurier Polski* on 26 November 1922.

Quotations in foreign languages, such as the expression *Pathos der Distanz* which I used in a recent interview on contemporary music, sometimes cause so much misunderstanding that I should like to state from the outset that my preferred Polish rendering of my beautiful English title[1] is 'wspaniałe odosobnienie' [splendid isolation], or even perhaps 'osamotnienie' [isolation].

Both macaronics originate in domains far removed from music, yet they illustrate clearly my position in relation to the majority of our critics today. Because in essence, the extreme 'pathetic distance' (and my attitude to musical questions in general and those of Poland in particular is marked by 'pathos') dividing my personal conception of musical values from the concepts that have currency among our critics must by its very nature lead to my being set apart in 'splendid isolation'. I call it 'splendid', because I presume that it is not open to doubt that when someone expresses certain opinions stubbornly and fanatically, he must be convinced to the depths of his being of the 'rightness' of those opinions. In a sense he must feel himself to be possessed of an absolute 'truth'. I do not for one moment doubt that my opponents also firmly believe their opinions

---

[1] The title is in English in the original. The expression was first used in a speech given in the Canadian House of Commons by Sir George Foster (1847–1931) on 16 January 1896: 'In these somewhat troublesome days when the great Mother Empire stands splendidly isolated in Europe.' It was employed shortly afterwards by Lord Goschen (1831–1907) during a speech given at Lewes on 26 February 1896: 'We have stood alone in that which is called isolation – our splendid isolation, as one of our colonial friends was good enough to call it'.

to be correct, and so I suppose it will be for posterity to decide the issue after we are gone.

For the present, however, the storms which have blown up over my recent interview oblige me to elucidate a number of fundamental matters to avoid further, highly disagreeable misunderstandings.

When I state that our critics overlook the musical 'distance' that of necessity separates them from myself, I mean that they base their judgement of my work on totally inappropriate premises. They simply do not understand it. Incidentally, I do not think it possible in general to make a valid judgement of a new work after only one hearing, yet in Poland this constantly occurs. Furthermore, it is an obvious naivety to believe that there is an unchanging mathematical formula, an eternal criterion, by which it is possible to evaluate every work of art or music through the centuries. The music of Debussy, judged by the standards of Palestrina, would be *pure nonsense.*[2] Yet there must be few, apart from our own little band of Polish critics, who doubt that Debussy's music really is Art with a capital A. In other words there is a certain degree of musico-intellectual consciousness capable both of experiencing an artistic feeling roused by this art and of conceiving its objective value in a purely rational way, that is to say, of forming a consciously critical attitude towards it. It is not a case of this level being higher or lower than the level on which we once based our notions of the value of Wagner; it is simply different. And this is really the heart of the matter. Mr Rytel refers with gay abandon to the question of 'spiritual values', and denies the existence of such values in the music of Stravinsky, Debussy and Ravel. But this is a debatable point, as the awareness of these values depends precisely on the ability to attain a particular degree of understanding. As far as I am concerned, Debussy's *Nocturnes* and *Pelléas et Mélisande* express greater 'spirituality' than Bruckner's Ninth Symphony, a vast musical monstrosity which, for my sins, I recently had to

[2] In English in Szymanowski's text.

sit through at the Philharmonia. Yet Bruckner's work is quite highly revered by our critics, and this I can only suppose is because it was born on the banks of the Danube rather than the Seine. Furthermore (and herein lies its 'spiritual depth') – it is dedicated to the unfortunate Almighty, to his everlasting ennui (*sic!*).

The problem then is how to attain an appropriate 'degree' of musical understanding. It is in effect a pointless waste of time to judge outstanding contemporary works, and especially those from Russia and France, by the standards of 'yesterday's' German music, since these works, quite apart from the extent of each composer's talent, were clearly written as a fully conscious protest against German music, as a categorical imperative in the discovery of a new musical base, founded on completely different principles.

We are approaching the heart of the matter. Obviously the objective value of German music during the period extending from Bach to Wagner is not open to question (although there is room for a 'revaluation' of certain judgements which have now become 'traditional'). But there is a difficulty here: we often have to deny ourselves the greatest treasures, no matter how marvellous they be, in order to discover our own. It is just such a denial that has resulted in the abundant development of contemporary music in France and Russia.

Admittedly, one could say that such a development is attributable to the simultaneous appearance of many outstanding creative talents. But this argument is only partially valid. First, a great creative talent is not just a machine turning out works of art; by the character of his works he expresses a fundamental relationship to art in general. Furthermore, many an outstanding talent, one which might have become distinguished in his field, has withered and fallen silent prematurely in the sterile, suffocating atmosphere surrounding him. And it is precisely such a stifling atmosphere which prevails throughout Polish society. Since I wish to clear the air, and since I fully recognise (and here I unmask myself completely before my opponents) the

sacrificial efforts of those in both the East and West who
have shifted music from its deadlock, I now declare that the
healthy development of Polish music depends exclusively
on the degrees to which we succeed in freeing ourselves
from the powerful embrace of that traditional 'better' and
'best' German music. For myself, and for those who understand me, that music with all its – *horribile dictu* – 'spiritual
depth' is useless, redundant, and a damming-up of all
possibilities of further development.

I say 'those who understand me', because individual
voices have reached me in my present 'splendid isolation',
agreeing with the position which I have adopted. Indeed, if
I regret anything, it is only that in my much discussed
'interview', I failed to state categorically that such sup-
porters now exist and are becoming more numerous. This is
my only 'démenti' concerning that interview, and I confess
to it with all due contrition. This apart, I have no pangs of
conscience, since I consider such pangs to be 'indecent', as
Nietzsche would have said.

Again I find I have written that famous name! And just in
time to remind my readers that fifty years ago that German
dreamed of a 'wicked, capricious, southern' music, a music
that had rid itself completely of the influence of the 'fatherland' – 'Europas Flachland' – in other words, a music which
had escaped from the dull flatlands of Germany, and dull is
an especially apt word if we go on to speak of modern
German music! Nietzsche centred his yearnings, not altogether aptly, on *Carmen*.[3] It is, indeed, a glorious work, but
how much more would he have rejoiced had he heard
Debussy's *Ibéria* or *Nocturnes*.

Nor is there any point in reproaching me on account of
those German influences which were evident at a certain
stage of my career, for I am more acutely aware of them than
any critic. I know all too well the story of my bitter struggle
with the vampire of convention, of how I finally succeeded

---

[3] *Cf. The Case of Wagner*, Preface, sections 1–3; *Beyond Good and Evil*,
Aphorism 254.

in strangling the spectre which had tried to strangle me. Yet
it is very strange that almost automatically from the moment
of my 'liberation', when I found my own two feet, I fell in the
esteem of the majority of our respected reviewers, who *en
masse* accused me of being subject to new 'influences', and
this time those of the Jewish-Russo-Franco 'futurists'.

This fact was clearly reflected in the rejoinder to my
interview published by Rytel in *Gazeta Warszawska*. In principle, I would prefer to say nothing about this article since
we use two different languages when speaking about music,
but the extent to which he misunderstands my music at
the present time is striking. As far as Rytel is concerned,
the content of my music (not, God forbid, its 'spiritual'
content – for this it certainly does not have – but just its
formal content) may be described in its entirety in terms of
influences which every so often change as it were mechanically from one composer to another.

In other words, Strauss, Reger, and even – just imagine
it! – Schoenberg, whose music I detest. Subsequently we
have the 'new phase': Debussy, Ravel, Stravinsky, etc., etc.

He does not see my real face behind these masks, which,
one after another, he would have me wear, and asserts that
I really do not have a face of my own at all. From such a
position, 'his' position, he is justified in speaking of 'my
indefinable aspirations towards ideally good music'. But this
is only from his position, for my aspirations are precisely
defined, and it is only a question of whether the greater or
lesser extent of my abilities will permit me to realise my
aspirations in my music. The only thing that consoles me is
that those contemporary composers for whom I have a high
regard are also out of favour with Mr Rytel. In the same
feuilleton, he declares Stravinsky's work to be 'beyond the
pale of music possessing spiritual values', while Debussy and
Ravel are 'merely interesting. Nothing more!'

The other response illicited by my interview was Stanisław
Niewiadomski's feuilleton, published in *Rzeczpospolita* on
the 19th of the present month and entitled 'Magdalena
Samozwaniec on Contemporary Music'. This admittedly

humorous article contains, however, a couple of rather problematic passages. For example, I do not understand the unequivocal allusion to a certain 'sheltered retreat', about which one does not speak in polite society.[4] What connection is there between that retreat and my undoubtedly extreme opinions on music? And then, why does this distinguished author devote so much space to Negro music; it has no bearing on my own work, although I find it 'enchanting'. It was Antonín Dvořák, a composer very much my senior, and, I believe, one quite highly esteemed by Mr Niewiadomski, who first drew widely on this music in one of his symphonies. It is now thirty years since that 'serious' musician turned his attention to it – so why shouldn't American composers do so today?! It did not occur to me that my rather superficial remarks about current musical attitudes in the United States would strike the author of that feuilleton as being so very funny.

Another observation, this time of a fundamental nature: I do not know to what extent Magdalena Samozwaniec, the authoress of an extremely witty pamphlet 'Na ustach grzechu' ('On the Lips of Sin'),[5] is musical. But I do know on the basis of this little booklet that she is a highly intelligent and cultured lady. Could it be possible that, along with Mr Niewiadomski, she believes that all my work falls into the same category as the *second-class*[6] literature which she so wittily and so wisely caricatured? Or has she been unwittingly drawn into a game going on behind her back?

---

[4] There is indeed no obvious connection between Szymanowski's views on music and the 'sheltered retreat' mentioned here. The expression appeared in Niewiadomski's parody of Samozwaniec's method because he could not resist cracking a lavatorial joke: 'Pathos der Distanz is the terrible emotion which arises in those moments when a man is taken unawares by a powerful compulsion to shut himself away in some sort of sheltered retreat and distance does not permit this [...].'   *Pisma Muzyczne*, p. 65.

[5] This was a parody of a pretentious novel, purporting to deal with elevated matters.

[6] In English in the original.

At least, I can have no doubt in this respect concerning Mr Niewiadomski. I would even go so far as to say that his objectively written article is the first frank critique, not only of my opinions, but also of my music. It cannot be taken in any other way.

And now my final observation – a footnote to the present article. I cannot understand why my determined and unambiguous stand against German music and its influence on our culture should not be recognised for its true worth by the reviewers of such papers as *Gazeta Warszawska* and *Rzeczpospolita.*[7]

---

[7] Both papers supported the nationalist stance of the Christian Union for National Solidarity.

'I Will Leave
My Rocky Entrenchment ....'
Gaetano di Gaeta[1]

First published in *Rzeczpospolita* on 8 January 1923

'I will leave my rocky entrenchment; I will descend unarmed to the valley and the camp of my grim enemies.' I do this, however, not because of a dangerous breach in my defences resulting from two recently unleashed high calibre projectiles in the form of feuilletons by Messrs Niewiadomski and Rytel. Nor do I carry a white flag and want to parley. Instead I am 'descending' to the valley, brimming over with audacity and demonic pride, or so my 'combatants' claim, but at any rate conscious of my impertinence in that I, a wandering tramp and minstrel of no clearly defined occupation, apart from an ability to scribble a note or two on paper if left in reasonable peace and quiet, am taking on two professors from the most elevated music college in the land! As befits an artist who is confronted by the nibs of his critics' pens, I descend unarmed, but not in fear and trembling, having learnt from the experience of history that a poisoned pen, for all its scabrous ink, has never inflicted a mortal wound on an honest artist!

Too much time has elapsed since the appearance of both the above-cited phillipics for me to polemicise further on

[1] Cajetan (Tommaso de Vio), known as Gaetano di Gaeta after his birthplace, was born in 1468/69 and died in Rome in 1534. He was a Catholic theologian of the Thomist school. He defended papal authority against the schismatic council of Pisa (1511), but urged church reform at the Fifth Lateran Council. He was cardinalised by Pope Leo X in 1517, and the following year was responsible for the examination of Luther at Augsburg. He issued the Bull *Exsurge Domine*, condemning Luther, in 1520. His most important theological work was a commentary on the *Summa*.

their factual contents and respective arguments. In any case, as I have already stated, it would be a fundamentally pointless exercise because of the diametrically opposed positions taken up by my adversaries and myself regarding the question of contemporary music.

I am concerned with another matter. The 'true likeness' of that passionate antipathy which my respected opponents feel for me is becoming increasingly clear from the mounting torrents of words fulminating against my 'revolutionary revelations' published in *Rzeczpospolita* and *Gazeta Warszawska*. This antipathy arises from a reaction against my insufficiently law-abiding musical convictions, opinions, predilections and intentions, as well as my seditious activities as a composer. It may even have to do with the shameful fact that I exist within Poland and within the context of Polish musical culture. Each word aimed at me seems to complain tearfully and peevishly that with the untimely emergence both of myself and my ideas, drawn from God knows where, I have dared to stir up and disturb the blissfully idyllic Garden of Eden which has existed here for centuries. Rytel's pronouncements in particular, with their smack of papal infallibility, leave the reader in no doubt as to the 'intrusive' nature of my presence in Poland.

At this point I must make it clear, and in so doing beg the pardons of both my esteemed 'antipathisers' (if it is possible so to term the converse of 'sympathisers'), that in spite of everything I by no means feel myself to be a musical intruder in Poland. And if, from sheer audacity, I am tempted to make one more sortie into the enemy-camp, it is not to defend myself, but only to show those increasingly numerous people for whom I am not an intruder 'the true likeness' of that antipathy in its proper light. It is possible to draw more than one analogy with the antipathy of those who try to fight the development of new, free forms of beauty in other fields of art. In the words of an Eastern sage: 'When you have identified your enemy, you have half vanquished him'.

Fate itself has placed between the esteemed critic of
Rzeczpospolita and myself an impenetrable wall, namely our
difference in age. We belong to two different musical generations. In short, the formative musical experiences of
Stanislaw Niewiadomski and myself took place in completely different atmospheres. It is in youth that so many of
the ineradicable lines which furrow the face of the artist
begin to appear. Although he often strays into distant,
foreign realms, he always returns to give a more perfect,
mature form to the same dreams and visions of a never-
fading beauty which did not flower fully in childhood.

Certainly it is with an increasingly melancholy smile that I
find myself beginning to accept the truly cynical compliment that I still belong to 'Young Poland in Music'. But it is
in just such flattery that the poisonous sting is hidden.
Polish custom seems to demand that, regardless of my
respectable and venerable old age, I be continually marked
down as a fractious futurist, an uncouth Józio, a bumpkin
who, in the words of Boy,[2] 'always gets it wrong' – some-one
like Wat and Mtodżieniec,[3] in spite of my obstinate and
dramatic assurances that I have never dreamed of such far-
reaching reforms in Polish life as dreamed of by these
promising young men. I should be completely satisfied if I
succeeded in breaking the deadlock of Polish music, and
shaking it out of its lethargy.

I fear that Niewiadomski has also undergone this futurist
hypnosis, and this very probably prevents him from coming
to an understanding of my music, which cannot be as
diabolically terrible as Mr Rytel paints it.

---

[2] Reference to a satirical verse by the poet, translator and critic, Tadeusz
Boy Żelenski (1874–1941), usually known simply as 'Boy'. The passage
which Szymanowski had in mind reads as follows: 'And Józio was a modernist. (A Modernist – a bumpkin who always gets it wrong; he sticks to every
stupidity and always likes to know better.)'

[3] Aleksander Wat and Stanisław Młodożeniec were futurists, active mainly
in the years 1914–20. Their work anticipated that of the Kraków avant-
garde of the 1920s.

But the dispute between myself and the critic of *Rzeczpo-spolita* does not just involve my music. The matter goes very much deeper. What causes offence here is contemporary music in its entirety, and in particular that music which so suddenly and abundantly flourished without regard for the inviolable 'taboo' of good old German music. We are dealing with an art that is not merely alien and hostile in Mr Niewiadomski's eyes, but one which seems to him to be rushing in a frenzy of suicidal madness towards an ominous abyss of certain self-destruction.

Even though he is able to place yesterday's modernists, Strauss and Reger, without difficulty within the framework of what I call the 'traditional musical aesthetic', that is the line extending from Bach, through Brahms to Reger, and from Beethoven, through Wagner to Strauss (what a sad decresqendo in these two series of names!); even though he is able to extend the lines to embrace the rather limited talents of Schreker and Busoni (and Busoni himself has admitted this limitation to a certain extent in one of his musical statements), and even – horror of horrors! – Arnold Schoenberg himself, that tragic Ahasuerus,[4] the Jew eternally wandering after delusive mirages of unattainable beauty;[5] even though he can accommodate all these composers, he finds the path to an untraditional art like Debussy's, which blossoms suddenly like a flower and which is so uncanny in its simplicity, barred for ever.

It is an art which is either understood and felt or is not – and that is the end of the matter. It is a seemingly dispassionate art the origins of which lie deep beneath the stormy, surging billows on the surface. It is an art which, unlike that

[4] Ahasuerus, the legendary Jew who refused to help Christ carry the cross to Golgotha, as a consequence of which he was condemned to wander the world until Judgement Day.

[5] It is an astonishing fact that Rytel, who sees a similarity (irony of ironies!) between 'Maurice' Ravel (who in spite of Rytel's declaration to the contrary is by no means Jewish) and 'Moritz' Moszkowski, is able to give his unqualified seal of approval to the German futurists, Schreker and Busoni! There is in this simple recital of facts much grist to the mill. –KS

of Richard Strauss, is not to be viewed through the hot, sooty spectacles of human temperaments and passions. It is an art which has some of the characteristics of natural pheno- mena: the deeps of the sea, the loftiness of mountain peaks, and the mysterious quiet of the forest, as one of our most subtle and cultured critics so beautifully expressed it recently.[6]

There can be no doubt that from the formal point of view Debussy's music is not indebted to any musical traditions, nor are there good or bad inherited patterns and habits in his art. In his originality and consciousness of his own style, he is unquestionably one of the world's most amazing composers. I suppose the only 'tradition' discernible in his music is his uncanny lucidity of thought and transparent depth, qualities peculiar to all French art, the art of the most cultured race in the world.

Fate has ordained that in Poland today, I am the only composer to express these 'liberating' ideas in his artistic works. But I play a dual role and am also one of the few theoretical guardians who speaks fervently on their behalf. In opposing my art and ideas in the way he does, Niewia- domski is fighting an outward and visible symbol of the musical 'futurism' he hates so much. When he aims the poison of his pen, often concealed by flowery compliments, at my heart, he seems to be pointing at the whole of contemporary art. But of course this is a groundless delusion!

Yet of my opponents Niewiadomski is the only one of any importance in that he undoubtedly is concerned with real and fundamental matters: the 'to be or not to be' of contem- porary music. Undoubtedly the well-nigh tragic shadow of the 'pathos of distance' falls across our mutual relationship (and I trust that Niewiadomski now understands that in employing this expression I do not intend to cause him any

---

[6] Incidentally he was roundly condemned by certain of his less subtle and cultured colleagues, for at bottom the guild hates its Hans Sachses no less than its Beckmessers! –KS

offence): he is not only an artist, but a gifted writer who is conscious of his metier and who takes complete responsibility for his written thoughts. Indeed, I believe that, apart from moments of impatience which befall me as well, his criticism flows from deep convictions and ideological motives.

The truth is that in a certain sense I foresee a 'Twilight of the Idols'[7] and also a twilight of the true gods whom this artist-musician, my senior, has worshipped all his life. It is also true to say that this senior artist-musician has closed his eyes to the true import of my work, as he does not wish to look deeply into the purity and honesty of my intentions. I am not just an exponent of the hated 'musical futurism'. I am also a Polish artist. From the moment that I was able to be objective about German music, from the moment I found my hands were happily freed from its influence (even though it is true that it has always inspired in me a deep, albeit cold admiration), a much purer stream of Polishness began to run through my music. I do not refer here to the Polishness of the painted wycinanka,[8] the nobleman's kontusz,[9] but to that sensitivity which is profoundly and quintessentially Polish. Yet Niewiadomski stubbornly denies that this attribute exists.

My works may be called *Métopes, Masques* or *Mythes*:[10] they may be good or bad music, but there can be no doubt that they were written by a Pole. It is precisely this characteristic

---

[7] A late work by Nietzsche: *Götzen-Dämmerung, oder Wie man mit dem Hammer philosophiert* (*Twilight of the Idols, or How to Philosophise with a Hammer*), 1889.

[8] *Cf.* note 12 on p. 84.

[9] Cloak traditionally worn by a Polish nobleman.

[10] Titles of three instrumental works composed by Szymanowski during the early years of the First World War. *Métopes* (Op. 29) and *Masques* (Op. 34) each consist of three piano pieces. The first cycle is based on scenes from *The Odyssey*, while the second consists of three very different character sketches. *Mythes* (Op. 30) is a series of three pieces for violin and piano, and evokes scenes from Greek mythology. All three works are splendid examples of Szymanowski's mature idiom.

which French writers have strongly emphasised. Some French critics have gone further still: it is they who, with uncanny perspicacity, sense that in each of my new clearly defined pieces, I pay hommage, humbly but fervently, to Fryderyk Chopin. It is his music which, with the dawning of each new day, I venerate ever more highly and with an ever deepening understanding, attempting, as far as I can, to relate my own work to what is for me the only Polish musical tradition.

Niewiadomski closes his eyes to my Polishness. Because of the inveterate confusion of artistic and political ideas which prevails amongst many of our critics, and not just our music critics, he cannot associate my Polishness with the seemingly extreme nature of my ideas. I on the other hand see that the only chance we have of freeing our music from its foreign fetters lies precisely in this extremism.

Consequently one should not seek to find cosmopolitanism, still worse, internationalism, in my music. It is possible only to find 'Europeanism' there, and this is not a negation of its Polish qualities; we have a right to be European. Today's Polishness is truly different from that of yesterday: it is free. The consciousness of that freedom penetrates to the depths of my being; it is the basis of my work, in effect my inner reality, and no traditionalism, born in captivity, can deprive me of it.

In the tangled web of contradictions and seeming inconsistencies, it appears that there is no one plane upon which our struggle over contemporary music could be settled in a rational, logical manner, in the way that one can solve an algebraic question. We have to go deeper, relying on intuition, that unerring instinct which cuts through the Gordian Knot of logical contradictions.

So let us try to go deeper. Reading between the lines of Niewiadomski's official indictments, I often have the feeling (although it may also be only an illusion), that at that deepest level, where his intuition as a real artist rather than a critic comes into play, Niewiadomski senses that which I shall call the deep seriousness of my work and the purity of my intentions – and is it possible to detect a note of sadness because rationally he does not want, or is unable, to answer the call of his intuition? Perhaps he even feels something akin to a quiet pang of conscience which, again, as a critic, he forcibly tries to stifle as he feverishly summons up arguments of enormous weight and unassailable proof, marshalling accusations and criticisms (both his own and those of other people), and leading his humble, obedient verbal army into battle against me, the exponent of a New Art that he finds alien and hostile.

For both our sakes, I sincerely wish my psychological excursion to be not just the illusory work of my imagination, but to be a help in bringing a hidden truth to light!

Part Two
ON FOLK-MUSIC
AND NATIONALISM

Antena
chez Karol Szymanowski

This was the last interview given by Szymanowski to a representative of the Polish press, most probably on the morning of 7 November 1936 before his final departure from Poland on the 'Nord Express' train in order to undergo medical treatment in France. His interviewer was Jerzy Freiheiter,[1] and the resulting text was published in *Antena*, the Polish equivalent of *Radio Times*, on 15 November 1936.

Karol Szymanowski's splendid ballet, *Harnasie*, which was a triumph in Prague and Paris, will shortly be staged in Hamburg. Polish Radio is broadcasting it in its entirety on 17 November at 20.00.[2] In connection with this event, one of our staff obtained the following interview with the composer:

'The literal quotations of folklore,' said Szymanowski, 'are an isolated case in *Harnasie*, and anyway are conditioned by the action. I don't suppose I shall do this again, as I am opposed to confining oneself to folklore.'

'But in your work it is not difficult to observe the tonal and rhythmic elements of Polish folk-song.'

'Yes, of course, but folklore is only significant for me as a fertilising agent. My aim is the creation of a Polish style, apparent from *Słopiewnie* onwards, in which there is not one

---

[1] Jerzy Freiheiter, a musicologist and music critic, trained with Adolf Chybiński and worked for Polish Radio until 1939. He was murdered by the Nazis in Lwów during the Second World War.

[2] This performance, by the Polish Radio Symphony Orchestra and Chorus with Maurycy Janowski (tenor), conducted by Grzegorz Fitelberg, was only the second complete concert performance of the work. The first had been given on 17 July 1936 at Kraków's Wawel Castle during a Festival of Polish Music.

jot of folklore,[3] similarly the Second Violin Concerto, Second Quartet and Fourth Symphony. In the mazurkas, connections with Tatra folklore appear, but these are loose, because in Podhale, there is no triple-time rhythm.'

'At this moment, you are not of course taking into account your elaborations of the *Kurpian Songs*?'[4]

'Of course not. They are elaborations of authentic folk-songs, and are similar to all the vocal sections and many of the instrumental parts of *Harnasie*, e.g., *Taniec Góralski* (*Mountaineers' Dance*) in the second act, with its traces of the Góral band. But artistic music must not necessarily draw on folklore. The national character of a composer does not depend on quotations from folk-music, the most splendid proof of this being the work of Chopin. This "drawing upon folk-music" which is attributed to me is much exaggerated, to say the least.'

---

[3] This is not strictly true. Apart from the use of the 'Sabała' motive in the first of the Mazurkas and the third song of *Słopiewnie*, Szymanowski also employed a Góral melody, exploited in *Harnasie*, as the subject for a fugue in the last movement of the Second String Quartet. In these instances, however, Szymanowski did not simply arrange the adopted folk-tunes, but made them the basis of sophisticated 'art' music.

[4] There are two sets of elaborations of Kurpian folk-songs, a set of six choral numbers (without opus number) and *Twelve Kurpian Songs* for voice and piano, Op. 58. Kurpie is a region of Poland, north-east of Warsaw. Szymanowski was not intimately acquainted at first hand with the culture of this district in the way in which he was with that of Podhale.

On Highland Music

This article, the autograph of which is dated 'Zakopane, 12 January 1924', appeared the following September in the Warsaw monthly *Pani* (*Lady*). It was commissioned by the editor of *Pani*, Stanisław Zmigryder (a pianist, music critic and the owner of the Warsaw fashion house 'Gustaw Zmigryder & Son'). The richly illustrated issue in which Szymanowski's article appeared was devoted to the mountain districts of Podhale and Zakopane, and also included a reproduction of the auto-graph of Szymanowski's elaboration of the mountain folk-song '*Idom se siuhaje*', later included in the ballet *Harnasie*.

During the initial discovery of Zakopane some thirty years ago, the first judicious newcomers from the Polish lowlands were so charmed by the Góral Highlanders' visual imagination, evident in their dress and adornments, and so enchanted by their unerring sense of architectural style, their rich and subtle dialect, not to mention the sheer poetry of their mythology, that they almost completely overlooked their highly characteristic and colourful music and dance.

In his magnificent books on Zakopane and the Tatra Mountains, Stanisław Witkiewicz[1] rarely mentions the songs, music and dances of the region. For him they are merely details of local customs, a dash of colour on the landscape, as in his inimitable description of the Highland Robbers' Dance and of the young shepherd's dance on the edge of a

---

[1] Stanisław Witkiewicz (1851–1915) was a painter and one of the leading representatives of the Polish impressionist movement. He was also a literary and artistic critic and writer. He established a style of architecture which is particularly associated with Zakopane. Szymanowski was friendly with his son, Stanisław Ignacy Witkiewicz (1888–1939), known as Witkacy, an artist and the author of several dramas and novels of a markedly futuristic character.

precipice (*In the Mountain Pass*); on the other hand, they are
sometimes subtle psychological observations, especially
when associated with the now mythical figure of Sabała.[2]

Kazimierz Tetmajer,[3] in his unique masterpieces *On the
Crags of Podhale* and *Tatra Legends* allows more space for
descriptions of music and dance, having due regard to the
customs and legends which form the background to his
books. And indeed the people of Podhale, probably more
than those of any other race, are inextricably bound up with
their dances, which, in their multiplicity of forms, almost
amount to 'pure art'. Tetmajer's books contain marvellous
pictures, the vividness of which attains visionary heights.
Naturally these exquisite poems are not the place for a
dry, analytical discussion of the properties of the music of
Podhale.

I must confess that what I know of the earliest notations of
these melodies (unless I am mistaken, the work of Oskar
Kolberg[4] and others, above all, Jan Kleczyński[5]) do not
inspire much confidence in me. When comparing them
with the originals, with the lively song of a highlander up in

---

[2] Sabała was the nickname of the legendary Jan Krzeptowski (1809–94), a
reformed highland robber who achieved fame and respectability as a
mountain-guide, story-teller, singer and violinist.

[3] Kazimierz Przerwa-Tetmajer (1865–1940) was born into a land-owning
family whose estates lay south of Kraków at the foot of the Tatra mountains.
He studied philosophy at Kraków and Heidelberg, and subsequently
divided his time between Warsaw, Kraków and Zakopane. His early works
were influenced by the ideology of Young Poland in Literature, and
Szymanowski set some of his poems to music in the Six Songs, Op. 2. It is
now generally accepted that his best works are those dealing with the life
and customs of the Tatra district.

[4] Poland can lay claim to one of the earliest attempts to collect folk material
systematically. In the first decade of the nineteenth century, Hugo Kołłątaj
drew up plans for ethnographic research, but it was not until 1842 that the
first volume of *Pieśni ludu polskiego* (*Songs of the Polish Folk*), compiled by
Oskar Kolberg (1814–90), appeared in Poznań. Kolberg descended from a
German family, and after studying with Elsner and Dobrzyński in Warsaw,
went on to train with Rungenhagen in Berlin in 1834. From 1839 he
embarked on a series of self-financed ethnographic investigations. His

the mountain pastures or the dance music played by Bartek
Obrochta's highland band, I cannot help feeling that these
notations are somewhat 'alien'. In effect they seem to have
been domesticated, and, divested of their original savagery,
have been reduced to the grey uniformity of the typical,
needlessly 'minor mode' sentimentalised 'folk-song'.

It is clear that the scales which form the basis of the
greater part of Góral song diverge markedly from our
'culturally' tempered scales. As Professor Adolf Chybiński
and I have repeatedly stated, they reach back to antiquity,
and it is only with some difficulty that they can be formulated within our tonal system.

In recent years a group of professional people, passionately interested in Góral culture, have energetically set
about saving the remnants of a once rich and original
Podhale music from what regrettably has now to be
described as final extinction. This really is the last chance,
because the 'denationalisation' of the highlanders and the
erosion of their indigenous art, especially in Zakopane,
proceeds with a rapidity that is simply frightening.

To begin with their clothing: the 'cucha', which is so well
tailored, has almost completely disappeared from the shoulders of the young highlander to be replaced by a hideous
smock and khaki-coloured waistcoat. Moccasins are now
only worn for show and at weddings for dancing. Only
embroidered 'breeches' and sleeveless sheepskin jackets
are still regularly worn. But worse still is the increasing
tendency for nasty little waltzes and polkas to be played at
weddings, and performances of such music by highland

---

earliest collections were scarcely scholarly, each folk-song being provided
with a piano accompaniment in an attempt to make it suitable for use in
the drawing-room. Subsequently, however, the songs were published
unadorned, and in the final series of volumes, Kolberg also provided
detailed studies of the people, customs and culture of the region in
question.

[5] Jan Kleczyński (1837–95) was a composer, critic and rather unscientific
folklorist.

bands is simply intolerable. Many of the young men now
dance the 'shimmy',[6] and 'lowland' music is determinedly
striving to oust the wonderful 'wirchowe', 'sabałowe' and
'ozwodne' melodies, those well-nigh mythical archaic
expressions of a culture which are now only preserved intact
in their traditional form as the priceless treasure they are by
the spiritual heir and successor of Sabała – Bartek Obrochta
of Kościelisk.

But the Podhale music 'rescue service' perseveres in its
work, and what is more important, is able to draw on a large
repository of information. In his summer vacations professor Adolf Chybiński rushes tirelessly from village to
village with notebook and pencil in hand, sometimes even
with a phonograph horn.[7] He has collected a truly enormous quantity of material which is undoubtedly authentic.
The curator of the Tatra Museum in Zakopane, Mr Juliusz
Zborowski,[8] has locked away in a cupboard in his office at
the museum, in systematically arranged note-books, practically the total poetic output of Podhale – a veritable
encyclopaedia of song-texts. Finally, one more work of
inestimable importance for the history of Polish folk-music
has appeared in recent times. It is a rich collection of Góral
dances and melodies, notated in a form identical to that of
the original, in other words, for the highland band of two

[6] The shimmy was a popular dance in the USA in the 1910s and 1920s. It
required no foot movement, simply the shaking of the shoulders and
torso.

[7] Mr Zborowski has been collecting Góral melodies since 1914 with the aid
of a phonograph. The collection, consisting of a hundred cylinders, is
presently housed in the Tatra Museum and has been turned to good
account by Professor Adolf Chybiński. Unfortunately the absence of
resources for the purchase of new equipment makes the completion of this
valuable material exceedingly difficult. A still sadder fact is the impossibility of making a more permanent record of the fragile cylinders by
means of zinc electroplating. The necessary techniques for setting up such
a long-lasting archive exist in America, Berlin and Vienna – only in this
country is it impossible for financial reasons. –KS

[8] Juliusz Zborowksi (1888–1965) was an ethnographer who was chiefly
concerned with the Podhale region.

violins and bass still in use today. Its author, Stanisław
Mierczyński,[9] has provided Polish folk-lorists with a document of prime importance, drawing not only on his skills
and expertise, but truly saintly reserves of patience. He has
culled his examples from the most authentic sources, from
the most illustrious of the famous musicians, namely the
above mentioned Bartek Obrochta as well as Jędrzej Tatar
and Józef Gąsienic of Las, among others. We can only
assume that in this work the source material has been
almost completely exhausted and preserved for ever in the
form of a three-part score with numerous annotations and
instructions for the performance of individual passages.[10]

[9] Stanisław Mierczyński (1894–1952), an ethnographer. Szymanowski provided a preface to Mierczyński's notations of Podhale music, published in
Lwów in 1930.

[10] The urgent preservation of Góral music was a theme which Szymanowski
developed further in an untitled article, probably written in 1924, but only
published posthumously in the Łódź periodical *Poradnik Muzyczny* in April
1947 (No. 2):

> Góral music is inexorably, albeit slowly, withering and dying, like
> almost everything to do with this once spontaneous, so colourful and
> lively culture. [...] The categoric imperative to preserve that historic
> musical tradition on cylinders, and the dance steps on film, becomes
> increasingly important day by day.
>
> Of course, it is a deed of almost funereal sadness to shut away in
> the cupboards and cabinets of a museum something which was once
> so very vital [...]. This deed is the responsibility of those of us who
> really can still love 'The Legend of the Tatras' in all its various guises,
> those who perhaps have succeeded in preserving in their childhood
> recollections a memory of old Zakopane, cut off from the splendours
> of the civilised world by the Obidowa Pass through which one
> travelled on a jolting mountain-cart [...]. [Szymanowski here drew
> on his own memories of his first visit to Zakopane in 1894, five years
> before the completion of the railway line.]
>
> We believe deeply that that seemingly so naive, yet so intense
> beauty [...], even when closed up in a museum, can remain a vital,
> creative force.
>
> Music is like the fragrance of a given culture's flower. When that
> flower withers, its dead form and faded colours may perhaps remain,
> but its fragrance perishes, never to return, with the disappearance of
> life.
>
> We are deeply moved when we stand at the foot of the Parthenon,
> entranced by the sight of the Hermes of Praxiteles, we read with

For an understanding of the intrinsic worth of this work, it should be noted that Góral dance music is composed of clearly defined melodic, harmonic and rhythmic patterns. It contrasts markedly with 'lowland' music in the constant retention of its characteristic features, and even departs in some measure from the style of the freely performed songs of this region, from which it draws only a fundamental melodic line which it then subjects to repeated, rhythmic changes and expressive adaptations. The technical difficulties involved in Stanisław Mierczyński's project were immense, as of course the local musicians play without music. Their performance then is rather in the nature of an improvisation à 3 which often creates the most unexpected 'modernistic' harmony which is, however, always controlled tightly through the iron grip of a specific rhythm. It was necessary to transcribe each instrumental part separately and often when, for example, the bass player was made to perform 'solo', he would play different notes from those he had played in the ensemble a moment earlier. Watching Mierczyński at work on more than one occasion, I came to appreciate the extent of the skill, perseverance, patience and utter devotion that he lavished upon this opus.

Fortunately *Tánce i melodie góralskie* (*Highland Dances and Melodies*) is not doomed, like so many other worthy works, to

---

deep feeling the words of King Oedipus: but the living sound of the chorus lamenting the fate of the king has vanished for ever. We conjecture about Greek music. Who knows now whether it was as deeply and as beautifully worthy a counterpart to the poetry or not?

We are fortunate today: we can preserve the fragrance for ever. The ethnological investigator, pencil in hand, can preserve only the word, losing the intonation or the pitch and timbre of the note. In contrast the phonograph needle and the camera lens in its dispassionate infallibility preserves life itself for ever, losing not the slightest, most elusive of tints!

[...] a museum [...] is perhaps 'art's' burial-place, but it is one from which eternally new, luxuriant flowers can spring.

Reprinted in *Karol Szymanowski Pisma*, Vol. 1, pp. 109–10, under the title 'O Potrzebie Ratowania Muzyki Góralskiej' ['On the Need to Save Góral Music'].

an eternal sojourn in the bottom drawer of the author's desk. The good will and initiative of a private consortium have made possible the appearance of this collection in the foreseeable future. It will be a sumptuous publication, splendidly put together, with illustrations by Zofia Stryjeńska[11] whose magnificent illustrations to several of the tales from Tetmajer's *Na skalnym Podhalu* (*In Rocky Podhale*) have shown so splendidly her deep, intuitive feeling for the mountaineers' way of life.

This is not the place for a technical analysis of the musical properties of the Góral style.[12] But I should like first of all to protest categorically against stories about the mountaineers' legendary lack of musicality, arising I suppose from tales put about by the first newcomers from the 'lowlands', scared out of their wits by the *yelling* (really!) of shepherds' songs from peak to peak and from valley to valley. Of course this way of singing has nothing in common with the caressing *bel canto* of Venetian gondoliers. But how can one describe as 'unmusical' a race who, besides possessing an exceedingly wealthy corpus of song, which so frequently captivates with its unusually capricious melodic line, are unique in Poland (and perhaps not just in Poland) for their creation of instrumental music built on original harmonic and rhythmic systems?[13]

---

[11] Zofia Stryjeńska (1894–1976), a painter, was the wife of Karol Stryjeński (1887–1932), the architect and sculptor. Both were close friends of the composer.

[12] I shall try to do this in the introduction to Mr Mierczynski's collection of dances. –KS [In the event, Szymanowski's preface ('Muzyka Podhala') contains no additional information about the mountaineers' musical techniques and is fundamentally a restatement and development of opinions already formulated in the present article.]

[13] In 'Muzyka Podhala', Szymanowski wrote:
Either one understands Góral dance music and has a feeling for it by way of the, so to say, mysterious instinct of race: then one loves it, yearns for its vigour, pulsating with a rapture latent in its rugged, angular form, seemingly fashioned from stone. Or else one does not understand it [...] and then one cannot bear it.
Reprinted in *Karol Szymanowski Pisma*, Vol. 1, pp. 251–52.

I am here deliberately avoiding a discussion of the effect of Slovak, Hungarian or whatever sort of influence on the moulding of the fundamental properties of this music, knowing from bitter experience that, as a rule, such a 'study of influences' explains nothing in a work of art, but only obscures its real essence. Consequently, I believe that to grasp the character of highland music it is necessary to contrast it with the radically different music of the 'Lowlands'. In all probability, two powerful local factors conditioned the overall form of the region's culture: first, extreme poverty and the pitiless, uncompromising harshness attaching to life in these parts in previous times,[14] and secondly, the equally extreme, intoxicating beauty of the surrounding landscape. These two contrasting factors

[14] In a touching tribute to Bartek Obrochta, 'List do Przyjaciół w Zakopanem' ('A Letter to Friends in Zakopane'), published in the Warsaw daily paper *ABC* on 16 February 1927 under the title 'Zakopane dziś i jutro' ('Zakopane Today and Tomorrow'), Szymanowski wrote at some length about the attractions of the mountaineers' old way of life:

It is certainly true that the 'good old days' meant 'ignorance, barbarism, superstition etc., etc.', and here we still go by the light of (often smoky!) oil-lamps. But the 'good old days' also meant courage, strength, vital power, the unyielding will to succeed, everything which once went to make such strange, vivid and beautiful forms of existence. And, ultimately, it meant 'freedom' – not one of those 'democratic' freedoms which are calculated on paper with the aid of compasses and dividers, but true freedom, the most personal of freedoms, one forged in hardship and through a superhuman effort for a life, a destiny of one's own moulding and which is one's own responsibility. [...] Isn't it precisely that vision of mythical freedom which has so inexorably drawn so many generations to the foot of the Tatras, those mercilessly precipitous crags which, in our Polish consciousness, have almost grown to be a symbol of spiritual uplands. [...] What could tie us contemporary, cultured people so strongly to that rough, but so admirably beautiful 'past', if not the yearning for precisely that magical, imperishable freedom of the solitary life in the mountains? Not long ago, a burial mound in Zakopane's New Cemetary was added to all those innumerable mounds at the foot of the Tatras. [...] There lies our common friend, who – until so recently! – by way of the living word, the living sounds of his fiddles, spoke to us of primeval matters and awoke eternal echoes which (let us not deceive ourselves) were silenced for ever the moment he died. There lies the greatest musician of Skalny Podhale,

forged the spirit of the old mountaineer, and affected all aspects of his day-to-day existence. The greatest individual effort was required merely to stay alive. Venturing out on to the steep mountain slopes and snow-covered uplands was a noble, age-old symbol of the hard, everyday life of the region, and I believe that this action was endowed with symbolic significance because the Góral is arguably the only peasant on earth who is sensitive in every way to the depth and beauty of nature. Of course, this sensitivity takes a form peculiar to the highlanders, and lacks the exaggerated sentimentality characteristic of lowland visitors. The everyday need for the greatest effort naturally means that one attains maximum results. In the artistic field this effort is translated into the desire for and pursuit of absolute formal perfection. This psychological property of the Góral is something which we artists can understand and sympathise with, and I think it accounts for the invincible force which, quite apart from the beauty of the natural scenery, draws us so strongly to the foot of the Tatras. In a certain sense, the highlanders have achieved this excellence of form in their architecture and decoration. My friends and I insist that they have also achieved it in their music and dancing. In both there is a primitive savagery, the schematic severity of something primordial along with the intractability of granite. At the same time, one detects the absence of any improvisatory incompetence in their works, endowed as they are with a positive inner value and laboriously forged in forms which allow for an innate plasticity of imagination and avoid drowning hopelessly in a sea of anaemic sentimentality. These attributes within the sphere of aesthetics enabled the Góral fully to achieve that which we call *métier* in art: steadiness of hand and the unerring selection of the most direct way of realising one's artistic ideas in any given material. This steadiness of hand is apparent in every

---

the visionary and poet, Bartek Obrochta, the Farmer from Kościelisk, the last link connecting 'today' with that mysterious 'past'.

architectural detail of those beautiful, old-fashioned wooden houses, and can be heard in every dance-tune, performed with such precise virtuosity by self-taught performers. Finally, it is to be seen in the dancers' well-nigh 'balletic' technique. The dance never depends on haphazard improvisation, but rather the individual temperament of the dancers for the realisation in movement of a certain 'form'.[15] In the Góral dance, the greatest difficulties are mastered with the utmost ease; it is always a solo display – hence the respect which the best dancers enjoy.

The true artist is characterised by his objective attitude to his own art, and the Góral is, or at any rate was in former times, of all the Polish peasants, the artist *par excellence.*

Delicate musical sensibilities and 'refined natures' flee from this 'cacophonous' music, seeing in it only a barbarous primitivism. Such it may really be, but in contrast to many of the not always subtle 'subtleties' of our contemporary musical culture, it is an envigorating force with its proximity to nature, the vigour and directness of its temperament and, finally, the unalloyed purity of its ethnic expression. I should like our young generation of Polish musicians to

---

[15] In 'Muzyka Podhala', Szymanowski wrote more about the notion of 'form':

> Undoubtedly Góral dance and its music, the melodic core of which is a rhythmically re-organised, but in essence 'singable' song, are a symptom of the customs of Góral life. It is striking, however, that both dance and music transcend those customs thanks to their formal values. [...] Each 'Krzesany' [Sparking Dance] or 'Zbójnicki' [Highland Robbers' Dance] is vigorously shaped and formulated within a vivid framework embracing not only melody and rhythm but also a full, characteristic harmony. May the devotees of classical music forgive me this outrageous blasphemy, but each dance is a 'symphony' of its kind, a 'co-ordination of sounds', a definite 'composition'. [...] Only when one comprehends the veritable Góral passion for investing artistic shapes on everything which surrounds him, only when one penetrates these [...] forms, will one perceive in this music the true face of the unyielding, hard, specifically Góral 'lyricism' [...].
>
> Reprinted in *Karol Szymanowski Pisma*, Vol. 1, p. 252.

understand how our present anaemic musical condition could be infused with new life by the riches hidden in the Polish 'barbarism' which I have at last 'uncovered' and made my own.

The Ethnic Question in relation to Contemporary Music

(A foot-note to Béla Bartók's article 'The Origin of Folk-music')

This article was first published in the Warsaw periodical *Muzyka* in October 1925 and was a response to an essay by Bartók published by *Muzyka* the preceding June.

Béla Bartók is without doubt one of the most interesting of today's composers. Although little known in Poland, he has for many years enjoyed a considerable reputation in the West where he is regarded as one of the most distinguished of contemporary musicians.

It would be a very good thing were we to become more closely acquainted both with his music and with his work in the propagation of Hungary's musical culture. Bartók is not only responsible for a whole series of very interesting musical works characterised by extremely modernistic (*passez moi le mot!*) tendencies. Because of the extent of his culture and intelligence, and thanks to his tireless work in society at large, he has also become the well-nigh archetypal and very eloquent exponent of ideals held by the younger generation of Hungarian musicians. Their ideals, or rather their single ideal, is the creation of a Hungarian musical school with its own style, capable of giving elevated expression to the nation's soul in the idealistic way this occurs in the great European musical cultures of Germany, France and Russia. We too are struggling to achieve this ideal, and so it is all the more important that we should become acquainted with Bartók's view of Hungarian music as expressed in his article 'The Origins of Folk-music'.

I should at the outset draw attention to a very characteristic, yet seemingly anomalous fact, namely that Béla Bartók, one of the most extreme 'futuristic' musicians of the present day, is at the same time a distinguished exponent of the extreme *nationalistic* aspirations of the young Hungarian musical school. So what is one to make of that notorious story about the International-Jewish-Masonic conspiracy that underlies all 'futuristic' music, a story which even today a critical faction here in Poland still stubbornly insists on spreading abroad?[1]

The story, as I shall now demonstrate, is a fiction, a mere scarecrow, for the following reasons:

The intensified musical activity that developed in certain European countries after the war, a movement which we were wont to baptise collectively as 'futurism' (a label that conveys nothing and which is as battered as an old penny) came about (strange to say!) because of unprecedentedly exuberant 'nationalist' feelings in various countries. Such nationalist movements purposefully sought their primary artistic sources in the defence of their cultural independence, and of necessity were strongly influenced by folk-music and in particular by its underlying concepts and aesthetic standards. But here we are not concerned with 'folk-art' merely in an ethnographic or picturesque sense; in any case, folk-art differs markedly from one European country to another on account of cultural diversity. The present

---

[1] It is exceedingly characteristic that, among the younger generation of Jewish composers (Ernest Bloch, Achron and Saminsky), nationalistic-folk tendencies appear evermore explicitly. This is certainly a very strong argument against the story about the levelling influence of Jews on contemporary music. –KS

[Ernest Bloch was born in 1880 in Geneva and died in 1959 in Portland, Oregon. Several of the works composed in his middle years, e.g., the Symphony *Israel* (1912–16) and *Schelomo* (1915–16) are markedly Jewish in subject matter and idiom. Joseph Achron (Akhron) was born in the Russian sector of Poland in 1886, and died in Hollywood in 1943. He was a violinist and composer, and his works include film scores, the *Golem Suite* and three violin concertos. Lazare Saminsky was born in Odessa in 1882 and died in Port Chester, New York, in 1959. His works include *The Vision of Ariel, Lament of Rachel* and *The Daughter of Jephtha.*]

author believes that folk-art clearly reveals the deepest primordial character of a given people in the sphere of aesthetics.

Contemporary concepts and aesthetics appear to be mounting a direct attack on the established and traditional dogmas of nineteenth- and early twentieth-century European music. It is as if they were destroying *incontrovertible* values and replacing them with revolutionary chaos. To the superficial observer it appears that the aesthetic instinct has lost its way and is straying helplessly through a wilderness which will eventually lead to the gloomy abyss of self-destruction. But a quick, objective glance at the heart of the matter reveals that, for the thousandth time, human history is repeating itself. In other words, what appears to be a new revolution in art during the epoch in question is in fact only a logical continuation, a natural consequence in the ineluctable transformation of the history of mankind.

The most interesting aspect of the whole fascinating question is that German music has become the obligatory 'pan-European' music for the cultured world. Thanks to its mighty breadth and its continuing irreplaceable value, the great century-and-a-half (from Bach to Wagner), while not ceasing to be, in the noblest sense of the word, a 'nationalistic' expression of the Germanic spirit, thrust upon all of us an obligatory aesthetic canon and universal ideal of such weight that it crushed individual upsurges of creativity attempting to evolve in their own way (Chopin), and became in fact the *international* musical ideal.

And here we encounter an unprecedented paradox: the Polish critic, who may, for example, be battling in the name of Beethoven's absolute values with the problematical (for him) value of Stravinsky, simply takes up arms in defence of true musical 'internationalism' as opposed to highly fanatical 'nationalism'. The extent to which that 'internationalism' is injurious to us is immaterial in this case. The Polish musician, in the name of his peculiar ideal, regards as anathema Stravinsky the Russian, Bartók the Hungarian and de Falla the Spaniard, all of whom are struggling on behalf of their own national ideals. He suspects them of Jewish-Masonic 'internationalism', and attacks what he realises – rightly! – is the only ideal of value on Polish terrain, the only safe redoubt to be captured – *coûte que coûte.*

Do we really need to repeat that beautiful German (how strange!) saying: *Leben und leben lassen!* Furthermore, should we not consider it our duty to study as meticulously and as impartially as possible, all paths leading to freedom, all roads along which others are travelling, and along which we too should feel compelled to travel? Is it really necessary for us to rely on the workings of a police state and a 'customs officer' for the defence of the basic freedom of Polish music from injurious influences? Are we terrified of foreign influences? Are we really that sickly now?[2]

All true development depends on courage and a wise and

---

[2] Szymanowski here touches on a theme which he had treated more expansively in two articles published six months earlier in *Kurier Warszawski*: 'Concerning the Aims and Tasks of the Philharmonia' (11 April 1925) and 'Is Polish Musical Creativity under Threat?' (14 April 1925). These essays were written in support of the Philharmonia Orchestra, then under attack in the press for the supposedly anti-nationalistic nature of its programmes. In Szymanowski's view, concert programmes could only be planned with artistic, rather than nationalistic, values in mind:

> [...] works which do not rise above the level of scribblerism and dilettantism should automatically be excluded from concert programmes, no matter how domestic the origin of that scribblerism and dilettantism.
>
> *Karol Szymanowski Pisma*, Vol. 1, p. 152.

Neither was the Philharmonia to be regarded as a branch of the educational system, a sort of 'incubator' for partially developed talents, since it existed primarily as an arena for mature artists capable of offering the general public 'the fullest and most artistic picture of the universal musical movement, taking into account native creativity, but only when it manifests itself in a truly artistic form, and as such does not suffer in a comparison with distinguished foreign works' (*ibid.*, p. 153). Cultural protectionism was counter-productive, especially in those cases involving music of little value, 'because all dilettantism, proclaimed *ex cathedra* from a major theatrical stage or concert platform serves only to bring about a lowering of standards in a national culture; no chauvinistic argument can save mediocrity from unavoidable extinction' (*ibid.*, pp. 153–54).

In the second article, Szymanowski set out to demonstrate that claims

thorough examination of life's depths – not on an ostrich-
like burying of heads in the sand.

*   *   *

The above thoughts have been only very roughly outlined. I
have tried to bring out vividly fundamental contours and
the most far-reaching disagreements in an attempt to reveal
the bare bones of the argument about contemporary music.

---

that Polish music was under-represented in the Philharmonia's programmes could not be justified:

> In the current season, works by 23 Polish composers were performed
> at the Philharmonia, representing a third of all composers featured
> in the programmes. The aggregate total of Polish pieces performed
> in the six-month period (October–March) reached the impressive
> number of 37 works, of which some were repeated two or three times
> (Karłowicz, Noskowski), making a total of 45 performances. I am not
> including Chopin or Moniuszko in this total, which would increase
> the percentage still more.'

Ibid., p. 158

Szymanowski went on to make merry at the expense of his old enemy,
Piotr Rytel, who had published a piece critical of the Philharmonia entitled
'Polish Subsidy of Russian Music'. Szymanowski acknowledged that such a
proposition sounded alarming, but then contemptuously ridiculed Rytel's
arguments:

> We read in the first sentence about the 'persistent propaganda of
> Russian music of a markedly revolutionary character' (political or
> artistic? One ought to dot the 'i's). [...] Later we are stunned into
> silence by the declaration that, amongst this revolutionary music, the
> author counts Rimsky-Korsakov's *Shéhérazade* and Glazunov's Violin
> Concerto. Some revolution! Next the author declares that public
> opinion is clamouring evermore vociferously for the right to enjoy
> Polish art. Up to now, alas, we have not been able to set much store
> by this feverish love for Polish music, especially as one concert in
> October, devoted exclusively to works by Polish composers, had to be
> cancelled because only 12 (*sic*) tickets were sold [...]. In conclusion,
> we encounter a totally unbelievable *salto mortale*, namely the claim
> that 'it is much more useful to perform even relatively poor composi-
> tions, providing they are Polish, rather than better, more celebrated
> but foreign works'. Sometimes one meets such unexpected argu-
> ments in discussion that one can only smile resignedly and hurriedly
> depart.

Ibid., pp. 159–60.

But on the surface the problem appears to be quite different in that other themes come into play, as if a function of those apparently centrifugal tendencies.

Above all there is the question of the common, generalised taste, characteristic of a given epoch. There is the question of style in the deepest sense of the word (namely in the way that Romanticism, for example, was the style of the first half of the nineteenth century).[3] We also have to take into account the ever-increasing reciprocation of interests that is undoubtedly taking place between the cultured classes of Europe, as well as the purely practical question of the influence exerted by stronger characters on weaker individuals. There can be no doubt that in this instance the unusual courage of his convictions has made the resolute figure of Igor Stravinsky the *deus ex machina*, whose work has led to a turning-point in the shaping of the contemporary musical style. Yet even though he exerted the strongest possible influence on European composers, Stravinsky as a Russian composer was a musical nationalist (see, for example, *Petrushka*, *The Rite of Spring* and *Les Noces*). The change that has recently taken place in his work can be attributed to several complicated causes, which for the present I shall not pursue.

In contrasting 'rural' music with 'folk' music, Béla Bartók immediately comes to grips with the heart of the question. (I have to say that I do not find his terminology to be completely satisfactory. By 'rural' music he means that which we commonly regard as 'folk' music, namely all that is the original and spontaneous creation of the people; whereas by 'folk' music he means the range of more or less successful attempts at stylisation – often superficial and theatrical – in works by composers. To avoid any misunderstanding, I will keep to our usual terminology, especially as in a subsequent part of this article my attempt

---

[3] These are all vital questions to which I should like to devote more space in the near future. –KS

at characterising the emergence of musical 'exoticism' will reveal the differences between these two types of music.)

In the Romantic era, authentic 'folk' elements (rhythmic and melodic) began to intrude increasingly strongly upon 'cultured', academic music in the form of an 'exotic' style. This exoticism, which was largely based on the absorption of the vast, mysterious wealth of original Eastern music, has, as is commonly known, yielded interesting results, especially in Russian and French music over the last few decades.

But in these endeavours, the prime concern was an artificial assimilation into European music of new, foreign rhythmic and melodic elements, aimed at seasoning European music with an interesting hot spice. A typical example of academic exoticism is Dvořák's *Symphony from the New World*, which makes use of original American Negro melodies. By way of this (superficial) exotic admixture with pure academicism, one's own folk-music could, and rightly had to come into play, as the most immediate and comprehensible type of music for any composer to produce (quite apart from idealistic, e.g., patriotic considerations). So developed the somewhat stereotyped and, of course, compromise 'folksy' academic style so characteristic of music at the end of the nineteenth and beginning of the twentieth centuries. There was a flood of great and small, more or less valuable works, in which authentic folk melodies and rhythms were exploited. Those birds, accustomed to singing freely over forests and meadows, certainly felt ill at ease inside their artistically crafted formal cages where they had to sing against an alien 'learned' background with its elegant harmonic progressions using a modern system of dissonance treatment.

I am not, however, opposed to that style, in spite of its artificiality. On the contrary: the introduction of folk elements from without initially enriched musical material automatically, and slowly paved the way for the development of a new style. Harmonic and formal structures gradually gave way before an invasion of barbarians. The day of liberation at last dawned with the escape from the

magic circle of functional chromaticism in which yesterday's music seemed to be suffocating helplessly as if in cold,
thin mountain air. The music of today looks to the people,
to the earth, to the fruitful, fecund soil.

The 'exotic' music of the folk-compromise was only a
bridge, leading from a lofty, and for a certainty, already
moribund 'academic' aestheticism to real life.

In fact, 'folk' music (or, as Bartók would have it, 'rural'
music) is not just an inexhaustible treasury of rhythmic and
melodic materials which can be ladled out and worked into
one 'symphonic' form or another. Its inner evolution (and
here I do not mean the far more striking and highly regret-
table degeneration arising from its unavoidable contacts
with 'civilised' life) is such an exceedingly leisurely process
that at any moment in history, it is possible to consider its
development to be almost non-existent. From this point of
view, the manifestations of folk-art (above all, music!)
appear to us to be fixed and unchanging, transcending the
limits of history and being the most direct expression of the
spirit of a race. The perennial problem of 'folk-art' has to be
understood in this way before one can appreciate the 'revolutionary' force which it can bring to bear on the stiff
decrepitude of a senile, moribund, academic aesthetic.

I willingly subscribe to the beautiful aphorism with which
Béla Bartók closes his article: 'Rural music is for the composer what nature is for the landscapist'. But I must stress
that this relationship has to be understood in as deep a
sense as possible, since it concerns a mysterious area that is
psychologically difficult to study, namely the inner dependence of a creative artist on his racial characteristics; his
dependence on a never-changing foundation which nevertheless permits one to detect the ever-changing features of
his style in each individual work of art, in each manifestation
of his inner experience fixed in the most objective and rigid
framework.

In fact, the raw material of folk music does not by our
definition constitute a work of art; when its elements are
imposed from outside on a work of art, a compromise

results, namely the hackneyed 'exotic' style which is familiar to us today.

So, apodictic aestheticism apart, we should be able to clasp that perpetually beating 'heart of the race' in the palms of our hands and by way of a perfect form which is comprehensible universally as a work of art, recreate the spontaneous, uncurbed creative force manifest in folk-music.

In my view, this is one of the foremost tasks of the great national artist, and in our musical history we had a brief but dazzling glimpse of such a visionary, creative genius. I refer of course to Chopin, and here lies the only area of disagreement between Bartók and myself.

In placing Chopin and Liszt on a par with regard to their relationship to folk-music, he has in my view committed a fundamental error.[4]

I regard Liszt as a typically 'exotic' composer, who, even though he was Hungarian, drew from Hungarian (or rather gypsy) folk-music rhythms and melodies for his famous rhapsodies with dazzling talent, adroitness and indifference. Had it been better known to him, he might have drawn upon the rich treasury of eastern music in exactly the same way. Besides, in his other works and indeed those of the greatest value, he emerges as a typical 'romantic' of the

---

[4] What Bartók wrote was:

> 'Chopin was to a certain extent influenced by the Polish, and Liszt by the Hungarian popular art music. Yet so much that was banal was incorporated by them with much that was exotic that the works concerned were not benefitted thereby. That is why it is not the nationalistic Polonaises that rank highest amongst Chopin's work, and the same applies to Liszt's Hungarian Rhapsodies and to his Tarantellas and Polonaises. In any case it is only these slighter works that have received what is after all only a nationalistic whitewash; the principal works of both composers are happily for the most part exempt from this influence'.

Loc. cit., p. 3.

By popular art music, Bartók meant those 'folk-songs' which the peasants had appropriated from townsfolk as opposed to genuine folk-music. He was of the opinion that neither Liszt nor Chopin had heard genuine peasant music at any time of their lives.

day: his music is nationally colourless and in taste somewhat eclectic.

Chopin, on the other hand, within the seemingly confined range of his work, with its stylistic homogeneity, never abandoned his 'Polishness'. This is true both of the polonaises and mazurkas, which in form are closely related to Polish 'folk-music', as well as of those larger works, even those which employ academic sonata form and so seem far removed from all folk references. These 'racial' subtleties are, of course, far easier for Poles to grasp than foreigners, and this perhaps explains why Chopin's 'Polishness' is not fully appreciated even by his greatest enthusiasts abroad.

A Footnote
to 'Stabat Mater'
Thoughts on Religious Music

This interview, given to Mateusz Gliński, was first published in the periodical *Muzyka* in 1926 (No. 11/12).

KS: A whole series of motives induced me to compose the religious work *Stabat Mater*, ranging from inner, personal experiences to external circumstances of everyday life which prompted me to lay aside other, already started, 'secular' works for the time being and devote myself exclusively to the *Stabat Mater*.[1]

MG: What were those 'inner' motives which inclined you to undertake this work?

KS: I do not think this is the place for a detailed analysis of the 'inner' experiences organically connected with my creative work in its entirety. I would have too much to say about this. Besides, as you well know, artistic 'exhibitionism' is in no way a part of my nature. The creative artist's inner 'mechanism' should remain secret. The only important thing is whether he 'produces' good or bad work. So let us try to confine ourselves to fundamental questions.

MG: Very well. Has the question of religious music previously been of interest to you?

---

[1] The work was almost completely sketched by November 1925, and the full score finished by 2 March 1926. It was commissioned by a Warsaw business-man, Bronisław Krystall, in memory of his recently deceased wife, Izabella. The 'inner, personal experiences' mentioned by Szymanowski were no doubt connected with the sudden death of his niece, Alusia Bartosze-wiczówna, the only daughter of Stanisława.

KS: For many years now I've been thinking about Polish religious music (I don't mean liturgical music, where certain formal canons are obligatory), and about this, I have certain opinions, too many to mention. In my view, it must have a directly emotional impact, and therefore must draw upon a universally comprehensible text: the emotional content of the word must be organically fused with its musical equivalent. I may be wrong, but I have the impression that · even those who know Latin best find this language elevated, to be sure, but also stiff and no longer open to further development because it has lost direct contact with the living. It has lost its emotional content and retains only a conceptual one. This probably does not apply to Roman (classical) literature, which in the nature of things used a language which at the time of writing was still living and capable of expressing directly the emotional content of the life of those times.

MG: What then do you think of those masterpieces of church music which draw on Latin texts?

KS: I must stress here that I am expressing a very subjective opinion: well, it seems to me that they affect us, above all, through the mysterious magic of a music based on a rather generalised concept of what the given passage means in 'words', while we take 'on trust' the already ossified poetry of the words of the text. Anyway, liturgical music is always based on those same texts which constitute a deeply idological, rather than specifically poetic, element of the given work. Perhaps because of this, and I admit it contritely, the singing in a country church of *Święty Boże* [*Holy God*] or my favourite *Gorzkie żale* [*Lenten Psalms*], every word of which is poetically a living organism, always rouses a religious instinct in me a hundred times more powerfully than the most artistic of Latin masses.

MG: In this case why did you select for your own work a Latin hymn?

KS: First of all, its simplicity had always captivated me. But in any case I would probably never have selected it were it not for my chance discovery of Józef Jankowski's[2] exquisite Polish translation of it some ten years ago in *Świat* [*World*]. Through the unusually primitive, almost 'folk-like' simplicity and naïvety of the translation, the poet managed to avoid the rather classical character of the Latin original (I am not an expert in this respect). But it does not hinge on this. The fidelity of the translation is of little account; it is its emotional content which matters. Here in its Polish vestments, that eternal, naïve hymn was filled for me with its own immediate expressive content; it became something 'painted' in colours which were recognisable and comprehensible as distinct from the 'black and white' of the archaic original.

That naïve opening:

> Stała Matka bolejąca
> Koło krzyża łzy lejąca
> [The grief-stricken mother stood
> By the cross shedding tears]

became so much more comprehensible emotionally than the no less comprehensible conceptually:

> Stabat Mater dolorosa
> Juxta crucem lacrimosa
> [The sorrowful mother stood
> by the cross weeping]

I tore the text out of the newspaper and kept in my 'archive' for later use as, at the time, I think I was working on the Third Symphony.[3] This 'archive', which contained so many valuable mementoes (e.g., letters from Żeromski and Miciński) as well as my own manuscripts, was destroyed in 1918 at the brutal, foul hands of the Bolsheviks.

---

[2] Józef Jankowski (1865–1935), poet, dramatist, translator and journalist working in Warsaw. His translation of Todi's thirteenth-century sequence was first published in the weekly magazine *Świat* (*World*) in April 1908 (No. 16, p. 7).

[3] Szymanowski was mistaken: he composed the Third Symphony in 1916.

Last Spring, I succeeded in obtaining from the author a handwritten copy of his translation, together with his permission to set it to music, and I should like to express my warmest thanks to him here for this.

MG: What can you tell me about this work?

KS: What can I say? Whether it is good or bad, I don't know. I tried here to give substantial expression to those ideas which underly my conception of 'national music', and in this case, religious music. In effect it had to be as far removed from liturgical music, with its lofty but, in my view, stiff academicism, as from the mechanical use of authentic 'folk' art (quite apart from my personal sentiment for it!), something which always leads to the saddest and least fruitful of all 'academicism', and which has, *nota bene*, an unpleasant habit of dressing itself up in a multitude of grand passwords. I was concerned with an inner experiment, of conferring mighty, concise shapes on something which in the mysterious life of the soul is both the most real and the most elusive. I repeat once again that the actual, tangible result of these efforts, i.e., the 60 pages of the score of *Stabat Mater*, is still for me an unknown *x* and I will only succeed in establishing its true position in the evolution of my musical work from a more distant perspective.

MG: But what form does the work take?

KS: It is scored for a smallish orchestra (double woodwind – the Mozart type of orchestra), a chorus (whose *qualité* is more important than its *quantité*) and three soloists: soprano, contralto and baritone. I divided the 20-strophe text (in tercets) into six sections, thematically unconnected and different in fundamental character. I was only directed by instinct in making these internal divisions: I attempted to isolate the most characteristic, contrasting moments and tried to place them in a certain perspective so that the breaking up of the whole into separate fragments (in musical terms, into separate movements) would not undermine the internal cohesion of the work. The construction of a work of art depends on the preservation of proportion between particular, often contradictory elements which stand in opposition to one another. In music, whose emotional content must run parallel to the poetic content of the words forming the text, preservation of these proportions is doubly difficult. More often than not, in place of the complete harmonisation of both elements (words and musical thoughts) we see a hopeless struggle, as a result of which one capitulates before the other: in effect, we have either a soulless declamation, helplessly proceeding through the ups and downs of a psychological intonation of the words or else, more frequently, the complete submersion of that intonation by an unfettered musical element. Thus the word loses its actual, conceptual and emotional content, and becomes only the underlying pretext, a mechanical syllabification, on which an *a priori* musical form is based. Hence the hundredfold repetition of one word or phrase, conceptually and emotionally absurd, bearable only in a foreign, albeit comprehensible language, but not in one which is in 'everyday' use. As an example, I cite Rossini's masterpiece, so well known here, his celebrated *Stabat Mater*, whose true religious content is lost in the naïve dramatisation of the text, in those masterly operatic finales, duets, quartets and ensembles, which last in total around three hours.

MG: So you are not a devotee of this work?

KS: No! But I am of the composer himself. His talent, the sureness of his technique and his genuine 'musicality' are truly dazzling. But it all stops at the point he begins to speak of matters of substance.

MG: I infer from this that your work moves along completely different lines of musical expression?

KS: I have tried to achieve this! Whether I have succeeded, I don't know. The essential content of the hymn is so much deeper than its external 'dramaturgy'! In the face of this, one has to remain calm and collected. As far as possible, one has to avoid the obtrusive and the garish. That artistic moderation, that absolute consciousness of the aims and purposes of a given work, is for the real artist the most difficult thing to accomplish.

Part Three
ON NINETEENTH-
CENTURY MUSIC

Romanticism
in the Present Era

This article originated in response to a request from Mateusz Gliński, editor of the periodical *Muzyka*, for the composer's opinions on nineteenth-century Romanticism and its impact upon his own work. It was published in the 1928 summer edition of *Muzyka* as part of a symposium commemorating the centenary of Schubert's death. Other contributors included Casella, Dukas, de Falla, Glazunov, Hába, Honegger, Malipiero, Prokofiev, Ravel, Roussel, Schreker, Suk, Tansman and Wolf-Ferrari.

I confess quite openly that *Muzyka's* questionnaire on the subject of Romanticism in the Present Era has caused me considerable trouble. One ought to start with a precise definition of the concept of 'Romanticism in Music', and on this alone it would be possible to write a fair-sized volume. Having done that I might then be able to ascertain whether, and to what extent, Romanticism has played a role in my work, this being the second and, in the opinion of the editorial board of *Muzyka*, the more important part of the enquiry.

Because space is short, I shall express myself as succinctly as possible, and therefore am advancing, without any supporting arguments or evidence, a handful of opinions, couched in a very simple, straightforward manner.

First of all, I am of the opinion that 'Romanticism' is one of those historical terms which, in spite of its intellectual 'breadth' and the vagueness of its outlines, is usually applied in discussions of artistic and literary matters as a *fixed, unchanging concept.* This approach has now become quite absurd in that Romanticism, understood in the simplest and crudest way, has now been dragged into the battle between the older 'pre-war' generation and younger musicians, who, at least in Poland's case, attempt with what can only be regarded as *unquestionable reasonableness* to reach a critical, objective view of the Romanticism of the past. The older generation regard Romanticism as a lost paradise, beyond the gates of which lie vast deserts of arid experimentalism. But in their senile obstinacy, they forget that it is only to madmen like Colombus that we owe a debt of gratitude for crossing oceans in order to discover new, golden shores. For the 'young', Romanticism is a stifling prison from which they have escaped to breathe invigorating, fresh air outside. They have regained freedom of action, and the possibility of new conquests lies before them, but they forget that their old prison could be a marvellous edifice with architecturally immaculate lines.

In bestowing upon Romanticism an entire, vital 'pathos', an entire emotional content in relation not merely to artistic questions but to life in general, both warring parties have confused the issue still further, so that it is well-nigh impossible to arrive at a precise definition of terms because of the constantly shifting ground. Consequently, I believe that the subject of 'Romanticism in music' cannot be considered simply from the point of view of the 'musical profession', but only as part of a wider survey, taking in all of mankind's cultural and philosophic activity within this particular epoch.

But to the matter in hand: let us leave these elevated regions behind and descend to the purely 'technical' level. Does a clearly defined Romantic 'musical style' really exist? It would seem that it does indeed, since we employ the term as a fixed constant in all kinds of predominantly sterile disputes. But what is the basis of this musical style? Not the least of our difficulties begins here. It is beyond dispute that it was precisely in this epoch that the development of compositional techniques, the intensification of expressive means and the singular refinement of the musical language all reached previously unknown heights. In itself this very richness hinders the search for a stylistic 'common denominator'. We must remember that within a very brief period of only a few decades, Chopin and Berlioz, Liszt and Schumann as well as Richard Wagner, on the threshold of a wonderful creative flowering, were all composing at the same time. What a marvellous variety and abundance of creative artists, so mutually exclusive and so frequently in conflict! How can we really determine a stylistic relationship between Chopin and Berlioz, Schumann and Wagner during his *Flying Dutchman* and *Tannhäuser* years?

Let us try another method. Let us leave aside the positive aspects which testify to the wealth of music at that time, and consider instead the negative elements, namely those elements which lead via the concept of style directly to the concept of mannerism and stereotype.

Even the most creatively gifted possess a weak spot, a sort of 'Achilles' Heel' by which they make contact with the earth, or the generally prevailing taste of any given epoch. The higher the creative flight, the weaker the link with the prevailing style. The lesser the talent (and character!), the more firmly is the work embedded in this easily worked, highly fertile soil. It is a truism that the genius works for the style of the *future*, just as it is also a truism to say that the artist of average ability is content to work within the established contemporary style. From these two truisms it is possible to arrive at a seemingly paradoxical conclusion, namely that the style of the epoch is essentially the sum-total of the 'Achilles' Heels' of all the artists working at the time, and that the common denominator of this style is more readily to be found in short-comings (and over-reachings), stereotypes and mannerisms, than in the impulse of truly gifted creative genius. I would say that this paradox, when applied to the music of the Romantic era, is also truistic. In effect, the variety and individual wealth of the creative figures of the era are something of a hindrance to attempts to assemble a perfect line of knights, fighting for a single common cause. As always those indispensable 'pupils', enthusiasts, acolytes, imitators, epigones, ideological pick-pockets and camp-followers enter the fray on their behalf, and it is to these people, on whose behalf Don Quixotes are

still tilting at windmills, that we owe the creation of the
'Romantic style'. Their contribution is of no further use, as
it represents everything that has been renounced, thrown
out and deemed irrelevant to contemporary life.

We are indebted to these people only for their unbear-
able 'emotional' verbiage, their pathetic sentimentality, the
naïve 'immediacy' of the connections they make between
dull, personal experience and musical 'expression', the
dilettante neglect of form in favour of 'ideological' substance, the lack of heed paid to music's self-sufficiency,
histrionic gestures which carefully conceal inner emptiness
and musical worthlessness, plus a hundred and one other
grievous faults which today I would rather not mention.

To recapitulate: various creative musical geniuses were at
work in the nineteenth century. In their artistic intentions,
they tended towards decentralisation, and so were unable to
create a 'style', in the sense in which we refer, for example,
to Baroque architecture or Classical music, where a certain
organic evolution is at any rate discernable. It is really not
possible to blame these composers for the terrible nightmare arising from the *epigonism* with which we are left and
over which such bloody wars are waged to this day.

What conclusions can we draw from all this? Since a
romantic style in music only exists *à rebours*, as a negative
phenomenon, then *eo ipso* it cannot have the slightest influence on the music of the future. We can only regard
'Romanticism' as the most widely embracing, historicophi-
losophical term for a certain, strictly defined period (the
middle decades of the last century). This 'term' comprises
thousands of exceedingly complicated historical factors,
and although as a concept it undoubtedly exerted a direct
influence on music composed during that period, it is
impossible to pick out those influences which would permit
us to define the 'style' precisely, a 'style' which, independent of other historical circumstances, could arbitrarily
reappear in music of some other century as if it were
revolving in a fantastic orbit around the sun of our artistic
culture. Such designations as 'neo-romanticism' or 'neo-

classicism', which are often found in critical literature and imply the possibility of such stylistic recurrences, are, let us be honest, 'clichés' – as Karol Irzykowski[1] would put it – and they do not correspond to any qualities really existing in music.

The development of music today in the direction of a deeply considered economy of expression, involving the restriction of content to purely musical elements and the search for new formal solutions in the use of a totally structural approach, suggests analogies with such ideal musical organisms as, for example, the Bach fugue or the Mozart sonata, and as a consequence the term 'neo-classical' is now being applied to the works of contemporary composers. But is it possible to speak seriously of a definite return to the classical style because, in one particular sonata by Stravinsky, what sounded like a distant echo of Bach was suddenly to be heard? These expressions are, I repeat, 'clichés', and I believe that the possibility of a 'return to Romanticism in the music of the future' (mentioned in the first of *Muzyka's* questions) is unlikely. History never repeats itself (thank God!), and old Ben Akiba[2] was simply being a boring, carping pedant with his aphorism to the effect that 'all that now is was'.

2. To all intents and purposes, the above disclosures make replies to the second question concerning the 'influence of Romanticism on my own work' superfluous. In reality, like every artist, I have been influenced not by Romanticism so much as by the succession of great composers living during that era, as well as those who lived in earlier times. At the same time, I must draw attention to two facts in particular: 1) From my earliest years right up to the present day I have fervently and humbly worshipped the 'classical' composers Bach and Mozart, above all others, and after them, Chopin,

---

[1] Karol Irzykowski (1873–1944) was a poet, dramatist, novelist and distinguished literary critic.

[2] Akiba Ben Joseph was a Jewish scholar of the first and second centuries AD.

who, as I have repeatedly remarked, cannot possibly be imprisoned in a tiny Romantic cage, no matter how gilded it be. 2) In spite of the deepest adoration I have for the genius of Richard Wagner, I have him to thank for all those bad musical habits of which I am today determinedly trying to rid myself.

One other matter: it often happens that my own art is described as 'romantic', albeit from two opposing points of view. First there are the 'ancients' who have already developed a liking for my music, but who use this term as if it were an absolution for their sinful, insufficiently law-abiding tastes. The others are the 'young' ones who no longer approve of my music and use the term to indicate their dislike. If we were in France they would dub me *vieux pompier*. In this rather comical fact, a minute detail in the picture of the development of contemporary music, one can ascertain the true value of those grandiloquent definitions when they are divorced from the events of the past to which they are usually applied, and used instead in connection with matters that are still *in statu nascendi*.

*   *   *

I should like to offer a few more explanatory remarks to all those who, having read my above comments and opinions, suspect me of being a devotee of Hanslick's musical aesthetic, encapsulated in the once popular *Vom Musikalisch-Schönen*.[3]

This little book has one indubitable virtue: it is a healthy, albeit naïve, reaction against all those derivative symptoms of Romantic music which I have already attempted to describe, and which, by the turn of the century, many found hard to swallow. Today there is no cause for surprise at this. On the other hand it is marred by numerous faults, of which the worst is the extreme shallowness of its assumptions. This is why it defends with the utmost enthusiasm outposts which are not so much fated to be captured as to be non-existent in

[3] *Cf.* note 2 on p. 74.

the first place. A philosophy of music which confined itself to the closed circle of acoustic phenomena that were more or less pleasing to the ear, thereby reducing the problem to the level of a survey of good and bad restaurants, obviously could not survive in the face of the immediate, psychological experience of even the average listener, an experience which occurs without reference to any particular 'style' or historical era. Today no-one doubts that the only source of real art, of a great musical work, is the profound, mysterious emotion of dread in the face of existence itself. The whole point is that this emotion springs from the *innermost depths* of the human psyche.

The naïve symbolism of the 'feelings', expressed in the work of the least important representatives of romanticism, also resulted from certain emotions, but today we cannot be concerned with such purely sentimental matters. On the contrary, the emotion that grips us when we listen to the *St Matthew Passion* (Classical!), *Tristan and Isolde* (Romantic!) or (*horribile dictu!*) *Pelléas and Mélisande* (Modernism? Impressionism?) always springs from the same crystal-clear source. How then can we use Romanticism as a constant, binding yardstick?

Any sensitive person who is capable of escaping from the superficialities of everyday life can experience this emotion: he does not have to be a creative artist. But a work of art has to be created with the basic, raw materials of the art in question (sound, word, colour, shape), and the true artist naturally has to learn how to handle them. The antithesis of the profoundly artistic, but, if we are talking of *métier*, 'unskilled' individual, is the superficial artist who is able to fashion his material competently without the necessary 'emotional' basis (in the most vital sense of the expression). This psychological dualism gave rise to the fundamentally false antithesis of 'form' and 'content' in art. It is false because *in a real work of art, form and content are completely intertwined,* this being a *sine qua non* in art of real value. We often meet with absurd statements in undistinguished music criticism to the effect that 'Mr X has thoroughly mastered symphonic form, but the musical content is insignificant and lacking in any real value'. It is a fundamentally absurd statement because the symphony cannot be regarded as a 'prototype' or 'Platonic idea'; it exists only in each individual instance as a successful or unsuccessful material expression of a particular creative idea. (We are not of course speaking here of the school-room classification of 'musical form' which serves a pedagogic purpose.)

A certain mental habit of 'classification', if so it may be described, has led us to apply this essentially non-existent dualism of 'form' and 'content' in the sphere of historical development. We habitually contrast 'classicism' (form) with 'Romanticism' (content), and so transport the whole affair into the realms of the exclusively artistic, and pass over those other non-artistic historical events which had a direct influence upon the shaping of the style of a given era. There is here, in my opinion, a purely dialectic misunderstanding; it arises from the confusion of stylistic concepts (perhaps even mannerisms) with the concept of the true value of an individual work of art, composed so to say *sub specie aeternitatis.*[4]

Let us come to a final understanding about the basic meaning of terms: if 'Romanticism' in music means an absolute unity and balance between form and content in a given work (disregarding its artistic-stylistic traits), then we are agreed on Romanticism. But perhaps I should remark that if we carry this ruling to its logical conclusion, then not only Bach, Handel, Mozart and Gluck, but Palestrina as well, must have seemed 100% Romantic to their contemporaries.

Romanticism! I refuse to conceal a certain dislike for this fine-sounding word. It has been much abused. All that is feeble, irresponsible, childish and immature in Polish art today has slipped in using it as a password, and such aspects form a sorry contrast with those organic, truly creative

---

[4] From the point of view of eternity; an expression first used by Spinoza in his *Ethics.*

undertakings which we have to tackle in our new-found freedom. Even the most abject contemporary 'experiment-alist' possesses one unqualified 'plus', namely the personal courage that leads him to burn his bridges and stake all on a single card. In contrast, solemn traditionalism and skilful juggling with the banners of a by-gone era go together to make a doleful, melancholy mask with hollow eye-sockets – a mask which carefully attempts to conceal a fundamental emptiness and creative impotence.

On Romanticism in Music

This article was written at the close of 1928 or early in 1929 in response to the symposium on Romanticism published the previous summer by *Muzyka*. It was first published in two parts in the Warsaw monthly *Droga* (1929, Nos. 1 and 2).

When I read with the greatest attention and concentration a recently published collection of essays entitled *Romanticism in Music*, a fair-sized volume which incidentally has been carefully edited and beautifully produced and which contains my own three-penn'orth, I found to my amazement that no solution was offered to the agonising problem which had so exercised all us artists: on the contrary it posed new, no less 'hermetic' riddles.

The fact of the matter is this: the contents of the monograph, which is highly characteristic in its expression of 'contemporaneity', consist of several dozen articles by people who are not only distinguished in the sphere of contemporary music, but who, and this is especially interesting, are highly cultured in a wider, more general intellectual sense. It was striking that in the various outpourings on the theme of 'Romanticism in Music', contributed by celebrated figures from such widely differing backgrounds, there was a fairly unanimous emphasis on the second and third-rate features of the period, and, especially in the case of the 'younger' contributors, the attitude towards these features was, on the whole, *negative*. But there was not one more or less *common formula* defining the deepest and most enduring basis of our relationship, that is the relationship of the representatives of contemporary art, to Romanticism as a historical concept. Such definitions cannot result from more or less vague psychological

154

enquiries which take the heart of the matter beyond the historical dimension.

In a significant measure this seems to offer confirmation first for my position, clearly stated at the start of my contribution to this monograph, namely that without a precise definition of terminology, any sort of discussion about the probability of a return of Romanticism in music, or of its continuing influence on particular contemporary composers, is impossible. Secondly, Romanticism as a basic 'common denominator', not in so far as the historical concept of the term is concerned but with regard to particular creative traits evident during that era, has to be established *à rebours*, in other words, by way of its *negative* manifestations.

In any case it is quite clear that the opinions of basically creative people can have a deeply subjective colouring, and so can tend in different directions. But in this case the divergence, or rather the 'eccentricity' (and I deliberately use the word here in its original sense) of opinions is so astounding (e.g., Hába,[1] Boughton,[2] Hauer,[3] Ravel and

---

[1] Alois Hába (1893–1973) studied with Novak in Prague before going on to Vienna where he took private lessons with Franz Schreker in 1918. He also worked as a proof-reader for Universal Edition, correcting scores by Schoenberg, Szymanowski and Janáček. From 1920 to 1923 he worked at the Berlin Hochschule für Musik, and during these years began to formulate his system of composition using quarter- and sixth-tones. From 1923 until his death he lived in Prague, working at the Conservatory where he established a department of micro-tonal music which, apart from an interruption during the war, functioned from 1934 to 1951, when it was officially closed by the Czech government. His quarter-tone masterpiece is the opera *Matka* (*The Mother*).

[2] Rutland Boughton (1878–1960), a 'Romantic' English composer, strongly influenced by Wagner. He planned an operatic centre at Glastonbury similar to Wagner's Festical Theatre at Bayreuth.

[3] Josef Matthias Hauer (1883–1959), an Austrian composer who developed a system of twelve-tone composition independently of Schoenberg.

Rathaus[4]), that one can only conclude that there was no profound, thorough consideration of the problem – and this, after all, is a problem which would appear to be organically linked with the contemporary development of art, which in turn is a kind of free, totally unrestrained improvisation on a given theme. And yet the majority of the contributors have their roots, at least *chronologically*, in this era! Whence the insuperable divide? The presence of the whole problem? There seems to be only one logical conclusion: Romanticism in its *definitive sense* (and we are concerned here with just such a definition) is undoubtedly a matter which is no longer relevant, worse still it is something which has *no organic connection* with the bases of art today, and is a domain best left to the exclusive attention of historians and philosophers.

It is worth reflecting further on the matter. Although I made my position unequivocally clear in my contribution to the monograph, I wrote in a rather aphoristic fashion and so I should like to discuss the matter more deeply here. But first, in order to amass suitable material and arguments, let us look a little more closely at the substance of this interesting book.

It opens with a remarkably beautiful introduction by Juliusz Kaden-Bandrowski.[5] His position is one of 'poetic agnosticism': 'Nobody knows anything about it (Romanticism). So little that they are forever renaming it. It changes its name as a snake forever sheds its skin', he says at the close of his poetic introduction. From one point of view, this position is closest to my own, and is the most 'synthetic' of the whole book because its author has the most profound

---

[4] Karol Rathaus was born in Tarnopol, Poland, in 1895 and died in New York in 1954. From 1913 he studied with Schreker in Vienna, and in 1920 joined Schreker, Krenek and Hába at the Berlin Hochschule für Musik. He moved to Paris in 1932, went on to London in 1934 and finally settled in the United States in 1938. He became professor of composition at Queens College, New York, a post he held until his death. His works are somewhat eclectic in style and include symphonies, stage and film scores, chamber music, piano pieces and songs.

[5] Juliusz Kaden-Bandrowski (1885–1944), a novelist and critic.

understanding of the subject. In effect it is within our power to choose this, rather than that name for that essentially mysterious something which is the age-old inherent property of the human spirit: the uncontrollable creative impulse, that sacrificial fanaticism which attempts to attain those heights and depths which reach above and beyond the confines of everyday existence and mundane experience. Suddenly, at some mysterious crossing of the ways of history, a mighty force erupts. In its white heat, precious metals are reforged, and treasures which will never be encrusted with rust created to be counted amongst the common property of mankind. The flame then dies down, scarcely smouldering for decades, or even centuries, before flaring up again for whatever reason. This creative, artistic power is beyond time and place: it cannot be confined to one place at a given time, at a fleeting moment of eternity. 'Romanticism', 'Prometheism' – all those fine-sounding words! This force 'changes its name as a snake forever sheds its skin', but it endures indefatigably, ever powerful, constantly aspiring to ever greater heights.

But it is not of this Romanticism that we speak, but of the dawn, flowering and twilight of the Romanticism which we have come to associate inseparably with the history of the nineteenth century. We also must consider the possibility of its 'return' and of its influence on contemporary art. I shall henceforth use the word in this precise and limited sense.

In the subsequent pages of the monograph we find still more abundant and thoroughly positive material upon which to reflect. First of all, Cezary Jellenta's[6] *Prolegomenon* establishes a historico-philosophical, poetic starting-point for the whole book. In a series of profound, penetrating observations, the author sketches a general background and reveals hidden connections linking music with both poetry and painting. It is highly characteristic of the author

---

[6] Cezary Jellenta, pseudonymn of Napoleon Hirszband (1861–1935), a writer, critic, poet and, in his youth, baritone singer.

that he should venture far beyond the chronological confines of the era in his search for substantiating artistic evidence. He goes back to Shakespeare, Tasso, Petrarch and even to the dawn of the Renaissance (represented by Dante). But why not go further? Are not the three great tragedians[7] classicists only because we have become obsessed with setting classicism against romanticism? Was not the whole of that era essentially a Hellenic Romanticism *sui generis*? The current notion of Classicism appeared first with Winckelmann,[8] seriously lost balance in the works of Goethe, and finally gave up any sort of notional value in the profoundly 'Romantic' aesthetic of *The Birth of Tragedy*.[9] Here again we have that vicious circle: is Romanticism an innate psychological property, a certain position adopted in the face of questions of life and creativity, or is it a means of classification, the title of one short chapter in the history of man?

The following articles (*Form and Art* by Dr Józef Reiss, *Sphere of Ideals* by K. Stromenger, *Problems of Form* by Dr Bronisława Wójcikówna),[10] as well as the lengthy series of contributions from various musicians, transport us properly into purely musical regions, and here the problem begins to become more complicated. First of all, almost every article cites the same traits as being characteristic features of the music of that epoch, while in my opinion these traits are of

---

[7] Aeschylus, Sophocles and Euripides.

[8] Jan J. Winckelmann (1717–68), German archaeologist, historian and author, whose chief work was *Geschichte der Kunst des Alterums*.

[9] *Die Geburt der Tragödie aus dem Geiste der Musik* (*The Birth of Tragedy out of the Spirit of Music*) by Friedrich Nietzsche, first published in 1872.

[10] Józef Reiss (1879–1956) was a Polish musicologist who, after specialising in renaissance music, played an important role in the general development of musical education in Poland. He was appointed professor at the Jagiellonian University, Kraków in 1949. Karol Stromenger (1885–1975) was a writer and critic, and Bronisława Wójcik-Keupralian was an expert on Chopin and the Romantic era.

secondary importance. In themselves they do not determine the value of a given work, but only its general
character. They reveal the direct link with the common
ideological currency of the day. They are the 'Achilles'
Heels' which I mentioned. The sum-total of which gives us
some idea of the mannerisms of the era rather than the
style. In this case the mannerisms consist of a direct link with
poetry and, stemming from this, the specific lyricism of the
sung word (the later *Musik als Ausdruck* of Wagner!), the
more immediate use of nature ('picturesque' in the
parlance of the painting profession), subjectivity, eroticism,
and the world of the 'supernatural' – hence those elves,
demons, devils and the rest of that often naive 'Fürchten-
machen' to be found in the operas of Marschner, Spohr and
even Weber. But if we want a fuller explanation of the
origins of these mannerisms, we have to make further
excursions into the past, drawing on names mentioned in
these articles, such as Bach, Handel, Mozart and even
Monteverdi! And this is certainly justifiable, for in the arias
(and sometimes even the recitatives!) of the above composers, is it not possible to perceive that essentially
expressive quality of the word which powerfully, and as if
magically, intensifies the musical element, raising it by the
power of 'x'?

Eroticism, then! But the author of *Sphere of Ideals* acknow-
ledges that the whole of Mozart's operatic output is literally
awash with it. Is it not he who also remarks that the appearance of the spectre of the Commendatore is a grim,
powerful call from a world beyond ours, the existence of
which is felt increasingly strongly right up to its final eruption in the divine grief of the *Requiem*? In other words, the
'supernatural' is not peculiar to Romanticism, neither does
it have a specific *made in* Romanticism patent. Subjectivity
then! But in the entire history of man's art, regardless of
style or epoch, only one great musical corpus sprang from
this fertile soil, although it has to be said that its greatness is
attributable entirely to its *objective*, self-sufficient mode of
expression. It is none other than the impressive longing of

Bach: '*abzuscheiden und bei Christo sein*'.[11] An unappeasable desire for eternity erupted from the depths of his soul. The intensity of his momentary, illuminating vision drew his eyes away from earthly matters, and permitted him to hear heaven's mysterious harmonies. In his perfect, objectively realised works, e.g., the Passions, the B minor Mass and some of the chorales, he gave *subjective expression to the most profound of human experiences*, namely confrontation of the self with God and eternity. What more could Mendelssohn say with his *Pauls* and *Elijahs*, Berlioz with his *Requiem*, to some degree even Beethoven with his *Missa Solemnis*, and Wagner with his *Parsifal*. I include Wagner because, in pursuing his particular mode of subjectivity, the late Romantic in general has been able to make histrionic play with even his religious ideas and his personal relationship with God. In so doing he has made of it a tool for wielding influence over his audience, an attribute of his personal power. This psychological trait of the *romantic artist* immediately becomes completely comprehensible when the upheavals and reconstructions at the heart of society, the result of catastrophic, albeit ultimately fruitful historical events, are taken into account. These ideological changes made it easier for the creative artist, unquestioned by any authority, to make his way up to the top of the social ladder. Such 'histrionics', based on inner experiences (often bordering on exhibitionism) were fruitful only in cases where there was creative genius, will and character. In the works of composers of 'lesser dimensions', the results were often intolerable. Either they lost themselves helplessly in the maudlin sentimentality of 'immediate' experience, or else their boring, personal affairs were pathetically inflated to assume the proportions of universal catastrophe. It is precisely this characteristic of romantic 'subjectivity' which

[11] Seemingly an incomplete citation of a line from a spurious Bach cantata, *Zu Mariae Reinigung:* 'Ich habe Lust zu scheiden und bei Christo zu sein'.

provoked a strong reaction among the present generation. Contemporary artists have experienced a multitude of catastrophic upsets and revolutions, and find themselves once more having to deal with a new, historical reality. In short, they are faced with the categorical need to change completely their attitude towards historical reality, and they fully realise that nobody today is going to be fooled by external, theatrical flourishes.

So, 'subjectivity, eroticism, poetry', etc., etc. Granted! But let us now peep behind the scenes of this huge historical stage and study the 'characterisation' of the various actors. And so, for example, is it not a cause for some degree of irritation that Berlioz composed the *Symphonie Fantastique,* that monstrous manifestation of *mauvais goût* and artistic immoderation, simply because he was in love with some totally irrelevant English woman? In that it suffers from the 'bad taste' characteristic of this epoch – a 'bad taste' which Chopin, for example, was able completely to avoid – this symphony presents us with a typical 'Achilles' Heel' of the period. This kind of 'eroticism' (very fashionable at the time) cannot on any account be included on the credit side of Romanticism's balance-sheet. Discretion is the mark of the gentleman, and it is also binding on the artist. In short, the vitality of any given work is determined only on the basis of its objective value, certainly not its autobiographical sources.

We should not forget that, in the case of Berlioz, we are dealing with a composer who was practically a genius. He created the modern orchestra, and when able to free his mind from erotic pre-occupations, he could compose such masterpieces as the greater part of *The Damnation of Faust* and *Queen Mab* (and it was not to the 'elves' alone that she owed her magical, sparkling intensity).

There can be no doubt that that soft-centred, vanilla-flavoured Jew, Felix Mendelssohn-Bartholdy, was also a 'subjective'. In truth, I have never been able to understand on what grounds this dull and boring composer came to be considered a 'genius' and a 'romantic'. Perhaps it was because his symphonies and overtures have names ('Scottish', 'Italian', and so on). Perhaps it was because his Shakespearian elves were made to dance a *majufes*.[12] There is nothing individual about his treatment of 'form', while the *Songs without Words* became an all-time prototype for sickly, sentimental, bourgeois salon-music. He was never able completely to free himself from the shackles of classical form, but I suppose we should really be rather thankful for this. Had he frolicked romantically after the fashion of Berlioz, the result would have been quite intolerable. He exerted a doubtful influence on such as Robert Schumann, who, although a great talent, became entangled in the web of this kind-hearted spider and was unable to free himself from the supposedly great man's simply manic suggestive power. Undoubtedly Mendelssohn played an enormous and very fruitful role in the propagation of musical culture in Germany, but this is to some degree incidental.

The 'supernatural world' is inseparably linked with the painted canvas backcloths and cardboard scenery of the theatre, or more precisely, the opera. This is only to be expected, since opera became the *most popular* form of romantic art, and although in conception it derived from the purely 'second-rate' traits of Romanticism, it also constituted a sort of embryo of the *synthetic* art-form eventually to be realised at Bayreuth. In itself opera provided an ever-growing public with an easily digested illusion of various ideological, extra-musical profundities, which became something natural and vital when presented by way of the 'histrionic' gesture inherent in drama. Of course this did not guarantee the staying-power and true value of the works originating in this era. And so the 'supernatural world' of Marschner, Lortzing and Spohr, inhabited by every conceivable sort of elf, demon and vampire (Mozart was content to make do with humans when he composed his masterpieces!), glimmered with a pallid, spectral light for a little while before suddenly flickering out at one wave of the

[12] Jewish ritual song.

'great sorcerer's' hand.[13] It was he who forced the lyric theatre on to achieve an unheard-of power, having first distilled in the demonic laboratory of his brain everything that was of any value at all in the legacy of the originators of the 'supernatural world'. Of that cardboard pandemonium there remain only some old stage-sets stored away in German opera-houses and a few charming overtures by Weber, which, in the nick of time, were smuggled onto the concert platforms of posterity where they still survive amongst the masterpieces of the orchestral repertory. When the concert-goer hears them today, he little imagines that once they were the gateway to a gloomy world of ghosts and sorcery.

Against this bustling, lively background, full of surprising, dazzling shafts of light, ideological dovetailings and criss-crossings, contradictions and naive enthusiasms, that great man, Fryderyk Chopin, appeared. He came almost like a being from another world in that he drew entirely on his own innate wealth of invention and stood independent of all other musical figures and phenomena. He stood above everything which was happening in music at that time. There was much which irritated and annoyed him. Against this background he seems so modern that there is simply no perspective by which he can be viewed in relation to his immediate surroundings. In spite of this, he often praised with a lordly gesture and gracious, benign smile the art of his time, interesting himself perhaps in an opera by Bellini or even one by Meyerbeer. But his 'modern' outlook is evident in the fact that he was only truly taken by the 'alien' music of Bach and Mozart. In spite of the many years that separated him from the temporal existence of these great composers, their art is related and has its mysterious origins far beyond the immediate surroundings of that feverish, manically lyrical 'Romanticism'.

In reality the secret of the amazingly imperishable quality of Chopin's art lies in this tiny phrase: 'beyond his epoch'. Let us reflect further on this point: Chopin's work is not

---

[13] A reference to Wagner.

only unable to serve as even a very general model for
'Romantic music', but, on the contrary, in its very essence is
a categorical denial of all those aforementioned traits which
in my opinion were a negative, albeit 'essential', part of the
musical works dating from that era, whether by second-rate
composers or stars of the first magnitude. The distinguishing trait of Chopin is undoubtedly his existing 'beyond his
epoch', and the enduring vitality of his art results not just
from his innate, inner creative dynamism, but from the
objective stand he took in relation to his own art. In the
music of the nineteenth century, there is only one other
composer whose aesthetic outlook is analogous for similar,
though not identical reasons, and that is Franz Schubert.
But the real pedigree of this type of creative animal goes
back much further, and once again we find ourselves talking
about Bach and Mozart and the secret of their marvellous
'craft', by which they were able to curb the flowing element
of a previously subjective experience, and forge it into the
objective, ever-enduring form of a work of art. Only through
such an approach are we able to solve the riddle surrounding both Chopin's vitality and the ever deepening abyss that
separates us from the other geniuses of the romantic era.

In striking contrast to Chopin's self-contained artistic
perfection, we have Wagner's truly gigantic output! It was
inevitable that, when taken to its logical conclusion,
Romantic ideology should give rise to the notion that a work
of art was in a sense a 'topical' offering on account of its
indissoluble union with the spirit of the era in which it came
into being. The inevitable ideological changes and alterations in our perception of the overall historical content of
our age have automatically undermined the aesthetic bases
that until so recently seemed intact. Today we find ourselves
face to face with a particular phenomenon of great force
(no one today would question that!) which is, however, like
a musical instrument played in a vacuum, so incapable is it
of producing a sound that we are able properly to perceive.
(If I use the pronouns 'we', 'our', etc., here, this in no way
means that I personally shall never find a way into the

aesthetic emotions of this particular world. But it is quite clear to me that the trend towards a fundamental revision or revaluation of our ideas about Wagner must answer to basic psychological facts, and not depend on snobbery or any similar second-rate contrivance habitually employed by critics of the previous generation.)

It is interesting to discover which of the many complex elements of Wagner's works now seem most alien to us. Logically we cannot object to his imposing concept of an all-embracing work of art which is synthetic in character, a work of art able to fill the aesthetic void facing the community of man in the widest sense of the word. We cannot therefore take exception to its extra-musical ideology, or rather, an ideology which is really supra-musical. We perhaps have reservations about the pretensions which are inherent *a priori* in such a concept. We are however dealing with works which have been in existence now for half a century, and which have become the object of almost fanatical admiration. On the other hand, we find that their purely aesthetic (musical and, to a certain extent, poetical) qualities were never fundamentally in dispute, even if they were open to criticism from one point of view or another. So that sense of 'alienation' undoubtedly stems from something else, namely the highly subjective relationship of the artist to his work. In this case it involves the 'histrionic' gesture taken to its utmost limits (an inevitable consequence of the romantic evolution), weighed down by the mighty burden of personal experience, and the victory of an all-powerful will over self–sufficient, objective artistic values. It is obvious that all those appalling Wagnerian epigones (with Bruckner at their head) show as clear as day the total impotence and helplessness of such a creative stance in relation to art. Seen in this light even Wagner appears to be some kind of huge mistake, but of such cyclopean proportions that by this very fact he aroused both admiration and something approaching dread!

To account for the origins of this, the last mighty chord of Romanticism which, like the rest of the era, has now died away, I must at long last mention a name that up to now I have intentionally avoided. I refer of course to Ludwig van Beethoven.

I must remark that in the monograph devoted to Romanticism his name appears only rarely, and usually in connection with the close of the classical era. At most he is credited with the first sporadic glimmerings of Romantic thought. The author of *Sphere of Ideals* ventures the furthest, describing him as the 'last of the classicists, poised on the frontiers of Romanticism, or else the first of the Romantics', albeit one who did not come to grips with the central problem. Mr Rathaus's view of the real significance of the finale of the 9th Symphony is to be commended. An insufficient awareness of the role of Beethoven in the history of Romantic music is, in my view, the reason for the difficulties encountered in the search for a general formula for this particular historical phenomenon.

I believe that Beethoven was the most profoundly eloquent symbol of his time. We know that he was born into the classical tradition, and that this was his starting-point in the quest for a new Ideal. As such he bridged two eras. The colossal burden of historical catastrophes and events of great power and consequence roared like a storm through his consciousness and channelled deep furrows in it. His music became a true likeness reflected on some mystical screen of the immediate historical substance (in the deepest sense of the word) of the fifty years that was his span on earth. Along with his contemporaries he searched for that new 'word which would become flesh', and his seemingly abstract art is clearly marked by the traces of his search and discovery of it. In effect his creative drive depended on the conscious breaking-down of the artistic forms inherited from his ancestors. The psychological source of this apparently destructive, yet in reality thoroughly *constructive*, work was doubtless a sensitive subconscious state that did not confine itself merely to the sphere of aesthetic matters. In their essence these aesthetic ideas were inherited from his great predecessors; we have eloquent testimony to this in all those works of his first period. Here we see living proof of how the inviolable inheritance gradually underwent a process of transformation in the evermore pressing search for a new 'form of expression', a new 'word' that would be the 'word', not just for creative artists, but mankind in the widest and most essential sense of the word. It means that we see here the gradual, mysterious crystallisation of the romantic idea. It constituted the entire substance of that creative artists psyche in its application to music, being the only means of expression which he had at his command. The full torment involved in the forging of new forms becomes increasingly evident in the late sonatas and quartets, where a secret 'password' always seems to be hidden away. The classical canons and formulae are broken down, transformed and re-arranged in a new order at the bidding of an unseen hand and for a purpose which seems far from obvious. Eventually this 'word' will resound clearly and unequivocally in *Fidelio*.[14]

But the operatic stage was not an effective platform for the thoughts of the great solitary. It was too limited and, in spite of its realism, too artificial. In any case he was not enough of an actor to be able to tolerate painted stage-sets as the living truth.

The inevitable moment was finally to dawn when that long suppressed inner force deliberately and wilfully set about its final act of destruction to unveil a new and boundless world of the most profound experience imaginable. After three symphonic movements, tragic histories of the cruellest human misery of one immured within the gloomy prison of bitter solitude, a sledge-hammer knocks down those prison walls and smashes the other-worldly, artistic edifice to smithereens, after which the magical 'word' is at last proclaimed from the rubble in joyous, disorderly song: *Alle Menschen werden Brüder!*

[14] The chronology of events implied by Szymanowski here is incorrect. *Fidelio* was first staged on 20 November 1805, whereas the late sonatas were composed between 1816 and 1822 and the late quartets between 1823 and 1826.

The choice of text for the finale of the 9th Symphony was by no means fortuitous, the result perhaps of purely poetic considerations. The decisive factor was undoubtedly the intellectual and ideological content of Schiller's hymn in which the full gravity and substance of the 'word' is positively and specifically expressed. In creating his greatest masterpiece, Beethoven was certainly far removed from purely aesthetic concepts. Instead he was at his closest to the very fountain-head of contemporary life, that internally glowing and uncontrollably coursing Life which is, day in, day out, posing questions of untold importance for those of course who are capable of understanding their full significance. Without doubt, Beethoven was one of those who 'understood' and who shouldered part of the ideological burden of his era, and perhaps his true greatness lies in his ethical qualities, rather than in the now slightly faded aesthetic qualities of his music.[15]

[15] Further evidence of Szymanowski's ambivalent attitude towards the music of Beethoven is to be found in a contribution to the Berlin paper *Vossische Zeitung* on 26 March 1927, one of a series of tributes published to mark the centenary of Beethoven's death under the title 'Die Welt huldigt Beethoven' ('The World pays tribute to Beethoven'). Other contributors included Ernest Ansermet, Alfred Cortot, Edward J. Dent, Manuel de Falla, Alexander Glazunov and Leoš Janáček. The complete text of Szymanowski's contribution is as follows:

What does Beethoven mean to me? Or rather, what did he mean? I need not say anything about his objective greatness. It is only a question of how I, subjectively, perceive his work.

He was a profound experience for me in my artistic youth. For the first time in the Kingdom of Art I understood how one could be consumed by the flames of one's own fire.

The unheard-of creative urge, the will to conquer a mythical world of heroes (in reality only a symbol), the will with which real music as a complex of sounding notes could scarcely keep pace, so often staggering along breathless, finally expressed itself in the super-human loneliness and resignation of the last quartets and sonatas.

The pathos of those gigantic, yet futile endeavours appealed to my romantic, youthful pessimism – and this had more joy than grief about it. At a certain moment however, when I moved from youth to maturity, the inhuman tragedy of the 'Joy' of the finale of the 9th Symphony became clear to me.

Today I am mature, rational, full of inner poise and composure.

Just as life does not come into being according to some pre-ordained aesthetic scheme, so art often reaches out beyond its proper sphere of influence. This happens at those sudden critical moments of history when a huge, seemingly destructive wave swells in the breast of humanity. In its essence, however, this wave proves to be creative since it aspires uncontrollably towards new, unknown shores; towards new forms and new ways of expressing social com- · panionship.

At times such as these, Art is threatened with divorce from the vital rhythm of life, and has to descend from its high pedestal of absolute value to mingle with the 'man in the street' in the struggle over his Fate on earth. In so joining the common fight, art becomes concerned with the greatness of that Fate. Already captured outposts are abandoned in order that new, altogether more elevated positions may be won. In the case of music, Beethoven affords the finest example of the supremacy of the ethical over the *aesthetic* in that he made himself responsible for shaping life as a whole rather than concerning himself only with a sublime ideal of abstract Beauty. This was in complete accord with Romantic ideology, which would be totally incomprehensible without this *ethical* factor.

In reality this struggle was concerned with the winning of the cause of man, with the establishing of his absolute value over a historical hierarchy of values that up to that time had been chimerical. It was to be based on one sure foundation: an individual's ability to create.

I try not to look back, horror-stricken at the presence of the so appealing but disturbing ghost from the years of my youth. Instead quietly, with measured steps, I go forward perhaps to find modest but individual qualities of my own.

Today the art of Beethoven is for me – in contrast to the eternally blooming youthfulness of Mozart and the immortality of Bach – one of Earth's most splendid tombstones.

Karol Szymanowski Pisma, Vol. 1, p. 206.

All mankind's thinking at this time was directed along various paths in the direction of this symbolic 'emancipation'. In social, political, philosophical and artistic spheres, sudden illuminating flashes of inspiration occurred and final solutions were discovered for thousands of pressing questions which were awaiting immediate attention. There were frequent excursions into back alleys that proved to be dead-ends, as well as constant breakneck searches for new routes through mountain passes. The only guide was that newly won freedom, born out of a sense of love, in the deepest, most transcendent sense of the word, for mankind in general. This gamble, with man and his hierarchy of real, creative values as the stakes, was played and won, and henceforth the artist was to be found at the head of society as a visible and indisputable symbol of those values. Once the modest producer and purveyor of that luxury article – objective beauty – at the courts of the mighty, he gradually became an active element in the life of society, indeed, almost a dictator in the ever-widening sphere of his own activities, since he was now dealing with matters that were not properly *aesthetic*, but delving ever more deeply into the volatile life of society as it was actually happening.

It is perhaps in the misunderstanding of this fundamentally different relationship of the artist to society that we find the source of that characteristic error, perpetuated so often in historical accounts whenever there is talk of the 'Romantic style' and the possibility of its return. I attempted to emphasise the nature of this error in my contribution to the monograph on Romanticism. The error arises from the isolation of characteristic types and traits, and the subsequent formulation of a general definition of Romantic art, whereas these traits were only the secondary symptoms of a general psychological attitude on the part of mankind when confronted with immediate historical reality, in the profoundest sense of that expression, as opposed to the much more limited, purely aesthetic field of action. In other words, we are today inclined to mistake for a *cause* that which was only a *result* of a whole series of factors which had nothing to do with true art. To all outward appearances it would even be possible to assert, paradoxically, that this whole epoch was not artistic *par excellence*, in the sense in which we describe the Italian Renaissance, but had such a richly vital, life-giving temperament that those initiatives which could not always be justified *artistically* nonetheless created in the artistic world the illusion of a mighty force that was overthrowing old idols and raising up new altars. But when we look at Romanticism today, coldly and objectively, its artistic atmosphere seems alien and irrelevant, apart of course from a few giants in the domains of music and poetry, and it is characteristic that – artistic qualities aside – these figures relate to us by way of our sense of 'then', and even 'now'. Of course this relationship depends upon a series of psychological factors which have nothing in common with pure art (as is the case with our Romantic trinity).[16]

[16] A reference to the poets Mickiewicz, Słowacki (*cf.* note 19 on p. 87) and Zygmunt Krasiński.

Adam Mickiewicz, regarded almost universally as Poland's 'national' poet and greatest writer, was born on Christmas Eve, 1798, in Nowogrodek in the Grand Duchy of Lithuania. After graduating from Wilno University in 1819 he became a school-teacher. A long-standing involvement with political and masonic youth movements led to his being imprisoned for six months in 1823, after which he was directed to work in Russia. He spent the next six years in St Petersburg, Odessa and Moscow before obtaining a passport enabling him to travel abroad, ostensibly for a health-cure. While in Rome he heard of the outbreak of the 1830 rebellion, and after unsuccessfully attempting to return to Poland, settled in Paris in 1832. He died of cholera in Turkey in 1855 whilst organising an anti-Russian force during the Crimean War.

Mickiewicz's poetry was so successful because of the relative accessibility of his language. His works include *Konrad Wallenrod*, the dramatic 'work in progress' *Forefather's Eve*, *Books of the Polish Nation and of the Polish Pilgrims* (a Messianic work concerned with the redemption and spiritual transformation of the western nations through the suffering of Poland), and most important of all, *Pan Tadeusz*, written in 1832–34. *Pan Tadeusz* was initially conceived as an idyll, but was eventually expanded to become a novel in verse. Mickiewicz here returned to the world of his Lithuanian childhood, setting the story at the time of Napoleon's invasion of Russia. Ironically,

When we approach the subject in this way, it becomes possible for us to understand both the heights to which romantic art could aspire and the depths to which it could sink. Everything that originated from this feeling of an individual's freedom to create appeared to be of value, especially when romantic philosophy (Schopenhauer) cast over the whole subject of 'liberation',the mystical, tragic radiance of the 'Absolute'. All artists. great and small, thronged the straight, wide highway that led directly from the moving, Christian idea of love for all men (*Alle Menschen werden Brüder*) to the proud, aristocratic idea of the '*Übermensch*'.[17] All were intoxicated by this sense of freedom; all bathed in the earthly brilliance of the 'absolute', which was now far removed from binding religious disciplines entailing contractual obligations to God, being rather a sense of individual self-esteem raised to an unknown power. (How far we are from that finely wrought, painstaking *métier* of Bach and Mozart who, with the most profound emotion, created in their work humble offerings both to God and all those various Electors and Kaisers!)

In music the suspension bridge, spanning the abyss from the *Hymn to Joy* to the final consequences of Romanticism, encapsulated in Wagner's work, which in turn was directly connected with the author of *Die Welt als Wille und Vor-*

Poland's greatest poet never set foot in the old Kingdom of Poland with Warsaw at its heart.

Zygmunt Krasiński (1812–59) was born into an aristocratic family. Although not compromised by the events of the 1830 rebellion, he chose to spend most of his life in France and Italy. Early in his career he wrote two dramas, both concerned with social decay, *The Undivine Comedy* (regarded by Mickiewicz as the finest achievement of the Slavic theatre) and *Iridion*. Later in life he published some poetry: *The Dawn* (1843) and *Psalms of the Future* (1845, enlarged 1848). He is now regarded as a markedly lesser light than Mickiewicz and Słowacki.

[17] The 'superman' was the embodiment of the ideal type of man in Nietzsche's later philosophy.

stellung[18] and indirectly (in that it revealed a psychological sense of its own *creative licence*) with the idea of the *Übermensch*, symbolises to a certain extent the history of the human soul during those few decades. But when faced with such far-reaching consequences, individualistic philosophy was unable to withstand the terrifying pressures of history as it unfolded. There is a strange irony in the fact that the year 1870,[19] the year that dealt the death-blow to Romantic ideology, should immediately set the scene for the work of the two great posthumous children of Romanticism, namely the stage-works of Wagner and the philosophy of Nietzsche. Unintentionally, these two figures became the spokesmen of the might of the German soul, but it was not the early German soul of Goethe, Schiller and Beethoven − it was rather that of the new historical reality, incarnate in the superior might of the modern state over the individual. At the start of the modern era, Romanticism flared up once again with a final, dazzling firework display of *absolute individuality*. It flickered out, but it left us with the greatest, indestructible trophy, *the freedom of man in the most profound sense of those words*. For no matter what direction history takes today, nor in what way the community and the individual relate one to another, no matter where conflicts over political and social ideals are waged, the *free man* is a constant, fixed quantity, the 'x' which is essential to the solution of the equation of history.

[18] *The World as Will and Idea*, first published in 1818, was one of the most important and influential of the works of Arthur Schopenhauer (1788–1860).

[19] This was the year in which the Franco-Prussian War started. Alsace and Lorraine were seized from the French and added to other German states which had come under Prussian domination. In 1871, the process of German political unification, engineered by Bismarck, was completed with the exclusion of Austria from the German Reich, the establishing of German frontiers as they were to remain until 1918, and the 'promotion' of King Wilhelm I of Prussia to the rank of German Emperor.

On this plane it is clear just how much Romanticism, in the most general sense of the word, belongs to the irretrievable past, even when we are concerned with questions of *style* in relation to purely artistic matters. What is the point of knocking on a door which has already been opened once before? It is perfectly understandable that art should occupy a position quite different from that which it adopted half a century ago in relation to its fundamental problems, and one which incidentally is analogous, though not identical, to that taken in the pre-Romantic era, because today's artists are in some measure free from the obligation to participate in the immediate 'making' of history. Their task, ideally, is once again the creation of an art which has a value *sub specie aeternitatis*, that is an art with a meaning which extends over and beyond the epoch in which it originates. It is precisely the type of art that Bach and Mozart created, and the only difference is, as I have already said, that instead of dedicating our art to the Almighty and all those Electors and Kaisers, we ought to ensure that the recipient of those artistic treasures, hard won in bloody combat, is the human fraternity. The responsibility of the creative artist in the face of society now assumes a quite different significance for us. Gone is the naive aristocratism of the beginning of the new era, expressed in the slogan 'art for art's sake'; gone too are all forms of sentimental, social philanthropy in the sphere of aesthetic emotions, expressed in the 'feeling' of the 'lesser' composers. That leaves us with a firm obligation to forge from the refractory material of reality, an art of the most profound, enduring value. The solution to this artistic question, taking into account our absolute freedom of creative action, is a personal matter for the conscience of each creative artist. That which is incapable of enduring the elements will be swept mercilessly away on the wave of life as it continually reshapes itself. That which is fundamentally indestructible, that which is organically linked to the very essence of existence will be raised on this same wave to exalted, *enduring* heights. My incurable optimism is perhaps psychologically dependent on the indisputable, historical fact that once, in the theatre of Dionysus, *almost the whole* of Athens listened, with the greatest concentration, to the *Oresteia* and *Oedipus* cycles. Does not that intensely beautiful vision of the past represent for us in particular, the artists of today, the highest ideal, albeit one that will not be immediately attained?

Whether the creative artist of today is capable of such a task is a completely different matter, and it is by no means a · fundamental argument against my assertion. First of all, the genuine artistic gift is always in a certain sense a *deus ex machina.* It would appear to result from the unexpected intervention of some mysterious force that operates beyond the normal sphere of human affairs. Furthermore, contemporary art, like all other elements which constitute contemporary life, has not yet entirely escaped from the state of ferment arising from the war. The unprecedented novelty and variety of the problems which arise day by day still do not allow us to discover an entirely safe way forward, but while that completely conscious, obstinate, well-nigh fanatical search for new ideas, forms and means of expression occupies so great a place in artistic opinion today, it is only irrefutable proof of the need to form a new relationship with reality and proof of the essential *vitality* of the present state of affairs. Now we only have an unmistakable sense of the vitality when it originates, not in 'romantic' individualism, but in the deepest possible 'universality'.

In effect today's attempts to create a new front in artistic affairs are proceeding along distinctly 'anti-romantic' lines. In the nature of things, these attempts must answer to modern man's unmistakable psychological make-up. The fashionable definition, *die neue Sachlichkeit,*[20] can be understood dialectically in two ways: first, it involves the application of art to the *commonplaces* of today's life (this

---

[20] The New Objectivity, a musical movement originating in Germany during the First World War as a reaction against the Expressionists. It was markedly anti-romantic in tone, its most distinguished representative during the 1920s being Paul Hindemith.

application has in any case existed at all periods of artistic life), and this in itself would indicate anti-Romantic tendencies. A second possibility is diametrically opposed to the first and is characterised by the aspiration towards the expression of *absolute* values that endure beyond the epoch in which the work was composed. This too is fundamentally *anti-romantic.* The inner drama of the creative artist as he searches out the most certain weights and measures in his pursuit of real values, is enacted between these poles, one a starting-point based on the trivialities of day-to-day life, the other a distant ideal, yet to be realised.

Perhaps it is true to say that in none of the arts is that struggle for the ideal expression of 'contemporaneity' so apparent as it is in music, and this is because music is the art that is most free of *conceptual* content. During the period of romantic intoxication, music was the exponent of 'thrilling' emotions, a magic lantern that shed an unearthly light upon the gloomy interior of the 'experiential' human soul; now she again aspires to peaceful mountain-tops where serene, transcendental castles of beautifully harmonised proportions may be built. Once more she is drawn to erect that idealistic superstructure that towers above the bitter fate of man on earth, namely that *unselfish* beauty which remains for ever mankind's most vital achievement.

Whether the contemporary generation of musicians will attain these heights is a matter open to debate. I have no doubt however that the right path, steep and stony though it be, has now been discovered.

Fryderyk
Chopin

First published in the progressive Warsaw literary magazine *Skamander*, in 1923 (Nos. 28–30).

What a lot we write, say and think about Fryderyk Chopin here in Poland! What an abundance of rhetorically coloured tributes we strew at his feet! And yet the questions that his work raises seem ultimately to be insoluble. We wallow in its profundities, but fear to break free from the magic circle we have so characteristically erected for ourselves around his superhuman heroism, a practice we habitually adopt with all those men of the past who tower above their epoch like mighty bronze statues.

That piety of admiration would be something quite respectable were it not for the fact that it gives rise to a phenomenon which in its effects is most undesirable, namely an addictive questing after markedly emotional regions that cannot lead directly to the secret of the work of a great artist, but rather to a stranding of itself in an inextricably intellectual labyrinth, the way out of which cannot be discovered. The inability to grasp clearly and objectively the nature of whatsoever kind of phenomenon in the field of our national artistic creativity hinders the formation within our society of what might be described as a sense of *national cultural consciousness*.

The anaemic state of that consciousness is most evident in musical matters. A synthetic view of its evolution, of the logical interdependence of individual facts, simply does not exist. The history of Polish music, especially of the nineteenth century, has yet to be written. At present it exists only in the form of a series of biographical studies of its various protagonists in which individual creative contributions are characterised more or less accurately. There is no overall

guiding idea, no ultimate demonstration of organic connecting threads, no robustly conceived, unambiguous
scheme of any sort. As if in quiet resignation, it passes over
the inexpressibly sad fact that here evolution took place
à rebours, descending slowly, step by step, from the lofty
heights of Chopin's genius, eventually to lose itself in a flat,
grey landscape.

It must be stressed that, to a great extent, the cause
for this lies in the wellnigh paradoxical fact that in spite of
the uncritical, almost religious cult of Chopin as a *national
hero*, he was never fully appreciated as a *Polish artist*, as a
result of which his precious work failed to bear fruit and so
remained a self-contained entity, peripheral to subsequent
developments in Polish music.

The work of a great artist only becomes an eternal
source of vital creative power when it takes its proper
place in the national cultural consciousness – a position
that is precisely defined and devoid of all forms of
sentimentalism.

* * *

An unusual and immeasurably fruitful phenomenon in our
cultural history is the 'rediscovery', as it has been called, of
Juliusz Słowacki.[1] His greatness and genius were never in
doubt, but it was only in the Young Poland era that he was
brought down from the misty heights and made to stand
among us. In so doing he lost nothing of his greatness, but
it was only then that we discerned the sparkling eyes of the
'man' behind the sublime, tragic 'seer's' mask. What is
more important, we were able at last to perceive the face of
the 'artist': we understood the marvellous secret of his
métier, we glimpsed his magical art and the true nature of
that wise, magnificent forging of weird, enduring shapes
from the intractable raw material of the 'word'. We were

---

[1] *Cf.* note 19 on p. 87.

even able to experience the rare moments when those hands, while carefully lifting up the superhuman burden of beauty, suddenly trembled under the influence of a heart filled with suffering.

It was at this time that the underlying organic connections between his work and the development of new poetry became evident. His work ceased to be merely a precious relic, an inanimate keepsake of past greatness. It now became something else – above all a 'living', driving force, the mainspring of new values. It became the equivalent of a feverishly coursing bloodstream which was able to nourish the flaccid tissues of the brain. The 'Awareness' of Juliusz Słowacki brought with it a new, previously unknown power that showed us how to proceed in new directions.

Incontestably, the most important question for a future Young Poland in music, indeed almost a *sine qua non* of its existence, would be an analogous 'rediscovery' of Fryderyk Chopin. This would involve the removal of his mummified corpse from the swathing bands of nearly a century's emotive rhetoric. It would lead to a real, practical 'awareness' of the roads leading to the independence of Polish music, roads along which no-one after him has been willing or able to travel.

Until now, Polish literature about Chopin, be it panegyric, biographical or technical, has often, it is true, shed an isolated ray of light on his life and work, yet who to date has been able to focus that ray of light sufficiently strongly and evenly so as to reveal his true face in a permanent, enduring form? Perhaps it is possible that one single writer will still be able to produce that combination of an ideal artistic biography with a creative critique of his work. The man who succeeds in doing this will fearlessly tread the path leading straight to the secret of Chopin's great work and, in the white heat of his ardour, will ultimately succeed in fusing into one knowledgeable rust-free alloy both the greatest admiration and the profoundest possible understanding of Chopin's music. It is becoming increasingly clear today how such a writer should set about his task, and I trust that the

present essay is justifiable in that it attempts timorously to
take a step in the right direction.

*   *   *

When 'revolutionary' musical circles – in effect, the people
who are engaged in protesting feverishly against the music
of the past – pose questions about which of 'yesterday's'
composers are really worthy of their high reputation, the
replies usually consist of rather short lists of famous names
which with two exceptions – Mozart and Chopin – are in a
constant state of flux. The unanimous choice of these
composers and their unwaveringly high standing are highly
characteristic. We are forced to the inescapable conclusion
that an internal relationship exists between the 'classicist'
Mozart and the 'romantic' Chopin. When all is said and
done, the choice of these composers is not dependent on
the scale of their individual talents, even though in both
cases it is considerable. After all, for many people the
'profundities' of Beethoven and the 'elemental power' of
Wagner are a hundred times more persuasive than the
strangely serene, sometimes cool music of Mozart. The
kinship must stem from deeper, spiritual sources, and for a
certainty it has to do with the most essential relationship
that exists between the artist and his work, in other words,
the way in which raw musical material is transformed into a
perfect work of art. In the light of this, we are faced with
grave doubts as to just how far the official tags 'classical' and
'romantic' correspond with reality. In the final analysis, can
the dogmatic classifications of creative individuals within a
pre-conceived historical framework, making them subject
to only the most general traits of various historical epochs,
be sufficiently capable of throwing any light on the deepest
characteristics of the work of any one composer? That
doubt is further intensified by yet another conclusion
arising from today's categorical division of the entire
musical past into two parts: namely, that the 'classicist' and
'romanticist', who are apparently diametrically opposed
because of the ideological nature of their historical epochs,

are of vital and absolute importance for the music which is being created today. Their works then are a signpost for, or perhaps even a firm bedrock upon which the development of today's music can rest firmly and confidently, music which for a few decades now has been developing energetically in spite of, and indeed beyond the bounds of Germany, which until then had been music's official home. Since it sprang up as a protest against 'romanticism', which attained its greatest achievements precisely in Germany, we must assume that it is not the specific 'romanticism' of Chopin to which we relate so closely today, but other features of his genius that in turn undoubtedly relate him to Mozart.

Neither the influences of historical perspective, which to a certain degree have a distorting effect, nor the deep differences that arise from changes in artistic ideologies from one epoch to another, are able to efface the deep kinship that exists between certain creative types, a kinship that is expressed in their most essential relationship to their work.

What about Mozart? There is no doubt that we cannot find in his art any trace of the concept of 'depth', a concept that appeared during the romantic era in Germany, and which still anachronistically haunts our critics in the guise of a threadbare, rather incommunicative symbol for anything of doubtful authenticity.

This music, although notable for its wonderful, almost southern delicacy, and the way in which it is steeped in its own transparent depths of absolute formal perfection, seems to be wrought from brittle metals that will never rust. Mozart's creative process took place, so to say, beyond the sphere of immediate inner experience. As in the case of Benvenuto Cellini, who was just as happy whether he was casting his Perseus or sculpting a golden goblet for his papal patron, it would appear that when Mozart had a work in hand, he modelled it carefully and critically, his eyes smiling with creative joy, conferring on the finished product a shape that was always sure – no matter whether the work was a symphony, *The Marriage of Figaro* or just a pleasing little song. It was always perfect.

It is in this 'objective' relationship of the artist to his work that the secret of indestructible formal perfection may be found. Such a work, charmed out of an unyielding lump of 'material' which expresses nothing but itself, is something that is infinitely 'plastic' and 'positive'. 'Organised' according to its own inner logic, and thus 'confined' within ideally harmonious proportions, the work enjoys a self-sufficient existence that has nothing to do with the stormy, eternally coursing currents emanating from the inner life of its creator.

It is here that we discover the fundamental difference between the attitude of Mozart to a work of art and – let us say – that of his antithesis, Richard Wagner. In the case of Wagner, the uncontrollably rapid, powerful current of his inner experience was not allowed to cool and solidify to form well-defined forms and shapes; it erupted explosively from an inner flame of passion, and the result was an art that was as if a perpetually flowing stream of red-hot lava. In a certain sense, Wagner's art is not 'pure art', but merely an objectively realised function of his admittedly titanic, creative temperament.

*   *   *

It is true that Fryderyk Chopin looked on the work of the great solitary, Beethoven, with esteem but also with a certain unease and unmistakable coolness. His (ungracious!) attitude to the music of Robert Schumann, the tender 'eternal youth' (*'Der ewige Jüngling'* as Nietzsche called him) was somewhat disdainful, but Mozart he admired and worshipped throughout his life.[2]

---

[2] Bach also. But I suppose it would not be difficult to find two musicians, no matter how different their convictions, who were not in accord on this point! –KS

That musical 'futurist'[3] of the romantic epoch (because in effect he created in his seemingly slight piano works the real foundations of the music which was to follow) looked with something approaching terror at Hector Berlioz, who at that time was pounding with romantic fury at the bronze gates of great art and creating those new monstrosities of genius, and instead summoned from the past the ghost of the graciously smiling 'cherubim' of music, and clasped him close to his heart. It seems that the two of them shared some sort of secret understanding of what constitutes the true essence of music!

Chopin's 'classical' predilections in the face of the pre-

---

[3] In 'Fryderyk Chopin and Contemporary Music', an essay first published in the Warsaw Philharmonia's *Concert Bulletin* on 17 and 24 October 1930, Szymanowski wrote more on Chopin's futurism in relation specifically to Schumann:

Above all [...] he [Chopin] was an incomprehensible, threatening 'futurist' a hundred years ago: [...] a real 'futurist', perhaps unconsciously creating the basis of the music of the 'future'. In effect he was [...] a revolutionary, the destroyer of eternal traditions and stereotypes, and the untiring seeker after new ways [...]. The opinions of many contemporary musicians, even when flattering, betrayed at every step of the way total misunderstanding of the fact that they had to do with the simply revelatory work of a genius. [...] As is well known, that celebrated German composer, Robert Schumann, was also a distinguished critic and musical activist fighting for the cause of new music [...]. At the same time he was a man of immaculately pure character, incapable of succumbing to such base motives as personal envy or racial prejudice. But that man, so uncommon in every respect, seemingly cut out to be the one who would understand in the deepest possible way the true value of Fryderyk Chopin's music, was incapable of following him to the furthest limits of his development. This is evident in a whole series of reviews devoted to Chopin, starting from an initial, unreservedly enthusiastic hymn of praise of the earliest works of our composer, and progressing inexorably with the passing of the years towards an evermore marked incomprehension and helplessness in the face of those works in which the true originality and power of the creator of the polonaises found its most profound mode of expression. He gives the impression of running out of breath in his hopeless pursuit of an eagle whose outstretched wings were constantly gaining in strength. Let us look at some of the simply unbelievable outpourings of this German musician [...] regarding the B flat minor Sonata:

vailing atmosphere of his time are very characteristic. Nevertheless the romantic ideology of the epoch has generally determined the background against which we usually perceive Chopin's psychological profile. Romanticism created *a priori* that insurmountable point of view which has governed all our judgments about Chopin and his art. It conferred on him a specific colouring which was further enhanced by the drab background of Polish history at that time.[4] Yet until very recently, a completely objective judge-

---

'Only Chopin could begin and end in this way, with dissonance, through dissonance and in dissonance'. And later, 'the Funeral March is cheerless, and there are even a number of repellent things there'. Finally, the most characteristic opinion about the finale of this sonata: 'It seems to give a sneering impression [...] we cannot praise it, because it is not music'. [...]

[Schumann had] misgivings that Chopin was too confined by 'nationalist' bounds, as a consequence of which he was obliged to lower his soaring flight. [...] 'Chopin's origins,' says Schumann, 'and the fate of his homeland explain his virtues to us, but also account for his shortcomings. When we talk of dreamy disposition, grace, presence of mind, warmth and nobility of feeling, who would not think of Chopin? But again one thinks of him when there is talk of strangeness, unhealthy eccentricity and even hate and savagery'. What a striking misunderstanding of the true significance of Chopin's art and its role in the history of music! One of his greatest claims, that he had the courage, will and strength to imbue music with national, racial elements, and in so doing discover new means of expression and open up previously unknown possibilities of development [...] leaves him open to the accusation that 'he confined himself within nationalist bounds'.

Karol Szymanowski Pisma, Vol. l. pp. 297–98.

[4] In 'Fryderyk Chopin and Polish Contemporary Music', published in *La Revue Musicale* (No. 121, 1931), Szymanowski stressed that the 'non-Polish' concept of Romanticism was significantly different from that prevailing in Poland, and this in turn led to radically different attitudes towards Chopin:

It has to be admitted that because of the complexity of elements which contributed to the formation of this epoch [...] the simple word 'romanticism' goes only a very little way towards providing an exact definition of any of these events. There is no doubt that the same formula provides the basis for the opinion of Poles concerning their greatest musician, but because of the exceptionally tragic

ment concerning the volcanic eruption of Polish artistic creativity in the middle of the gloomiest years of our history was wellnigh impossible. It was as if we tried to perceive the true objective value of his art through a black veil of mourning. But now that the national tragedy of the last century is a thing of the past, the true reality of Chopin's art is thrown into a new perspective. At the dawn of our new era, Chopin now appears much fresher, much more youthful, and his relationship to his surrounding circumstances also seems to have changed. Because of the essential qualities of his art, he seems much closer to us today than do all the other figures of his epoch. He was then more 'isolated', more 'misunderstood', and in turn perhaps even less 'understanding' of the feverish artistic atmosphere of Paris than it would now appear. He certainly seems to have been more 'fashionable' than 'understood', as so often happens when the snobbery of a large town comes into play.[5]

---

conditions in which Poland then found herself, the interpretation itself of the word 'Romanticism' differs in some degree from the sense in which it is habitually and currently used by foreigners. A certain sentimental exaltation, a fierce and heroic grandeur by which we are still accustomed to adorn 'Romanticism' in Poland goes far beyond the precise notions of a certain style in art and poetry, of certain philosophical and social ideas which elsewhere constitute the entire content of 'Romanticism'. It seems to me that it is precisely in this two-fold interpretation of Romanticism that a certain divergence between the opinion of foreigners regarding Chopin and that which is held in Poland originates [...]. For the foreigner, Fryderyk Chopin [...] is a sublime monument of the past, with a value strictly 'fixed' and catalogued in the inventory of universal art. But for Polish musicians he is a still living reality, an active force which exerts a direct and spontaneous influence on the evolution of our contemporary music in its entirety.

Karol Szymanowski Pisma, Vol. 1, p. 315.

[5] In 'Fryderyk Chopin and Contemporary Music', Szymanowski wrote in more detail about Chopin's reception in Paris:

[...] one has to admit that in such a highly cultivated centre as Paris then was [...] he was surrounded by a truly fanatical circle of people who well-nigh adored him and had a profound understanding of his true greatness. But this circle was not the public at large [...]. There

The 'Romantic' pathos of many of his works often seems *from the outside* to be the reflection of the flames of some great conflagration, or the echo of a lament sung far away in the distance. But the essential magic of his music does not lie in this pathos, even though it gave rise to stories about a mysterious man who dwelt within a magic circle of spiritual isolation that was misunderstood even by Adam Mickiewicz[6] – isolation which was beyond dispute even though he appeared to be a man of the world and *petit maître.*[7] This pathos also gave rise to fantastic stories about the 'literary' basis of his art, stories which led to its being disfigured by all manner of intimacies and shallow gossip

---

can be no doubt that today we are inclined to exaggerate the fame which he enjoyed in his lifetime. [...] Apart from that by no means numerous group of truly cultured individuals who realised that his relatively slender piano masterpieces were in effect a new start, Parisian society in general, even those more cultured layers of it, knew him as a magnificent pianist, a teacher of great ladies, a man of the world and a witty conversationalist, and his works, which seemed to contemporary opinion to be strange, capricious and unhealthy, were more often tolerated rather than really admired.
Karol Szymanowski Pisma, Vol. 1, p. 297.

[6] *Cf.* note 16 on pp. 171–72.

[7] In 'The Myth of Fryderyk Chopin in relation to the Polish Soul', an introductory address given at the Warsaw Philharmonia at a concert mounted in commemmoration of the seventy-fifth anniversary of the death of Chopin, Szymanowski discussed at further length the failure of even the most distinguished of his fellow Polish exiles in Paris to understand the true significance of his work:
By all accounts, the other three [Mickiewicz, Słowacki and Krasiński] did not understand him. Perhaps they expected action from him, action beyond the sphere of the inner life in which he was Sovereign Lord. For in superhuman despair, in inconsolable irresolution, they seemed already to have forsaken their ivory towers of dreams in order to save that which seemed to have perished without trace [...].
And that descent from solitary heights, that elevated heroism shown in the surrender of their inner freedom, left in the priceless crystal of their works strange refractions, flaws and imperfections which are clear and comprehensible only to us [Poles]...
Fryderyk Chopin stood by them in quiet, apparent calm. Perhaps

from old women – the 'pupils' pupils'. These people imposed alien, banal content on individual pieces of music: a mazurka might be described as a 'tavern scene', while some people heard the 'fluttering flanks of hussars' in the A flat *Polonaise*. Others heard 'Janek's cymbals' in the *Polonaise-Fantaisie*, and there always was much talk about the 'Revolutionary' C minor Study.[8]

---

it was with regret and reproach that they looked on Him as, in that terrible time, in self-contained solitude, he perfected tirelessly and patiently his finely-wrought works.

'Why aren't you composing a national opera, Fryderyk?'

Fryderyk smiled in silence and with quiet determination did not compose a national opera.

Instead he avidly amassed his seemingly slender and tiny trinkets, but nobody knew then how far he had to dig into the depths of the earth – his earth – for the priceless ore from which they were forged.'

Karol Szymanowski Pisma, Vol 1, pp. 134–35.

[8] In an address on Chopin, given at the University of Warsaw on 9 November 1930, Szymanowski launched a ferocious attack on those who persisted in finding extra-musical elements in Chopin's works:

What poverty of imagination it would be to perceive in [Chopin's music] only the wandering shades of past events never to return! Whether the richly coloured, vividly prideful nobleman's kontusz [cloak] and fur-lined coat, the chivalrous clash of swords in the polonaises, or the rustle of coarse, stiff, home-spun peasant's cloth, the stamping of feet, the echo of tavern-songs in the mazurkas! This music is neither a memento of the personal, painful experiences of its creator, [...] nor a black, dismal vision of the nation's grief at that time. Perhaps you will object: 'What about the undoubted tragedy of the music, ringing like the blows of a heavy hammer?' To which I reply: 'What truly great assignment, aiming at a final fulfillment of a destiny played out beyond the confines of that "Aeschylean" stage, could avoid hammer-blows in the forging of eternal shapes?' Perhaps you might say: 'What about that bitter sadness concealed in his melodies?' To which I reply: 'Is it really a faint, pallid sadness of disillusion, of barren melancholy, a pathetic mask hiding powerlessness and dejection? Is it not instead a creative sadness of yearning for a destiny of real greatness? Not even sadness, but surely that immortal and, for us, omnipresent "Melancholy", that magical, fundamentally Polish Sovereign, who leads us pensive towards our common destiny [...], the wide expanses of free creative action?' You may finally object that, in the grip of my musical enthusiasm and inexhaustible wonder for Chopin's enchanting, matchless

These fundamental aspects of Chopin's relationship to the problem of his own creativity are expressed in so characteristic a way that he stands out against the general background of his epoch and the artistic ideology of his time. It was during this era that the range of Life's activities expanded immeasurably and the content of Life enriched in an unparalleled way. The artist, the creative man, found himself standing, as it were, right at the heart of these processes. It was as if he were an actor on stage, taking an active part in and directly influencing the dramatic action of life. In this way he regulated the course of events. But with this increase in his active role in life came the binding of the artist to the purely dramatic content of his own epoch. The artist, as never before, became above all the exponent of the epoch. In the face of this, the problem of pure art and its formal, objective value had to give way to the exceedingly intense experience of the substance of life, and this was quite without regard for metaphysical profundities introduced from without during that same era – particularly in German art. The artist performed on the stage of art and in the forum of life, striving, often in vain, to convey life's all-embracing substance through his work. We can see now how far art of that period had strayed from the objective creation of well-defined forms characteristic of eighteenth-century composers such as Mozart and even Bach, whose

---

'craft', I perhaps see [...] non-existent characteristics which in their very essence are alien to the work in hand: something in the nature of the divinations of a mystical prophet [...], the solemn bombast of which negates the crystalline, transparent simplicity of the originals? Perhaps – but I counter with the deepest conviction possible that this precious corpus of work in effect encapsulates a certain lesson, precept or testament of feverish effort bequeathed to posterity which aims unswervingly at the conquest of perhaps the highest values in its sphere of action. That lesson is not delivered in muddled thoughts or misty words [...]. On the contrary, it is [...] there in [...] the perfect assembly of its content and form.

Ibid., pp. 259–60.

unfathomable pathos soared to the furthest bounds of the reality that surrounded him.

That active-actor element of the creative artist was most clearly exemplified in the work of Wagner, who regarded music merely as a means of expression. When conceived in such a way, the notion of a work of art as a self-contained form had to take second place, not so much on account of its external theatricality, but because its creator took the lead as protagonist, providing evidence of his own life-giving role on the stage of art. It is possible then that these histrionics of the soul, which were certainly expressed with great genius, constitute an individual trait, but I believe that Wagner's work in general provides the clearest example of the relationship existing between the artist and his own work during the Romantic era. Chopin's work is completely devoid of that histrionic element; it would appear that his psychic individuality, the *spiritus movens* of his creative will, retreated into the shadows surrounding his art, shining as it did with its own unearthly light. There is in this a strange sorcery that creates worlds of beauty pulsating with their own life. His work appears to us to be a play of pure and perfect forms, free from all immediate contact with the psychic experience from which it developed, a play of forms that are above all expressive in themselves through the imperturbable harmony of their individual elements. It is our belief that the freeing of the powers of creativity from all coincidental connections and the unswerving will to create absolute forms together constitute Chopin's own type of 'profundity'. But in using such terms as 'depth', 'profundity' and 'absolute', I must caution against their being applied in the way that they were until quite recently in those fashionable aesthetic-cum-metaphysical pronouncements concerning music as a means of expression. On the contrary, I consider that the 'depth' of a great composer is dependent only on the extent to which he adopts a positive attitude to problems of what we might call *métier*. The critical and aesthetic judgments of the French, which are usually clear and to the point, often make use of this word.

Such a positivism that brings the notion of 'craft' into the sphere of the most elevated questions of art can only be a healthy instinct, since it is an unambiguous declaration of the fact that a work of art can only be genuinely valuable if the basic material has been thoroughly mastered. In the creative process, what is most important is how; only then comes what, and here no extraneous element should be added to magnify the 'spiritual value' of a piece of music.

I am here deliberately dealing with solemn notions of 'depth', 'spiritual value', the 'absolute' etc. They are words which crop up almost every step of the way in critical judgments about music. I have the impression that musical opinions here in Poland have evolved in the last few decades to a markedly lesser extent than those in the fields of fine art and poetry, and consequently, criticism today – with a few exceptions – still draws for its judgements and pronouncements on the guiding ideas of the past. A factor in this state of affairs is perhaps the Wagnerian dogma of music as expression, since musical opinion today finds difficulty in freeing itself from the suggestive influence of that powerful personality. 'Music as expression' is an ambiguous principle, leading to a series of misunderstandings in the definition of the absolute musical content of a work, since in itself it implies a negation of formal, constructive values. Besides this, the idea 'expressed' by musicians was in any case a self-contained 'idea', and already stood outside the sphere of music. That was how the matter stood in nineteenth-century Germany. That mysterious 'x' in the musical equation could be an externally imposed 'literary' content, whether religious, philosophical or historico-tragical, and this content had to provide the supposed 'depth' or 'spiritual value' of the work in question. Yet regardless of the 'absolute nature' of the particular idea with which the musical essence of the work was saturated, the method itself is tantamount to the binding of a work of art to the dramatic substance of an historical epoch, entrusting its fate to the perpetually flowing currents of historical reality. For 'musical expression', in contrast to normal musical values, is only as if a function of values that are extra-musical, and as such it is an idealised reflection of that fast-flowing reality.

But surely the great artist yearns instinctively and profoundly to create a work the solid structure of which stands in marked contrast to the unceasing movement and eternally flowing currents of life? And surely the intensity of that will to create such structures determines the final value of the work.

In introducing a line of demarcation between Chopin and the artistic atmosphere that surrounded him, I have tried to show that 'romanticism' does not account for the most vital substance of his work, and that thanks to this indestructible creative urge, and also to his admirable objectivity with regard to questions of artistic creativity, he succeeded in forging positively valuable works which in their absolute, 'innovatory' nature were far ahead of their time. In addition, the positive qualities of these works were so constant and enduring that even the richly varied and highly eventful history of music at the turn of the nineteenth century was unable to obscure the radiance of his work. On the contrary: the 'revolutionary' changes that have occurred in artistic affairs in recent years have, if anything, intensified that radiance, demonstrating fully the inner vitality of Chopin's art. It is all the more striking that he is much closer to us now, while Wagner's enormous *œuvre* seems increasingly to be of the past, not of course in its simply unparalleled manifestation of musical genius, but as a concrete expression of the fundamental position he adopted in relation to the question of music.

Today the reaction in the world of art against the immediate 'yesterday' is an indisputable cultural fact. But we are compelled to play too great a role in the living reality that is in process of development all round us to be able to form a completely objective, critical evaluation of today's art. I believe that it is not at all the case that we are dealing with an absolutely 'revolutionary' new beginning. Our art is too organically connected with that of 'yesterday', even if only in the negative form of protest. It seems to be more like the 'next instalment', part of the ebbing and flowing of the tides of a mighty ocean in accordance with unchanging natural ordinances. The present period is also considered by a number of melancholics to be the final boundary, the tragic *Ultima Thule*[9] so extreme in its effects that the incoming tide will never turn! Yet such extreme pessimism does not fundamentally change our position. In the abstract formalism of today's fine arts, e.g., in the extreme intellectualism of those aspirations to the ultimate solution of the problem of form, there smoulders assiduously somewhere beneath those creative emotions a faith in the suprahistorical, absolute value of art (which to be sure seems paradoxical against the background of 'futurism' as a 'philosophy of life' *sui generis*), a faith which perhaps is not sufficiently borne out in cogent argument about real works of art. Yet this state of affairs does not warrant such dark pessimism. The contemporary artistic world is a chaos of conflicting ideas and notions, of apparent contradictions, disputes, enthusiastic claims and counter-claims, yet the enormous vitality of art is perceived to be a fixed constant, and the ways in which it can develop are just as clear. These ways are easier to discern in music, the evolutionary rhythm of which is subject to its own particular laws. From this point of view, the role of Chopin has a clear, decisive significance both in the history of music and in the creation of today's 'new' music. The psychological basis of that 'new' music is the undubitable, gradual liberation from the spell of 'Germanicism'. This is not to say that we must disregard the undisputed, colossal, aesthetic qualities of German music. We are only interested in exploding the myth of its 'universality'. I here state categorically, once and for all, that great music can be based on foundations other than those of the ever-shrinking circles of

[9] Ultima Thule: 'farthest Thule', the extreme limit of travel and discovery. Thule was the ancient Greek and Latin name for a land six days' sailing-time to the north of Britain. It is not known whether Shetland, Iceland or Norway was meant, but Polybius believed it to be the most northerly region in the world.

German 'emotionalism'. That liberation must rest first upon the elevation of the artistic qualities of ethno-musical traits of other national groupings. This involves not only 'formal' qualities, but the very 'spirit' of the music, its deepest substance. This process has already been accomplished in France and Russia, and what an enormous role Chopin's music played in this process! For there can be no doubt that a century ago he had already understood fully the profundity and 'organic nature' of the question of basing one's own compositions, not on established aesthetic canons but a canon of one's own devising, building his music up from foundations which in the nature of things constituted the most vital relationship possible with a musical element derived from his own racial properties.

Chopin was one of the greatest 'revolutionaries' in music, for in destroying formal and 'spiritual' traditionalism, he opened the way to freedom. Yet his unerring instinct and elevated culture permitted him to discover his own, steadfast 'discipline' straight away. His flexible imagination delineated the bases and limits of his art, and it was only those self-imposed chains that his *métier*, that marvellous 'craft' dealing in terms of formal perfection, had to develop.

The 'Polishness' of Chopin's work is beyond question, but it has nothing to do with the fact that he wrote polonaises and mazurkas (this is to misunderstand his attitude to folk-music as the basis of creativity!) upon which, as we have already observed, ideological or literary material was imposed from without. In the absolute 'musicality' of his work he rose above his epoch in more than one sense of the expression. As an artist, he sought forms which could stand independently of the literary-dramatic character of the musical aspirations of the romantic era. As a Pole, he mirrored in his works not the actual, contemporary, tragic collapse of the nation; instead he instinctively aimed to express himself, on behalf of his race, in suprahistorical terms, in other words in terms that were the most profound possible. In so doing, he realised that only by freeing his art from the limited sphere of dramatic history as it happened could he be certain of conferring on his art the most enduring, truly Polish values.[10] Such an attitude to the question of 'national music', realised with genius in his own work, accounts for the reason that Chopin's music (unlike Moniuszko's) is understood beyond the frontiers of Poland, and as such has been elevated to the heights of universal art. His music also became a starting-point for today's endeavours, and herein lies the strange riddle of his eternal contemporaneity. Perhaps, today, we do not perceive with sufficient freshness the innovatory qualities which affected the musical materials of his art most strongly. Nonetheless, every individual element – whether it be harmony, modulation, melody or rhythm – was the result of a deeply conceived creative experiment and gave the impression of sprouting up in furrows which had not previously been

---

[10] In 'The Myth of Fryderyk Chopin in relation to the Polish Soul', Szymanowski explained the suprahistorical significance of Chopin's work thus:
   [...] how is it that his spiritual legacy [...] has lost nothing of its divine radiance and still glows continuously [...] like a transparent diamond in which there are no flaws, no refractions which speak to us of the now bygone days of captivity, days full of terror, torment and despair? On the wings of an unwavering faith in the future, the works of Fryderyk Chopin transcended the tragedy of the Nation as it was happening so as to outlive it, to ring out with unyielding, irrepressible life and creative joy.
   I have named it the Myth of the Polish Soul [...]. For at the heart of this magical beauty, in its opulent formal diversity, it always glows with the unchanging, indubitable truth of his Polishness. Similarly, historical myth is not a fairy-tale [...]; within it lingers precisely that which now stands beyond the elusive, unstable reality of History as it forever comes into existence. The most profound truth of a nation is crystallised in immaculate form within myth, reflecting, as if in a magic mirror, the nation's true likeness. [...] The works of Fryderyk Chopin possess precisely this trait of immutable Polishness – a Polishness existing beyond this or that historical event, concentrating in itself, as if through a lens, all that which is Light and Beauty in it, not 'speaking', but 'singing' out the Myth of the Polish Soul from the most profound depths of the heart.
                                   Karol Szymanowski Pisma, Vol. 1, pp. 133–34.

ploughed by man. He possessed such characteristic objectivity and balanced wisdom, as well as the true courage which distinguishes those who, in their creative work, fearlessly abandon terrain that has been explored safely any number of times, terrain where traditional 'aesthetics' become addictive and ideological fashions quickly change. After a century that has seen, on the one hand, the Romanticism, post-Romanticism and contemporary music of Germany, and, on the other, the antithesis of German music, namely that of France and Russia, a music that has developed so abundantly mainly as a result of Chopin's unprecedented art, it is at last possible to understand fully the tremendous significance of Chopin's work in the evolution of music all over the world. I should like the 'transformation of values' which Chopin initiated a century ago to become at last an accomplished fact in Poland.

We do not wish for an uncritical ladling-out of what has already become in some measure an aesthetic traditionalism, but for the deepest understanding possible of his position in relation to Polish music in particular. In effect we are concerned with the ultimate destruction of the alien fetters that are impeding the development of Polish music. We are concerned with the courage 'to renounce', and with the will to create a Polish music that rests on foundations of its own making. Fryderyk Chopin is an immortal example of what Polish music can become, and also one of the greatest examples of Europeanised Poland, a Poland that loses none of her racial peculiarities yet at the same time enjoys a high standing in European culture.

Part Four
ON TWENTIETH-CENTURY MUSIC

Karol Szymanowski
on Contemporary Music

Text of an interview given to Jerzy Rytard, first published on
12 November 1922 in the Warsaw journal *Kurier Polski.*

As we were interested in the contemporary musical movement in the West, we approached Karol Szymanowski who
provided us with some interesting facts together with his
personal views about this fertile area of artistic life.

In reply to our question as to whether there had been a
fundamental shift in concepts of musical values in general,
so accounting for the multiplicity and variety of recent
happenings in contemporary musical composition, Mr
Szymanowski said:

I believe this to be the case; for example, my own general
impression is that the German musical hegemony which has
lasted for so long has at last come to an end. A thorough
investigation of this phenomenon would take us too far
afield. Naturally the War played an enormous role here.
One of the indirect, superficial causes was of course the
growth of a nationalism which was not just politically motivated in the case of those nations which were at war with
Germany, but was evident in the conscious desire to create
an autonomous national art.

But there are more immediate causes organically connected with the very nature of art. In general they have to do
with new ideas breathing life into contemporary art (fine
arts and poetry), which an insufficient sense of reality and
insufficiently profound critical and public opinion (especially here in Poland) have up to now dubbed collectively
with the threadbare name of futurism. Fortunately, contemporary music is much less encumbered with the use of
defining 'isms'. Even the so much discussed problem of

pure form does not exist at all as a 'problem' in the case of music, as music in essence is already pure form.

JR: So should we approach the phenomenon of new music from a different point of view?

KS: Of course. And first, one must begin by recognising that music not only exists, but is beginning to blossom luxuriantly in France and Russia, as well as in Italy, Spain and even England and America.

In my view, the general, underlying cause of all this is a sense of 'liberation', 'a protest against that which was' and which is now inessential for 'us' today. This apparently negative basis becomes totally *positive* for composition under certain conditions.

JR: How do you mean?

KS: I shall try to explain. There is no doubt that the German music which developed so strongly from the seventeenth century onwards created such a stupendous burden in the form of an 'obligatory aesthetic', erected all manner of academic pyramids and put so many of its disciples in fetters, that all creative movements standing outside the enchanted bounds of the German psyche and emotional world, seemed to be almost completely exterminated. That first, marvellous rebellion instigated by Chopin, though eternally precious in itself, ironically brought us no liberation. A better organised movement, rebelling against that 'obligatory aesthetic', originated in Russian music of the second half of the nineteenth century. This not entirely 'free' music, based strongly, albeit a little too academically, on folk-music, brought forth many works of great value, and alas these are too little known here. Above all, the masterpiece *Boris Godunov* by Mussorgsky.

JR: What influence do you think this had on the West?

KS: That breath of Russian fresh air reached France first of all, fortunately at the time when Claude Debussy's marvellous, precocious talent was maturing. One has the impression that, with a refined but determined gesture, he suddenly opening eyes in stifling, fetid concert halls to the existence of enchanted gardens and a boundless landscape of mountains, seas and clouds. His pantheistic investigation into the essence of the experience of nature is far removed from the brutal naturalism of Richard Strauss. Claude Debussy, regarded as 'superficial' by many of our critics, is one of the most harmonious, self-aware and hence profound artists: a true expression of the never-to-be-extinguished '*génie latin*'.

After him came the very great, spiritually related talent of Maurice Ravel. But this was before the War. Russian composers on the one hand, and Debussy and Ravel on the other, created new, formal musical values, and indicated new ways to be followed. Today in France, the younger generation already regard them as 'academic', and are protesting against their 'impressionism'. Their marvellous subtlety of sound is being countered by more powerful, masculine accents.

After the War, a similar 'liberationist' tendency also appeared in England, Spain and Italy. (I am deliberately not saying anything about the pre-war barrel-organ music of the Puccinis, Leoncavallos *e tutti quanti* as it cannot properly be regarded as being proper art to any real extent.) That tendency very nearly became a postulate, more than once bringing in its train distasteful, chauvinistic fancies. (But is it not strange that from this point of view our chauvinism is rather forbearing?!)

JR: How do you see those nationalist tendencies of which you spoke earlier?

KS: Here one must immediately correct a misconception. We are not at all concerned here with the more or less academic elaboration of folk-music which in Poland is stubbornly, but unjustifiably, termed 'national art'. (And digressing to Polish terrain for a moment, it was with some astonishment that I observed just how far removed Paderewski's *Album tatrzańskie* [*Tatra Album*] was from the true spirit of Góral music; it is nothing like a musical equivalent of the admittedly marvellous *Skalny Podhale* [*Rocky Podhale*] of Tetmajer.[1] In truly national music, as represented by Chopin, one is not concerned with folklore. One is concerned with the formulation of the most profound racial characteristics, without doing damage to the formal unity of the work of art as such. Folk-dress is no help here.

Musical creativity is too immediately connected with an artist's individual traits for it to depend ultimately on a racial basis.

With regard to the nationalising of western music, Igor Stravinsky's powerful work has played an enormous role here. This man, who stormed all the stereotypes and official aesthetics of music with real fury, plumbed his racial properties to the depths (in *Rite of Spring*) like no one else.

JR: Do Stravinsky's nationalist traits arouse special interest in his work?

KS: In a certain sense. At present, on account of its particular, exciting exoticism. But one must not forget that in pursuing his own breakneck way, he creates unusual formal qualities in his own music (if only his totally new concepts of instrumentation). It was precisely these aspects above all which dazzled western professional musicians, even before the War. Later they were to come to a deeper understanding of his true position. He is an uncompromising figure, whom it is impossible to ignore in any consideration of today's music. His powerful, somewhat barbaric touch, which nonetheless is endowed with invigorating strength, has left its mark on western music. It began with adoration and a certain amount of plagiarism on the part of the young. Now something of a protest movement against his pre-eminence has developed, but it is a protest full of profound admiration and quiet gratitude for his revelation of new

---

[1] *Cf.* note 3 on p. 116.

approaches. I shall speak more widely about him else-where.[2]

JR: Apart from Stravinsky, is there anything else of interest happening in Russia?

KS: Alas, I do not know enough about this. A significant number of Russian composers are presently in the West, and I should mention Sergei Prokofiev who, apart from Stravinsky, is undoubtedly the most distinguished of Russian composers.

JR: Where then, in your view, is there the liveliest musical activity?

KS: France, or rather Paris, still occupies pride of place. Even we in Warsaw have heard of 'Les Six',[3] and as the individual members of the group mature and their talents develop, it will increasingly lose the character of a 'group' and consist of diverse personalities. They have already become more distinct, not only on account of the extent of their individual talents, but because of certain differences of intent. Darius Milhaud and the still very young Poulenc appear to be their leaders, and their work is characterised by a truly Latin transparency and formal clarity. In general the idea which prevails so much over here, namely that musical futurism (!) has to do with a continual move in the direction of Germanic entanglement and aural congestion initiated by Strauss and Reger, is mistaken. The true 'simplicity' of today's good music poses problems only for those who regard simplicity as 'vulgarity' or dilettante primitivism. Of

[2] Szymanowski may have had in mind an unpublished article on Stravinsky, drafted in 1921. Another article was written and published in 1924; *cf.* pp. 223–27.

[3] The members of 'Les Six' were Louis Durey, Darius Milhaud, Arthur Honegger, Germaine Tailleferre, Georges Auric and Francis Poulenc. They were united initially in their stance against late romanticism and impressionism, and sought a return to simple, direct, unemotional modes of expression, appropriate for an art which was based on the happenings of everyday contemporary life.

course the formal framework of today's music has broad-
ened considerably. It embraces a multitude of surprises
which disturb the unfortunate Philistine. But within that
framework, today's good music has a clear, broad outline
which is markedly more transparent than that of the
German music of the recent past.

Spanish composers, such as Granados, Albéniz and,
above all, Manuel de Falla in the younger generation, are all
under the prevailing, beneficial influence of folk music.
They are fortunate that they have this folk music to draw on
as it is truly magical and exceedingly rich, rhythmically and
melodically.

A similar evolution is occurring, it seems to me, amongst
the youngest Italian composers (Malipiero, Pizzetti, Res-
pighi, Casella and others). That really would be marvellous,
because for too long the Italians have compromised themselves with that dull cosmopolitanism so favoured by our
public when it appears in the operatic works of the
Verismo!

In essence I do not consider the English to be endowed
with excessively profound musical talents, but a few interesting composers have appeared there (Lord Berners,
Goossens, Bax and in particular the still very young, but
exceedingly radical, Arthur Bliss). In this music one detects
the undoubted formal influences of the French impress-
ionists on the one hand, and of Stravinsky on the other.
There is, however, a certain nationalistic note, deriving
from the use of Scottish and Irish folk-songs.[4]

JR: What musical impressions did you form during your stay
in America?

----

[4] The eccentricity of these opinions leads one to suppose that Szymanowski
moved in fashionable rather than musical circles during his stay in London
in 1920, a view confirmed by remarks in a letter to his mother, dated
26 December: 'I know lots of interesting people, lords, ministers, etc., for
example I've been to the Asquiths (I very much like Lady Asquith, a very
interesting and intelligent older woman). In general we are leading the
most wordly life possible, and I am in my dress coat every evening [...]'.
                                    Karol Szymanowski, *Z Listów*, p. 198.

KS: America finds herself in a rather isolated and interesting position as a consequence of her post-war attempts to detach herself from Europe in all cultural fields. Because, in the nature of things, she has an exceedingly diverse mixture of races, she does not possess any true folklore. Everything which is 'folk' was imported at one time or another from somewhere in Europe. In the absence of anything better in the musical field they have turned to the negroes! This despised race, an essentially unstable social element, is wonderfully gifted from the musical point of view. Their subtle dance rhythms are astounding. This music, which is essentially dance, albeit in the best sense of the word, has begun to acquire greater rights of citizenship. 'Serious' composers are paying close attention to it, discovering it to be an extremely rich and distinctive material. I am not surprised at this. While in New York, I myself went to one revue, composed, performed and sung entirely by negroes, eight times in all: it really was fascinating music.

JR: In the face of the so very many fruitful musical changes you have just described, do you consider that an appropriate musical criticism has developed yet?

KS: Of course, the conservative camp, both here and in the West, is not short of invective when it comes to new art. But thanks to a higher general level of culture, attitudes in the West perhaps assume a more balanced form than they do here. Over there, there really does exist a criticism which has adjusted splendidly to the achievements of contemporary composers. Each unexpected event in the field of artistic culture arouses first of all curiosity, and then interest; understanding follows and finally acknowledgement and often admiration. This process happens so quickly that even the most extreme tendencies are readily discussed and defended. A whole series of musicological writings is concerned, technically and impartially, with the question of new music. I by no means wish to neglect the increasing depth of those studies which are devoted to that which 'was', but I must mention here an exceedingly interesting monthly – *Nouvelle Revue Musicale*[5] – as it is thanks to their initiative that my name has become so well known in the West. This is proof of their impartiality and lack of chauvinism.

JR: What do you have to say about our critics?

KS: It's like being 'in the condemned cell, etc., etc.', and I'm the one who usually gets executed. I'm not going to go on about this at great length as I am by nature submissively patient. Naturally I cannot give way to an access of rapture when, for example, Mr Stanisław Niewiadomski, in writing about my Violin Concerto,[6] attempts to assure his readers that my rather beautifully cultivated flowers are simply garish. It's difficult: there are many different flowers, not just innocent little forget-me-nots.

There again, Mr Rytel looks at my work from the point of view of the ballet as up to now he has generally been incapable of conceiving the purpose of my 'zigzagging steps'. I can assure him, once and for all, that my one and only aim is good music, and that by all accounts, especially those of foreign commentators, I am not so far from achieving this.

Nietzsche has a beautiful expression: '*Pathos der Distanz*'. Our domestic critics often forget it in relation to me, but I never forget it in relation to them. This accounts for my tender-hearted forbearance in this matter.

---

[5] Szymanowski here was referring to the Parisian monthly *La Revue Musicale*, founded in 1920 and edited by Henri Prunières. In the May 1922 edition it contained an extensive article by Alexander Tansman about Szymanowski, along with a supplement containing two studies for pianoforte, Op. 33, Nos. 2 and 8, and the first and third of the *Three Lullabies*, Op. 48.

[6] Concerto No.1 for Violin and Orchestra, Op. 35, written in 1916 and first performed in Warsaw by Józef Oziminski with the Warsaw Philharmonia, directed by Emil Młynarski on 1 November 1922.

The Highways and Byways of Contemporary Music

This text, finished in the early months of 1926, was originally intended to form the introduction to a book on the subject of contemporary music. A number of sketches for later chapters were written, but this was the only section to be published in Szymanowski's lifetime (*Muzyka*, May 1926).

When one is swept along by deep, but fast-flowing, currents created by the actions of the human spirit, shaping and reshaping itself with a relentless inevitability from day to day and from hour to hour, one's awareness of eternally enduring forms, raised aloft through the operation of a creative will to the noble station of immortal symbol, is lost in the feeling of immediate reality. One is only aware of the unceasing, merciless course of life as it destroys the indubitable values of 'yesterday' in favour of the more problematical values of 'tomorrow'.

As they developed, the exact sciences, operating upon absolute concepts that create an inevitable continuum in our view of reality, have been compelled, on more than one occasion, to retreat from previously held positions and seek another way out of their increasing difficulties. How much freer is the 'science' which deals with artistic considerations in their fullest and widest sense. First, we leave behind the misty, lofty, stifling confines of transcendental aesthetics. Then we abandon the history of art, in the true sense of the word, i.e., the critical examination of bygone facts, their mutual dependencies and general pattern of evolution. Finally, as we give up our somewhat arbitrary scale of values, we at last find ourselves dealing with critical judgements about contemporary art. These judgements are free of necessity, for the simple reason that the artistic 'reality' presently surrounding us does not present any fixed, defined forms. Instead, it is in a state of continual ferment that at the most betrays the general direction in which contemporary artistic thought is moving. These directions, labelled for easy reference by all manner of decorative 'isms', are applied as part of today's critical method in judgements on the works of various artists. In this way the 'isms' are endowed with the qualities of absolute concepts. It is here that the most serious error arises, because these 'isms', whose real significance can depend only on sanctions derived from a particular genius, who in the nature of things is endowed with the qualities of a *deus ex machina*, cannot under any circumstance serve as a yardstick for absolute values. It seems then that the only certain mainstay for critical ideas are norms which were applied in the past. In effect, the aesthetic canons of the past pave the way for the art of the future, and at the same time define the boundaries beyond which uncharted aesthetic regions lie. The eternal conflict between academic, critical thought and the creative licence of the genius originates within this vicious circle. It is a conflict between artistic 'stasis' and 'dynamism', and it inevitable leads to unbalanced judgements on both sides. Critical thought obstinately holds to values investigated and recorded a hundred times over, and on principle is opposed to the creation of new values which are based, not on continuity, but the apparent negation of everything which has gone before. Creative thought undoubtedly recognises elements of continuity, even when evident in apparently extreme contrasts, arising from the artist's happy illusion that he is creating everything *ab ovo*.

I believe that this eternal dispute, arising from artistic laws of 'supply and demand' which I have here sketched very roughly, has existed since the dawn of artistic history. Now, however, the problem is a hundred times more complicated.

The intellectual atmosphere of life today among the cultured classes, that stage upon which are enacted fierce battles over new forms for the expression of reality, has now been made much more complicated by the bringing into play of ever more subtle and finely differentiated concepts. In the nature of things this process gradually led the creative artist into the very centre of ideological conflict in that his intuitive, impulsive reflex was pitted against art as an objective, purely aesthetic issue (Bach, Mozart and even, in a certain sense, Chopin). By the time we come to Wagner, theoretical discussions on the subject of what made a music drama long preceded its artistic realisation in those works which proved to be his most valuable. This famous example is an incontrovertible argument against that (conservative) section of the critical establishment which attributes the (apparent) failures in contemporary art to its inevitable over-intellectualisation and abstraction which supposedly result *a priori* from artistic theorising. In reality there is here a very elementary misunderstanding, namely that notions of form and content have been confused, more or less consciously, and their organic connections ignored. Indeed, the battles about new forms in the fields of both the fine arts and music could be reduced to a few fundamental ideas, each having only a relative significance in any judgement about the real worth of a given work of art. For example, it must be stressed that tonality, atonality and even polytonality cannot serve in substance as the starting-point for a critical evaluation of a musical work, the inner logic and formal elements of which will automatically become independent of all pre-conceived, imposed disciplines if they are to achieve their fullest expression. The theoretical foundations on which the work of today's most distinguished composers is based result from historical necessity. When one penetrates the consciousness of the creative artist pitted against the harshness of today's existence, it becomes clear that the 'over-intellectualisation' of art is a defensive instinct in the face of the inevitable mechanisation of contemporary life. The *a priori* abstract nature of art results from an attempt to raise it to a 'suprahistorical' level. It is a way of making certain of its absolute value and of saving it from the grinding routine of social utilitarianism – in which direction it is being thrust more or less consciously by the leading journalistic critics of the present day. Here there is an opposition of creative licence and pseudo-scientific norms, which in reality are no more than the passing expression of the current pleasures and tastes of one or other social group. There is no doubt that factors beyond the bounds of art (e.g., political) often have a decisive influence on the character of the judgements propounded by our critics. Of course, this none-too-flattering evaluation of journalistic criticism refers only to its character in general, and is by no means intended to be an attack on those individuals who are able, thanks to their erudition and integrity, to attain a genuine objectivity.

I am firmly convinced that no discussion of contemporary art can take place without triggering immediate repercussions in the press. The press now has the power of moulding public opinion to an extent it has never previously enjoyed in history, but its treatment of matters which ought grandly to be designated *sub specie aeternitatis* has degenerated into a more or less consciously 'mixed hand' of distorted ideas and opinions. Accordingly this has led to the unprecedented confusion of notions, so characteristic of the present age, with its labrynth of ideas and ideologies in the face of which the modern artist would be defenceless were it not for the 'shield and buckler' of his deeply considered creative thoughts.

The above thoughts are intended to define the fundamental character of the present work. It does not have pretensions to 'scholarship'. It will be the improvisations of an explorer, forever searching out new shores and new lands; it will be an attempt at a conception of phenomena in their totality, and will concern contemporary music from the point of view of its inner dynamism. In this respect, the well-established 'academic' scale of values will be of interest only in as much as it forms a spring-board – a point of departure for ceaseless forward movement. These writings will be the 'letters of a traveller' in a strange land, addressed to those who, though they remain timorously behind, are attempting, on the basis of their insufficient experience, to paint for themselves the distant, inaccessible landscape of the future.

On the Work of Wagner, Strauss and Schoenberg

This text is the most substantial remnant of Szymanowski's
sketches for his proposed study of contemporary music. It was
first published in 1958 under the title 'Regarding "Contemporary Music" ' in *Z Pism* (*Selected Writings*).

The starting-point for the most recent phase in the history
of German music was Richard Wagner's truly massive output. This figure is surrounded by an aureola originating in
his incalculable creative mastery, but a number of extra-
musical factors have conferred a particular, exceedingly
characteristic colour on the work of *der alter Zauberer* of
Bayreuth.

First of all there is the political factor.

The apogee of Wagner's work coincided with the triumph
of German imperialism, symbolised in the unification of
the Reich, so conferring artistic sanction on political
events and deepening their ideological significance by
way of association with mystical, gloomy German myth.
Siegfried, the German hero, in spite of his tragic fate on
stage, was elevated to the honourable position of symbol
of romantic individualism, the philosophical substantiation
of which was ultimately revealed in the 'Superman' of
Zarathustra.

Wagner's work was in the nature of a philosophy of
history, and this aspect of his achievement was given dialect-
ical expression in Nietzsche's *The Birth of Tragedy*, a work
which became the gospel of German artistic ideology in the
final years of the nineteenth century (much to the subsequent annoyance of its author).

Under these circumstances, Wagner's work, which artistically was merely the resplendent, albeit late, crowning
achievement of musical Romanticism, became the starting-

211

point for the 'New Art'. From our point of view, it is
particularly interesting to note that psychologically he was
typical of the modern artist in that his astounding awareness
of his mission found expression in a whole series of theoretical and aesthetic works which in turn exerted a powerful
influence on the moulding of the aesthetic ideas of his
German contemporaries. Small wonder then that the
almost uncritical epigonism which characterised the subsequent era lay both in the Master's mighty creations and
his aesthetic opinions. That epigonism gradually became a
suffocating nightmare, and in order to escape its absolute
power, another road to freedom had to be discovered.

This 'liberation', like every other revolutionary movement in the history of mankind, bears ineradicable traces of
latent traditionalism. The constant development of forms is
often reflected in ideological dialectic which introduces
more or less consciously the deepest organic connections as
a series of categorical contradictions originating *ab ovo*.

And so the 'liberation' movement was initially concerned
with conventional aspects of external gesture and with all
those bad habits which so distinctly mark all artistic epigonism. This apart, post-Wagnerian German music constantly reveals the deepest possible interrelationships. It
travels relentlessly along new roads which, though diverging
widely, still lead back to the massive achievement of the
composer of *The Ring*. This divergence is not only obvious
but inevitable. Wagner's powerful individuality, through
which a whole epoch of German culture found expression,
encapsulated in potentia all the possibilities of subsequent
development. At the same time, the development took the
form of 'disintegration' – in the way that a huge tree-trunk
forks into branches, boughs and twigs . . . .

The works of Strauss, Mahler, Schreker and Schoenberg,
although so apparently different in character, spring from
the same powerful source of Wagner's art, both in their
form and underlying ideology, categorically expressed in
Hans Sachs' affirmation of the indestructible might of *die
deutsche Kunst* in Act III of *The Mastersingers of Nuremberg*.

Richard Strauss' compositions most obviously reveal inner dependence on the work of his great predecessor. Notwithstanding the dazzling 'novelty' of his mode of expression, his music is marked throughout by latent 'traditionalism', rigid discipline and (despite his semblance to an *enfant terrible*) musical 'good breeding'. It was only the unusual daring of his gesture and, let us be honest, his tremendous genius which saved him from becoming hopelessly lost in the epigonism that is so evident in the youthful *Guntram*.[1]

As for the raw material of Strauss' music – its actual substance and the means by which he manipulates it (e.g., his style of instrumentation) – it is the fruit of an exceedingly courageous and resolute development of elements already present in the work of Wagner. The most interesting aspect of his innovations (e.g., the numerous and, chronologically, the earliest glimmerings of polytonality) originated not in a pure feeling for sound in its own right, but as a result of extra-musical speculation, stemming logically from the psychological content of the work. We are dealing here with what, as in Wagner's case, was a very typical expansion of the musical vocabulary in that it went beyond the bounds of key for the sake of dramatic tension. In this way the state of the soul could be expressed through the opposition of consonance with a highly skilled treatment of advanced dissonance. It was in the atmosphere of this musical 'psychology', the underlying basis of Wagner's art, that Strauss began his career as a composer.

The 'theatricality' of the content of his works (and it matters little whether we are concerned with stage-music or symphonic poems) means that the fundamental, normal state of mind is conveyed by a well-defined key and that even the most distant deviations from this key arise from the intensity of the psychological conflict. In substance we are

[1] Early opera by Strauss, composed in 1895.

dealing here not with a resolute 'revolutionary' stance, nor
with a ruthless change of the musical system (e.g., in the use
of atonality or polytonality as the basis of the musical structure), but merely with an unusually bold 'evolutionary'
enrichment of existing modes of expression.

In essence Strauss' work in its entirety developed from a
Romanticism upon which twenty years of literary 'modernism' (analogous to that of our 'Young Poland') had made a
strong but superficial impression, and it is here perhaps that
the causes for the comparatively transitory qualities of
Strauss' work lie. Because it was connected too directly with
life, and with the dramatic expression of life, because – let
us be absolutely frank – it neglected to some extent the most
vital qualities of musical form for the sake of literature, it
now finds itself unable to survive in the light of the fundamental revaluation now taking place in our thinking about
music.

Today, Strauss' music seems to us to be inescapably pre-
war – the art of yesterday. Here again, in a striking way,
the political factor becomes evident. The superficial expansion of large-scale resources taken to its limits (a legacy from
the composer of *Tristan*), the absence of introverted inti-
macy, an official, frequently noisy pathos in the guise of a
gala display, the festive presentation of the mighty German
soul – all these aspects are uncannily bound up with the
underlying psyche of pre-war Germany, with the implacable
affirmation of German achievements, with a fanatical faith
in individualistic heroism, represented first by Siegfried,
then Tristan, Walther, Hans Sachs and ultimately Zarathustra. These heroes gave way to the pretensions of *Heldenleben*,
and finally the rather dull caricature of the self-satisfied
bourgeois in *Sinfonia domestica.*[2]

---

[2] *Ein Heldenleben* (1898) and *Symphonia domestica* (1904) were the two tone-
poems which glorified Strauss's own exploits as composer and family
man.

Here there is almost paradoxical corroboration of that malicious phrase 'Wirkung ohne Ursache' – activity without cause – coined by Wagner in connection with the work of his rival and enemy, Jacob Meyerbeer, now an almost forgotten mediocrity. It is strikingly apparent in many of Strauss' later works in the aspiration towards external 'greatness of form', the artificial broadening of proportions without sufficient 'internal' bases. That degeneration through 'elevation' (*des Erhabenen*) is an inevitable result of an historically out-moded attitude towards artistic problems, and it speaks volumes about the nature of its true sources. Two appar-ently incompatible philosophies of life – the stylised pessimism of Schopenhauer in Wagner and Nietzsche's uncompromising assertion of life in Strauss – became mutu-ally complementary, binding the creative thought of both composers together ideologically.

The historical significance of Richard Strauss, who has to be numbered among the great musicians, will become patently clear once we have comprehended the role played in his career by *Elektra*[3] – undoubtedly his finest and, characteristically, his least understood and valued work. He drew on ancient tragedy, or rather, if one takes into account Hoffmansthal's interpretation of it, a structurally modern-ised ancient Greek myth which, in this form, became an elevated symbol that transcended history and which required considerable courage in its realisation. A poetic masterpiece, stripped of all superficially aestheticised Hellenism, it stood on the abyss of a most profoundly conceived realism. It marked a catastrophic turning-point in Strauss' development. It was the highest, indeed, the only peak he was to scale, in the course of the career he had elected once and for all to pursue. It seemed that in this unique work he had slammed the doors on the past epoch

---

[3] For the libretto of this one-act opera, composed in 1909, Strauss used Hugo von Hofmannsthal's reworking of the tragedy by Sophocles.

and its far-reaching quest of 'musical psychology' born out of the romantic conception of life. In creating, apparently spontaneously, a music drama with formal qualities, he opened up new horizons for future musicians. In reality, the innovation of *Elektra* most positively lies in its musical 'substance'. Its formal wealth is simply astonishing, yet it seems that Strauss himself drew no positive conclusions from this invaluable achievement. After this supreme creative effort, he permitted himself to sink into the aesthetic quietism which typifies *Der Rosenkavalier*, the *Alpine Symphony*, *Ariadne auf Naxos*, and a whole series of increasingly weak works in which there is a distasteful resting on laurels and the decking-out of bourgeois complacency in the ceremonial robes of a profound and refined culture.

The last gleams of the romantic concept of 'Germanness' flared up once again in the work of one of the most gifted epigones of this past era, illuminating with incredible brilliance the depths of the abyss on which German music then stood; only by bridging this abyss could the future progress of German music be assured.

During the period immediately preceding the Great War, a period of the most acute ideological crisis, we were witness to a feverish, determined search for new paths and new problems. In the forum of public opinion a whole series of names appeared, and the interests of various groups of musicians were focussed upon them. They often aroused premature enthusiasms which inevitably led to dashed hopes, disappointments and bitter scepticism. It seemed that the mighty spectre of a magnificent past haunted this activity. *Noblesse oblige*: German music had to remain 'great', it still had to be universal, it could not withdraw from its celestial fortress. From this attitude stemmed the tendency towards an artificial 'elevation', that broadening of proportions apparent in Strauss' work. But the differences which existed between the various attempts and the centrifugal nature of their aspirations are now an accomplished fact. We are faced with a vast range of phenomena which give the illusion of our entering upon a new era with a new set of principles. The classical bearing of the music of Reger,[4] which is related via Brahms to a Bachian tradition, stands in marked contrast with its *sui generis* neo-conservatism to the

---

[4] Max Reger (1873–1916) exerted some influence on Szymanowski during the 'Germanic' phase of his development. To many of Szymanowski's contemporaries, and in particular Adolf Chybiński, Reger-like complexities were self-evident in such works as the *Concert Overture*, Op. 12. Szymanowski knew and admired some of Reger's works, e.g., the *Sinfonietta*, the first performance of which he attended in Berlin.

In the rough notes Szymanowski made for his projected study of contemporary music, there are some additional illuminating remarks headed 'German Music, Reger and Cyclic Form':

a) The return to constructionalist-formal music in Germany was always connected with reactionary tendencies – Brahms. It always involved a return to the template of classical form.

b) Reger gives the illusion of constructionalism, again returning to the classical tradition for form, which he filled entirely (in a literal sense) with non-constructionalist matter. It is a strange language, having recourse in a downright disorderly and alogical way to the elements of the classical language, deformed to some extent by the introduction of new harmonic and modulatory concepts. This more remarkable mixture at first glance gives the impression of novelty; but very quickly one senses the lack of uniformity and the artificiality of the basic musical elements and the complete absence, unfortunately, of any sort of framework able to embrace that somewhat exuberant lyrical element in a clearly defined shape. (I am not referring to the small-scale works, especially the very many, very beautiful songs.)

c) It should be understood that German musical thought to this day almost automatically connects the concept of constructive form in music with 'form' bequeathed to us from the classical tradition, in effect, sonata, symphony.

d) One should ponder over cyclic form in music and its suggestive influence on our psyche. Without doubt it arose quite coincidentally and mechanically in the linking together of a few dances with different rhythms (partita, suite). At some time or another, that linking of several entities, different in character, into a musical work with the apparent unity of a work of art and the sense of that composite unity as a constructional-formal value stole into our consciousness. What sort of analogies are there with the 'unity' of a work of e.g. fine art? (The tryptich, so common in painting, has in general only a thematic connection.)

Karol Szymanowski Pisma, Vol. 1, pp. 487–88.

apparent 'innovations' of Mahler.[5] Yet these contradictions are contained within a traditionalism, the true sources of which are constantly open to investigation. The same may be said of Schreker,[6] who appeared to be searching out new solutions to the problems of music drama in a long series of stage-works. In the end he did not discover a new approach at all, but remained faithful to the example of his great predecessors, even though he incorporated elements from the works of non-German composers (e.g., Debussy and even Puccini). So the innovatory work of these exceedingly interesting composers depends basically upon the logical development of pre-existing elements and the enriching of

[5] Szymanowski heard Mahler's Symphony No. 8 in 1912, and found it 'invigorating'. In a letter to Stefan Spiess, dated 21 March 1912, he went on to say: 'Of its musical values I am unable to speak; perhaps there are some ugly things there, but overall it is marvellous and moving'.
Karol Szymanowski, *Korespondencja*, Vol. I, p. 335.

[6] Franz Schreker (1878–1934). Szymanowski heard *Das Spielwerk und die Prinzessin* in 1913. In a letter to Spiess, dated 18 March 1913 (*Korespondencja*, Vol. I, p. 374), he wrote: 'The critics were real swines. The only people who acquainted themselves with it properly, evaluated it and who attended every performance were of course Ficio [Fitelberg] and myself. In essence, in spite of many obscurities, inconsequentialities and weak pages, it is most beautiful. Full of poetry and expression. The music at times fabulous, the instrumentation sometimes simply amazing.'

Along with Paul Bekker, Alban Berg, Oskar Bie, Julius Bittner, Grzegorz Fitelberg, Robert Heger, Joseph Marx and Arnold Schoenberg, Szymanowski contributed to a series of 'greetings', published in *Musiblätter des Anbruch* (1928, Nos. 3/4), commemmorating Schreker's fiftieth birthday. The text of Szymanowski's contribution is as follows:

I became acquainted with Schreker in Vienna many years ago. It was at that time that *Spielwerk*, then still in its original version, was staged at the Hofoper, to the excitement of public and critics alike. For me and for many other young musicians, this performance was a startling, still vivid experience which I can see in my mind's eye even now. I was present at all the performances and it was then that I became possessed with a love and regard for Schreker as a composer such as I had had previously for him as a man and poet on the basis of personal contact and readings of his poetry. Here I should like to express my esteem and reverence for Schreker – among whose friends I am proud to count myself – both as a man and as one of the most distinguished composers of our times.

Karol Szymanowski Pisma, Vol. 1, p. 226.

their means of expression. It does not involve a single, fundamentally new idea, nor a basic change of position with regard to the problems of music.

I have just mentioned the three most important names in German music, but have said nothing about the many other composers who produced countless works which, for the most part, are excellent when it comes down to a consideration of *métier*. This in itself is symptomatic of German integrity in creative matters, and is testament to the well-established, truly profound musical culture of a nation which has long had an awareness of fundamental artistic questions in the blood. Further evidence of their musical culture is reflected in the huge literature devoted to the subject, a literature which is notable for the depth and extent of its scholarship.

After the period in which Richard Wagner enjoyed a well-nigh absolute hegemony (I deliberately leave aside the noble, solitary figure of Johannes Brahms,[7] whose art, regardless of its absolute value, has played almost no part in the evolution of recent music), the ideological war broke out again, the chief combatants being Wagner's most distinguished followers. In the years immediately preceding the war, the conflict of differing opinions, along with increasingly vocal protests against the pre-eminence of Wagner, and, finally and characteristically, the awakening of interest in the musical modernism of other nations (chiefly France and Russia) led one to sense the threat of an approaching storm, with its relentless ideological crisis and the fundamental, internal reconstruction that would inevitably follow in its wake.

In these circumstances, amidst the truly tragic conflicts and struggles over the right to a hearing, the fame of Arnold

[7] Szymanowski retained a deep affection for Brahms' music throughout his life. Even when forging his most characteristic, non-German style in the war years he played through the Third Sonata for piano and violin with Kochański several times.

Schoenberg, modern Germany's most amazing composer, slowly developed.

Here we come to the heart of the problem. Many of Schoenberg's distinguished colleagues, the representatives of pre-war musical 'modernism', are alive to this day, but Schoenberg was the only one among them who not only survived whole-heartedly the terrible historical cataclysm which the Great War was for Central Europe, but who held his ground as the standard-bearer of ideas that were to lead German music from the stifling, pre-war atmosphere which enveloped it to new triumphs and conquests. In the opinion of most of those in Germany today, he is the long-awaited builder of bridges spanning the firmaments, the man who has opened up a path to the future. His name, which is on an equal footing with that of Igor Stravinsky, has become a symbol of revolutionary musical modernity. The psychology of this phenomenon must be thoroughly investigated.

Schoenberg's immense creative energy, his fanatical faith in his mission and his unshakable fidelity to his own ideals inspire respect for this extraordinary personality and require of us the utmost caution and objectivity in the formation of critical judgements concerning his work. There can be no superficial, laconic dismissal of an artist whose work counts for so much in the history of contemporary music.

In his work the internal reconstruction of the basic means of expression is seen at its most explicit, moving centrifugally, so to say, from an ideological nucleus towards a total revaluation of the basic premises of music's formal elements.

The most striking feature of Schoenberg's development was that his creative point of departure was post-Wagnerian epigonism. *Gurrelieder*, the Romantic bases of which are not open to dispute, is eloquent proof of this. The characteristic subordination of particular musical dynamic elements, necessitating a relaxation of the organic cohesion of form for the sake of extra-musical content, is evident at every step. It is precisely in those mysterious links with Wagner and

German Romanticism in general, symptomatic again of the undeniable traditionalism of a deeply-founded culture, that the starting-point for any sort of critical judgement of his work is to be found, even though, paradoxically, his work has travelled far from its natural sources. Let us consider in what direction the formal elements of music, in accordance with their notional basis, tended. It was during the Romantic era, especially in Germany, that the 'horizontal' style of the classicists, implying in its very premises the construction of purely musical 'forms', changed gradually to a 'vertical' style as a result of the 'dramatisation' of the subject matter and increasingly clearly defined bonds with immediate psychological truths. An increasingly varied and enriched harmonic practice became the starting-point for the Romantic style in music for reasons which are totally understandable. The intensified saturation of music with the lyricism of an immediate living reality, the basing of music on a psychological rhythm, the formal framework of which was, strictly speaking, the rhythm of the spoken word, with all its improvisatory freedom and deeply felt pathos, gradually dragged music away from the natural course of its development. The rigorous control of rhythm, music's exoskeleton by which the proportions of the individual particles of a musical work are made comprehensible, was gradually relaxed. At the same time vertical (harmonic) sounds came to the fore, acting as frontier-posts and creating (from the formal point of view) arbitrary resting-points which provided a general background for the saturating lyricism of the music. Furthermore, harmony (divorced from other musical elements) provided a grateful framework for that so-called (*horribile dictu*) 'mood', that formal 'nothing' which abandoned musical dynamism in favour of an 'emotional' dynamism and produced a new, fundamentally static sensation of 'colour' in music.

So long as harmony was based on tonal principles, so long as it was subject to movement, the concept of modulation could exist. Harmony (consonance) became increasingly varied with regard to its component parts, and there came a time when dissonant harmony created the concept of a chord as a self-contained value, an unresolved dissonance that came from and went nowhere: the absolute in vertical harmony. In the history of this type of chord, the chromaticism of *Tristan* was a turning-point. The chord evolved further in the works of distinguished composers of the post-Wagnerian era (i.e., Strauss, Mahler, etc.). But in these cases such chords were used to express psychological conflict, as colour, as 'mood'; they never existed as a formal, absolute value in their own right. Such a chord was a deviation, a digression, an aberration, but by the very possibility of its existence it indicated the right, purposeful way forward. The notion of an absolute, vertical sound which constitutes a self-contained value as opposed to a function of musical 'expression', is the highway which leads to atonality proper. Arnold Schoenberg crossed the Rubicon, separating himself for ever from his past. He did this with a sense of complete responsibility for his actions and in full consciousness of the significance of his decision. He found himself in a spacious, open land in which all things were possible and, in the words of Nietzsche: 'Nichts ist wahr, alles ist erlaubt'.[8]

We should be completely mindful of the gravity and the consequences of that step.

---

[8] 'Nothing is true, everything is permitted.'

Igor Stravinsky

First published in *Warszawianka* on 1 November 1924 in celebration of Stravinsky's arrival in Warsaw to play the solo part in his own *Concerto for Piano and Winds*.

For Warsaw's musical world the arrival of Igor Stravinsky is an even greater sensation than the guest appearance of a tenor with a ravishingly beautiful top C sharp. But in this case it must be said that the sensation results not from tawdry, strident publicity aimed at the superficial, unpleasant snobbery of townsfolk. The Russian composer's reception is a natural, justly deserved response to the truly remarkable role that his *œuvre* has played in the history of European music during the last decade or so. Indeed for some people it is a tragic harbinger of the decline of musical culture; for others it marks the start of new, fruitful developments. But all agree that no matter how extreme the views of the character of his work may be, it is quintessentially a phenomenon of the utmost importance, a decisive turning-point which cannot be ignored in the terrifyingly rapid evolution of our conception of the art of music.

Quite apart from the immediacy of its expression and its purely objective value, Stravinsky's art by its very nature demonstrably and definitively 'revalues' established ideas about musical aesthetics. We can easily discover analogous traits in the work of Pablo Picasso, and the role it has played in the history of present-day painting. Picasso's work also appears to be 'revolutionary', but in essence it is a courageous and unhesitating foreshortening of the evolutionary path along which today's art is relentlessly travelling. But there is a difference: Stravinsky's creative powers and 'specific gravity', together with that fascinating faith in the rightness and importance of his own work, are much more pronounced than they are in the case of the famous painter, and consequently have evoked a much stronger response in the 'birth-pangs' of modern music.

There can be no doubt that today Igor Stravinsky really is the greatest living musician in so far as his inner will and impulse to create a world of beauty attain concrete and perfect expression in objectively realised works of art. He deals with the problem of form in the simplest, most direct way with unerring, well-nigh mathematical precision. His incredible craftsmanship, pushed to its furthest bounds, almost permits us to place him alongside those classical or renaissance masters in whose music a beauty of great vitality sprang directly, as if organically, from the very concept of 'craft'. This is not the sort of beauty which strays through the dark recesses of the soul or lurks amongst the restless spectres of 'expressionism', 'impressionism' or any of those manifold 'metaphysical' banalities which often led, especially in the post-Romantic era, to tragic and sometimes comic conflicts between 'form' and 'content', between the creative intention and its artistic realisation. In Germany a classic example of such inner confusion is to be found in the work of Gustav Mahler, and in Russia, to a certain extent, in the music of Aleksander Skryabin.

Igor Stravinsky, a singular man, whose appearance and European manner seem to suggest a more 'distinguished' profession than that of dangerous musical 'revolutionary'! Although Russian, with a strong lacing of Polish blood (he descends from a Russified branch of the Strawińskis, well known and still numerous in Poland today, and his grandfather, a Catholic, spoke good Polish),[1] his life-style and the externals of his career are, in contrast, markedly European, not to say Parisian, for Paris was for many years his home and the real birth-place of the world-wide fame he enjoys today. His art, however, has remained fundamentally

[1] Confirmation of these facts can be found in Igor Stravinsky and Robert Craft, *Memories and Commentaries*, Faber and Faber, London, 1960, pp. 17–18.

Russian, the majority of his stage-works, especially those of his first period, being based on subjects taken from Russian life, e.g., *The Firebird, Petrushka, The Rite of Spring, Les Noces, Mavra* and others. It would appear that in deserting his grim fatherland and determinedly bringing his art 'to the West', where the atmosphere of freedom and respect for the individual better suited his spiritual system (which from his early youth had been in conflict with Russian officialdom), he took with him an idealised recollection of his homeland. His vision was undisturbed by the pain and humiliating grind, by the spectres which have persistently haunted recent Russian history. His pure, unstained youthful memories formed the mainspring of a great talent which, freed from casual, immediate experience, scaled ever greater heights and took in the broadest horizons possible, so finding perfect expression in works which were to shake the whole of Western musical opinion to its very foundations.

And here we have to face an extremely interesting question. We are dealing with an art which is characterised by a very specific ethnic colouring (at least in most of its manifestations), an art which from the outset was regarded by public opinion in the West as the fruit of an almost paradoxical exoticism. How was it that such an art gradually became the ideological point of reference for groups of nebulous, diffuse concepts, and for individual, unco-ordinated efforts both to create a new music, clear and unambiguous in form, and to discover a new way through the rubble, splendid though it was, of yesterday's art?

In those transitional periods which occur in the course of the evolution of artistic ideologies, a powerful, creative figure of great intelligence will suddenly appear, as if conjured up by magic, to concentrate within himself, and also to express in concrete form, the gradually maturing but as yet unvoiced moods and yearnings of the masses. Such works indicate with unerring certainty the direction future evolution will take. The ethnic qualities which colour a work so specifically are superfluous in an assessment of its true worth. They merely provide an indisputable warranty of the artist's integrity in relation to his own creativity, constituting the essential, natural atmosphere in which his work is to develop if it is to be a genuine 'creation' and not just something which is helplessly wrapped around in worn-out aesthetic rags. This, then, is the origin of the time-honoured label 'revolutionary', with which every great artist is traditionally branded.

A striking example of this process is provided by Richard Wagner. He was probably the most 'German' of German musicians, but by sheer force of genius he compelled the whole world to rush blindly into the fantastic abyss of his art, the extra-musical, ideological atmosphere of which was, in many cases, as it was for us in Poland, downright alien, if not inimical.

Fanatical 'integrity' in the creation of one's own world of beauty, and a complete breaking away from the chains of accepted aesthetic canons have, at various times in the history of art, meant 'self-sacrifice' for the sake of attaining elusive objectives which seem forever to be vanishing into the distance. Yet it is only in such conditions, requiring the surrender of immediate success as well as intense inner concentration, that real, enduring values are created.

Stravinsky has always trod this hard, stony path of inexorable artistic duty. Since escaping from the remnants of foreign influences, he has travelled rapidly in seven-league boots to create and perfect his personal style. He has never been deterred by hostile demonstrations, and even his kindest critics háve been thrown into a state of confusion when, having reconciled themselves to the 'aesthetique' of one work, have found themselves helpless when confronted with the next. Each new work seems to be the ruination of all established, approved theories about the nature of his talent, but in actual fact is only another stage in a development that is proceeding with great rapidity. Such was the case a decade ago with *Petrushka* – now officially regarded by all the great critical moguls of London and Paris as a masterpiece. It was followed by *The Rite of Spring*, which provoked unprecedented protests from public and critics alike at its premiere in Paris in 1913. Yet now, in that same city it is recognised – and quite rightly so – as perhaps the greatest of contemporary works.

There is no doubt that it is precisely this tireless search for the shortest and most direct route in the pursuit of inner development which holds the secret of Stravinsky's psychological influence over the younger generation of composers in the emergent, newly autonomous musical cultures of the West, such as England, America, Italy, Spain and even young Germany (Hindemith).

This is not the place for a detailed, 'technical' characterisation of the inner mechanisms of Stravinsky's work, nor of his commanding influence on the music of the present day. My concern has been solely to outline the extent of this distinguished Russian composer's achievement in European art. It must be said that there are few people in this country who are aware of his reputation, and those who are seldom approach his work with much understanding. I have already read one highly critical piece in the Polish press, and its author has never heard Stravinsky's work in its orchestral form! Unfortunately, information obtained from such sources will be as helpful as a blind man's description of colour.

But I have no doubt that as the greater part of the Polish public greets even suspect pieces of surrogate Russian art with open arms, they will appreciate all the more enthusiastically the work of that nation's greatest living composer.

On the Musical Life of Paris

First published in two parts in *Wiadomości Literackie* on 20 and 27 July 1924.

'Les Six' and Erik Satie

Stefan Żeromski's beautiful book *Snobbery and Progress* is concerned with spheres of thought beyond the range of this article, but its title provides us with an apt, logical formula around which to concentrate our often unhappy thoughts about contemporary art. It is possible to travesty the phrase and speak of 'the snobbery of progress', or worse still, 'the progress of snobbery', in other words, that strange but threatening evolution of taste in the field of art which is making what had been a simple, direct relationship between 'manufacturer' and 'customer' increasingly complex.

Paris is such a vast battle-ground over new ideas that everything assumes proportions which are well-nigh monstrous and deeply disturbing for the unassuming newcomer from the provinces.

I am trying to close my eyes to the enormity of this struggle, to the multitude and variety of its component parts, and if possible narrow my horizons so as to concentrate on music alone, since it is of music that I have the most sympathetic understanding. But here I find myself having to deal with problems which are all the more difficult to solve as nowadays the autonomous study of any single field of art is out of the question: everything is inextricably interlinked by the often elusive, but no less binding, chains of what are fundamentally psychological and sociological developments. A shift in one's point of view on artistic questions in general has now become a matter of course in pronouncements regarding any sort of contemporary work. In effect,

228

we here have that inescapable 'progress', which would be a much esteemed word if only it did not bring in its wake the insolent, boring shadow of form without any real content, negation for the sake of negation and the deceitful 'creativity' of the uncreative: in other words 'the snobbery of progress'.

On hearing recent works by the youngest and most famous of today's French composers, I was aware first and foremost of the application of 'theory' rather than the intrinsic content of each piece of music, and present-day tastes persistently taking precedence over the subjective will of the creative individual – everything indeed which makes for the hopeless monotony of a predetermined style. I confess that I was deeply disillusioned because it was not a question of one single abortive work, but of the work of a whole group who had until now represented certain ideals, a group of young artists[1] to whom we are indebted for several fine works, notably ballets, some performed by Diaghilev's celebrated Ballets Russes[2] (Auric's *Les Fâcheux*, Milhaud's *Le Train bleu* and Poulenc's *Les Biches*), others by a rather peculiar theatrical company ('Les Soirées de Paris'), whose artistic intentions are not totally comprehensible to me (Milhaud's *Salade*).

To complete the picture, two more ballets must be mentioned: *Parade* and *Mercure* by Erik Satie.[3] In my view these 'works' should be given short shrift, as the incomprehen-

---

[1] *Cf.* note 3 on p. 203.

[2] Serge Diaghilev (1872–1929) was the founder of the 'Ballets Russes'. His name is inextricably linked with that of Stravinsky, whose reputation he was largely instrumental in establishing. After the Great War, he was based chiefly in Paris and there commissioned works from de Falla, Poulenc, Milhaud and Ravel. Debussy and Ravel had also composed ballet scores for him before the War.

[3] Erik Satie (1866–1925) exerted a powerful influence on some members of 'Les Six' as well as the composers of 'L'École d'Arcueil', a group of young French musicians which he brought together in 1923. The most prominent members of this group were Henri Cliquet-Pleyel, Roger Désormière, Maxime Jacob and Henri Sauguet. The name of the 'school' derived from the suburb of Paris in which Satie resided.

sible course the career of this most unusual of composers
has taken originates entirely in the vast reserves of snobbery
to be found in this correspondingly vast city. Unfortunately
he has also played a major role in what I would frankly
describe as the 'corruption' of the younger generation of
French musicians.

Erik Satie is an eccentric creature of slender musical
talent but considerable *esprit* and intelligence. He also has
the temperament of the typical *camelot*.[4] Throughout the
whole of his long life, he has distinguished himself by always
being 'younger' than the 'youngest'. At one time he was
younger than both Saint-Saëns and Chabrier; subsequently
he was younger than Debussy and Ravel, and now he is
younger than the members of 'Les Six', who in reality are
younger than he is. (Today, to the annoyance of all old folk,
he leads yet another group of even younger composers,
L'École d'Arcueil,[5] reserving for himself the role of a
musical Socrates of unhappy memory.) Truly, what indestructible youth! A malicious old man has now frightened
three generations of really gifted French composers with his
terrifyingly virulent wit and the spectre of the *dernier de
derniers cris*, and to this day, in spite of his sixty-odd years, he
keeps going, light as a hollow buoy, bobbing on the cease-
lessly rolling waves of snobbery. *Parade* and *Mercure*
constitute an extremely depressing spectacle when viewed
against the rest of present-day Parisian music (I emphasise
music, because the *décor* and stagecraft of these ballets
contain a number of interesting features, thanks chiefly to
the participation of Pablo Picasso). On hearing these works,
one is filled with *ennui* and repugnance, but in any case it is
best to ignore them, as they will fall from the tree of art,
without prompting, like faded, rotten leaves.

The saddest aspect of the whole affair is the direction now
apparently being taken by 'Les Six' in their musical works.
In point of fact, these composers are no longer grouped

[4] Literally, a hawker.

[5] *Cf.* note 3 on p. 229.

together under a single ideological banner. The group has now split, and though some of its members are still connected, it is only by business interest and the desire for a taste of publicity. The sad thing is that in spite of their undoubted talents (and a series of works from the not-too-distant past provides ample proof of this), their creative gifts are already beginning to betray symptoms of decay. The root causes of this lie deep in the psyche of post-war society and in the Parisian atmosphere, which unfortunately becomes, during certain months of the year, markedly less 'French' in the true sense of the word, a high price being paid to satisfy the tastes of a crowd of tourists from various countries with a degree of culture which is obviously not of the highest standard. It is for this reason that one can clearly detect a vast difference between the French novel, which has recovered so beautifully from its post-war decline, and the theatre, which in many cases is intent only on seasonal displays.

It is especially during the *grande saison*, namely May and June, that the great impresarios mount extraordinary attractions and pack to over-flowing huge halls such as the Théâtre des Champs-Elysées. One of the greatest of these impresarios is Serge Diaghilev, the founder of the celebrated Ballets Russes. There was a time when this man, who succeeded in canonising the genius of Stravinsky, was inflexible in his artistic idealism. But today that idealism, which is no longer bolstered by the huge personal fortune he previously enjoyed, and possibly even the patronage of the Tsars, is becoming flawed. Erik Satie was able to exploit this weakness a couple of years ago with his exceedingly weak *Parade*, and it seems that in the style and general standard of their recent ballets, Milhaud, Poulenc and Auric have been affected by Diaghilev's decline.

Snobbery and Talents

What is the basis of the 'style' of the younger French composers? Without doubt their works are linked by certain

common features, but alas it has to be said that these
features are negative in nature. As far as individual, positive
qualities are concerned, a certain hierarchy amongst these
composers can be established. Indisputably the most valuable of the four ballets which I have heard is Francis
Poulenc's *Les Biches*. Its music is youthful and indeed almost
naive (which is all the more striking as the events on stage
are, to say the least, *équivoque*). It is charming and fresh, with
a pleasing, unsophisticated sound, and betrays sporadic
traces of this composer's previous, revolutionary 'polytonal'
tendencies. Its pleasant, easy-going melodies importune the
ear like pretty girls whom even highly moral gentlemen find
difficult to resist. After that comes Auric's *Les Fâcheux*. Quite
apart from its purely musical qualities, namely dexterity,
lightness of touch, and the genuine humour and freshness
of its harmonic ideas, it impresses with its skilful control of
stage situations, its characterisation of individual figures
and the logical construction of its dramatic plot. The composer is aided in the realisation of this drama by a judicious
'balletic' travesty of Molière's comedy and a skilful staging,
which makes use of beautiful *décors* and costumes by
Bracque. On the other hand, Milhaud's *Salade* (in spite of
the one or two really beautiful numbers it contains) and,
above all, his wretched *Train bleu* put even the most sympathetic listener in a difficult position.

Is it really the case that in France, the classical land in
which, as all the *raffinements* of the great Debussy and Ravel
demonstrate, *métier* has always been obligatory, the ideal,
the *dernier cri* to which her composers now aspire is that
awful-sounding, vulgar tavern music which not only lacks
any innovatory tendencies, but hankers after the most
mundane trivialities? This is the heart of the question. The
young of 'Les Six' were originally united beneath a banner
of protest. Protest against what? Surely not against the
marvellous skills of their predecessors? They were concerned with principles, with theories, with the ever-fickle
'spirit of the times'. They had had enough of all those
subtleties, almost dissolving into a twilit non-existence;

enough of those sophisticated soft sounds; enough of that aristocratic isolation within the subjective experience of an infinite gamut of different feelings in which it appeared that the 'construction' of musical form was abandoned. Gone were the dreams of idealised exoticism originating in the 1,001 nights, of that refined representation of the world of external objects in an 'aesthetic' individual experience. Instead, they turned their attention to the 'reality' of life, and the strong positive 'material' values of existence. They would propagate these values, filling day-to-day life with them; indeed, they would exploit the fantastic events of everyday life which present themselves to the imagination, raising them through the power of their subjective creativities into the realm of artistic expression. Agreed! The basing of art on a par with everyday life and all its undeniable wealth is a characteristic development in the evolution of modern art. In this process a powerful influence was the urbanisation of Paris, perhaps the only modern city in which an artistic existence (as such) is truly warranted. There is the 'realism' of the town, its ensnaring dynamism, and its own unbelievably disparate poetry, be it the poetry of a music-hall, a circus, or a fair at Neuilly. Such a huge organism, so overwhelming in its complexity, has thousands of nuances: an incredible gamut of sounds exists alongside the 'dreams', and all intrude upon the mind with the power of real, indisputable fact. This is one sphere of influences, and others of a subsidiary nature exist. There are newcomers from America, terrific Negroes who sing really beautifully and who play a music wonderfully enlivened by syncopation. They have an exceedingly refined sense of the musical value of noise,[6] and undoubtedly contribute new formal values which can be transformed and exploited even

---

[6] Unfortunately in Warsaw we have no idea, believe me, of jazz in its ideal, essential form! Would that some of our Warsaw musicians could hear, e.g., the four Negroes who play in the relaxed atmosphere of 'Jardin de ma sœur'. What bliss! –KS

in the most serious musical conceptions, as the latest works of Igor Stravinsky demonstrate.[7] Furthermore there are ideological factors, and in particular the hatred which existed even before the war for the Germanic concept of music as a means of conveying idealism – in other words, the nebulous metaphysics that dilutes a work of art into anaemic dreaming about itself. There is also the enormous influence exerted by the truly mighty, uncompromising and compelling art of Igor Stravinsky, an art which storms all citadels, and with a truly Russian passion first destroys and then builds colossal edifices through which his amazing genius can express itself. In addition there are the 'theoretical' justifications of Jean Cocteau,[8] a cacodemon of considerable *esprit* and talent who, especially in his most recent books, is capable of producing an art that is well-nigh classical in its poise and sense of beauty. In his spare time, and for reasons best known to himself, he amuses himself by baffling those of lesser musical intelligence than himself by paradoxical jugglings with ideas and ideals. Admittedly he does this with abundant grace and wit, as we can see in his book *Le coq et l'arlequin*. Finally there is the 'bad example' of that old immoralist and *farceur,* Erik Satie, of whom I have already spoken. Add to this the feverish, almost unhealthy atmosphere of artistic Paris, the impossibility of concentrating one's thoughts there, the pressures arising from the composition of a commissioned work to meet an impressario's deadline in time for the season, and the need to adapt such a work to suit the capricious whims of director, ballet-master and designer,

---

[7] *Ragtime* for eleven instruments (1918) and *Piano-Rag Music* (1919).

[8] Cocteau's influence on French music at this time was considerable. His book *Le coq et l'arlequin* (1919), which provided 'Les Six' with an underlying theory for their work, was strongly anti-Romantic, anti-Wagnerian and anti-Debussian. It called for the creation of a national music which was truly French in spirit and praised Stravinsky, particularly for his rhythmic and harmonic innovations.

and finally (let us be frank), the snobbery of keeping abreast of the latest fashion, a snobbery which plays such an important role in the assembled chaos of the Parisian 'Season' – take all these factors into account, and we have some understanding of the general background against which the latest stage-works of France's young composers have come into existence.

As for their musical talents: do they possess any at all? What they have has been shamefacedly hidden away for the time being. They have yielded to the excessive demands of fashion and theories imposed *a priori* which have resulted in today's chaos, or at least a labyrinth without an exit. Or perhaps I ought to say a labyrinth with only one exit, and this, as it always has, requires fanatical, naive, absolute faith in the rightness of one's own art, and total independence from whatever else may be going on round and about. It is in essence the creation of a scale and hierarchy of values of one's own. (Incidentally it seems to me that so far only one of 'Les Six', Artur Honegger, the composer of the beautiful *King David*, has discovered this exit.)

This exit now really is like 'the eye of the needle, through which etc., etc. . . . '. Even the most sincere of today's artists must bear an intolerable, almost tragic burden consisting of everything which ought properly to lie beyond the bounds of pure art. By this I mean the infernal tangle of loops and coils arising from generalisations, theories, 'isms' and the whole quasi-intellectual bag and baggage that stands between the artist and his intended work, illuminated in the cold spotlight of contradictory, divergent critical opinions. Every impulse of genuine inspiration is poisoned by the venom of these uncreative, vindictive conceits.

In Paris, where opinions are forged as if in the white heat of a steel foundry, one needs superhuman strength to retain one's integrity.

Even the strongest talents betray passing weaknesses, and so, in spite of my recent, rather unhappy experiences, I have not abandoned hope for the future well-being of Milhaud, Auric and Poulenc.

The impression made by their recent ballets was exceedingly interesting. I was prepared (from the names of the composers) for all manner of uncompromisingly radical writing, unprecedented dissonance and a markedly futuristic musical apparatus. Instead of this, one was confronted with a strangely submissive, tame, well-schooled and – *disons le mot* – rather trivial music. There were no surprises, even in the sheer sound of the instrumentation. On the contrary, even here the previously obligatory *métier* was 'below standard', especially in Milhaud's case. Perhaps this veritable abnegation can be justified by one of their numerous 'theories', but on no account by true Art (with a capital A). Putting aside the forces operating from without, I believe that I have succeeded, in so far as I can, in formulating the internal mechanism of this particular 'musical evolution' with its so very striking results.

Maurice Ravel on the Occasion of his Fiftieth Birthday

First published in *Muzyka*, March 1925

When listening to Ravel's music one often has an almost visual impression of the sun, weaving a dancing, golden net over the waves of a southern sea. It is full of the open air, of mysterious, glittering lights, of an azure sheen, of movement and life. Sometimes one feels quietly pensive, attempting to hear mysterious melodies floating on the far away air. There again the sky might cloud over and the sea darken, taking on a steely brilliance. There is a moment of self-contained melancholy, without complaint or reproach, without blatant gesture. Suddenly there is a stronger gust of wind and the waves billow as if in tragic anticipation of a storm which never arrives, so as not to destroy in a senseless outburst of passion the beauty and order which prevails here. And then, once more, the peaceful rays of the sun glitter bewitchingly over the nimbly playing waves.

It may appear from this that Ravel's music is a superficial play of light, colour and shade – a cold, soulless 'aestheticism'. Not at all! For beneath this 'surface' translucent, peaceful, concentrated depths lie concealed, and it is to these depths that the 'surface' owes its magical play of light and colour.

I believe that herein lies the characteristic 'depth' of French art in its greatest and most typical manifestations – whether it be poetry, the fine arts or music. The depth is apparent not in the pious intention of 'creating' a great work in line with one idea or another, often alien to art, but is, as it were, 'self-contained', in the very fact of the work's 'perfection', in the joyous sense of an independent 'organic' existence beyond the constantly flowing currents of everyday reality and spheres of immediate experience and the intricate play of passion and feeling. The art of Maurice Ravel possesses this transparent 'depth' to the highest degree possible. Whether he composes *Rhapsodie Espagnole, Greek Songs* or the well-nigh Viennese *La Valse*, he constantly remains one of the most fascinating exponents of the French genius. He embodies all the fundamental elements of what is perhaps the world's most beautiful artistic culture.

But his faultless technique, with its lively controlling intelligence, does not lead to his work being confined within the rigid, speculative formalism of an intellectualised art: on the contrary, it is merely the powerful, faithful ally of an unerring instinct, emanating from the depths of creative emotion.

This art teems with fervent, intense life, but it is not given to 'histrionic' over-acting, nor does it waste inner energy on superficial, clamorous gestures. It is typified by that strange 'reticence' regarding emotional displays, characteristic of all noble artists.

I believe that the creator of *L'Heure Espagnole*, unquestionably one of the most distinguished of living composers, is insufficiently understood and esteemed – and not just here in Poland. Undoubtedly one reason for this is in some measure the fact that he was overshadowed by his great predecessor, Claude Debussy.

The composer of *Pelléas* really was the first to succeed in breaking free from the fetters of the many different influences and suggestions coming from the other side of the Rhine. He also liberated himself from the stereotyped eclecticism that flourished in French music during the second half of the 19th century, and in *Pelléas* created a great work, not so much in size as the decidely innovatory nature of both its form and content, on account of which it became epoch-making in the development of the French music of the future.

It is only natural that the sudden opening up of new, almost boundless possibilities initially dazzled and enchanted Ravel, a man more than ten years younger than Debussy. But the younger composer, once he had started to investigate this new, hitherto unknown world, rapidly began to make his own way with complete certainty.

Ravel and Debussy together formed a glorious, emotional brotherhood, fighting for a great, original French music, freed once and for all from foreign influence. They are linked by an identical attitude to fundamental artistic quest- · ions, a result of their racial character and common spiritual culture. But in matters of individual creativity, important differences and divergences between the two artists soon become apparent. It is the early, exceedingly superficial critical assessments that are to blame for the banal label which to this day stalks the pages of reviews and for ever links both names together as the representatives of 'French Impressionism in Music'.

I believe that this is fundamentally a 'cliché', created *ad hoc* by music critics (on the basis of some superficial analogies with the contemporaneous movement in painting). As so often happens, these critics did not know in which already prepared pigeonhole to place a living, impulsive eruption of truly French music. The term lacks all *raison d'être* in the case of Ravel's music, where formal, structural elements always predominate over that direct, improvisatory 'sensibility' which so often swamps the clear, defined outlines and internal architecture of a work of art.

In spite of the undoubted presence of innovations in Ravel's music, innovations resting fairly and squarely on his unfailing technical mastery, we discover no trace of the 'revolution' which wants to 'destroy' rather than 'build', and therefore only rejects all the values of 'yesterday'.

On the contrary, at the very heart of his artistic sensibility lies a deeply conceived traditionalism originating in his racial, cultural consciousness, and this is something which I find sympathetic and totally comprehensible.

Ravel's exceedingly aristocratic 'genealogy', which can be traced back to the great French masters of the sixteenth, seventeenth and eighteenth centuries, has enabled him to

arrive at a new understanding of their marvellous, sunlit art.
It is surely for this reason that the composer of *Daphnis and
Chloe* shows himself to be a genuine 'nobleman' in all his
works: never descending from the heights of true culture,
he persistently shuns the vulgar demagogy which unfortunately is so prevalent in the art of the present day.

*   *   *

I will never cease to declare that familiarity with French
music, together with a real, deep understanding of its
content, of its mastery of form and of the ways it may
develop in the future, is one of the pre-conditions for the
development of our own music in Poland.

In the present superficial sketch, I have attempted to
characterise the essence of Ravel's art from the point of view
of its most profound, evolutionary value.

So these words are not merely a common courtesy,
addressed to the composer on the occasion of his fiftieth (!)
birthday, but an expression of genuine, warm admiration
for his music and its great, enduring qualities.

Paul Dukas
'Tel qu'en lui-même enfin ... '[1]

This obituary, the last piece which Szymanowski prepared for publication, appeared in the May–June 1936 edition of *La Revue Musicale* as part of a series of tributes to Dukas, who had died on 17 May 1935.

Although I did not know Paul Dukas personally, I realised that he possessed a refined nature, both on account of his work and also because of what I have been told about this noble artist and honest craftsman. I can appreciate the extent of the loss which French musicians in general, and his friends in particular, have suffered, and I wish to associate myself with the unanimous hommage presently being paid to his memory.

I heard *Ariane et Barbe-Bleue* twice, but it was only after hearing it for the second time, some ten years after my first encounter with the work, that I was able to appreciate it fully.

At a time when I responded enthusiastically to an aesthetic which gives us masterpieces, but which has more to do with the emotional expression of the moment, my first contact with *Ariane* failed to make a profound impression upon me. I noted the fine technical qualities of the work, but took pleasure from it without enthusiasm, the pleasure which one takes in all works which are well executed, balanced and endowed with noble, elevated traits.

After going through many experiences and a process of development which moderated certain of my enthusiasms and instilled considerable scepticism into my judgement, I again heard Paul Dukas's lyric drama. My previous regard

[1] 'Such as he is in himself at last . . . ' is a quotation from the opening line of Mallarmé's *Tombeau d'Edgar Poe*.

for it, far from being weakened, was changed into a profound, warm admiration. Compared with so much which lies in ruins or has lost its value, *Ariane et Barbe-Bleue* appeared to me to be the most powerful, most definitive, most perfect and moving work of the French school after *Pelléas.*

These few words must suffice to express the extent of my esteem and the warmth of the sympathy which I feel towards this grand, well-ordered work, the orchestration of which (one of the most sumptuous scores I know) has as much power as it has transparency and as much brilliance as ingenuity.

The Future
of Culture

This is the text of a contribution Szymanowski made at a
conference held in Madrid between 3 and 7 May 1933,
devoted to the future of culture. It was organised under the
auspices of the League of Nations and chaired by Marie
Skłodowska-Curie. Other contributors included Jules
Romains, Miguel de Unamuno, Paul Valéry and J. B. S.
Haldane. Szymanowski was the only musician present at the
proceedings. Contributors were invited to define culture, if
possible differentiating between its individualistic, national
and more general human aspects; to establish a hierarchy and
relationship between these aspects; to state whether they
believed that representatives of the intellectual world were
now immersing themselves more fully in everyday life; to
comment on the clash between the soul and technology and
problems arising in the civilising of the masses; to discuss the
possibilities of creating a code of cultural values which would
be applicable to all people and nations, and to discuss the
future of culture in connection with developing international
relations. Szymanowski's contribution was published in
Entretiens, Vol. 2, 'L'Avenir de la Culture', Paris, 1933,
pp. 188–95.

In an article on Fryderyk Chopin in which I sought to
express the essential significance of his music in its most
profound sense, I made the following statement about him:
'he resolved the basic problem of all great art: how to
achieve in his work the perfect expression of a profoundly
and universally human grandeur and dignity without losing
anything of his innate characteristics and nationalistic
originality'.[1]

---

[1] 'Frédéric Chopin et la musique polonaise moderne', *La Revue Musicale*
(No. 121, 1931); reprinted in *Karol Szymanowski Pisma*, Vol. 1, pp. 317–20.

If I call on the name of my great compatriot here, it is because it seems to me that this statement about his art, generalised and inadequate though it be, is relevant to the fundamental problem which here concerns us, namely the relationship and links between individual, national and human culture in general.

On the one hand, it is true that a composer of genius cannot be looked on merely as something of an exception, a happy accident, but on the other hand, is it not true that it is in the profound instinct, in the spontaneous intuition of the artist, that so often the definitive solution to so many of the tragic problems facing the whole of mankind is revealed?

And it is precisely music, with its abstract, transcendental element, which, acting in the most direct of ways upon the human sensibility, creates this unique atmosphere in which hidden truths seem to be revealed. Was it not Beethoven himself, the greatest of German composers, who just over a hundred years ago intoned that joyous and mighty hymn: 'Alle Menschen werden Brüder...'? Was this because he was Flemish by descent and had scarcely anything in common with the 'pure race'?

If I insist on the importance of the role of intuition, it is because it is almost impossible to discover in a new state of affairs in process of formation a definitive formula for pure, abstract reasoning based on a more or less exact knowledge of past events. As we have been able to establish in the course of our discussions, the search for such a formula often leads one to refer too often to various historical mythologies, to aspects of a perhaps glorious, but now irretrievably faded, past. And the wild spectre of some sort of return to the middle ages fills us all with terror.

Is it not then more justifiable for us to turn boldly to face the future and to rely more in our investigations on the creative *élan* of modern man, on his undoubted achievements in the realms of spiritual life, those achievements which have led to the excavation of a fathomless abyss between us and the 'men of history', the men of preceding epochs, no matter how much they may have contributed to the formation of our civilisation?

For it seems that this *élan*, this creative force, is for us the only real basis on which – in spite of the tragic chaos, confusion and desperate contest of seemingly opposing ideas – the vital contours of the spiritual life of future humanity are already taking shape. The ideas which already outline these contours for us are born in the most elevated, most abstract of thoughts, but once conceived they are already living and immediately begin blindly to find the path which leads towards their total realisation – like a work of art which is born in the artist's subconscious but is infallibly realised in a definitive, concrete form.

It seems to me to be beyond doubt that were we to penetrate the most profound depths of human consciousness, in spite of appearances to the contrary, we should be convinced that we were on the way to a grand synthesis.

These tendencies are immediately obvious in the realms of science where huge advances have set us completely apart from men of previous epochs. I do not feel it would be right for me to speak in its name, but another sphere of the human spirit remains open to me: art, and in particular, music – the field in which I work. That clandestine but powerful *élan*, striving for the creation of new forms, a new state of affairs, appears to us there in its purest aspect, freed of all constraints and controlled only by an objective concept of external reality.

Let us try then to come to some understanding with those mysterious forces which seem to determine the destiny of contemporary music. One of the most significant phenomena to have occurred this century is the prodigious development of the nationalist schools. The whole of the preceding century was fundamentally dominated by the mighty flowering of German music. Its inordinate sense of proportion, its romantic and transcendental pathos, suggested to us a vision of a unique scale of values, a certain universality of style, by the side of which all other concepts of music seemed pointless and naive. It was only in the last

few decades of the preceding century that we saw the birth
of a movement which reacted against this state of affairs. We
saw initially the Russian school liberate itself gradually from
the traditional aesthetique imposed upon it by the great
German masters. In the west, the sudden appearance of the
genius of Claude Debussy presented us face to face with a
completely different aesthetic concept.

The work of Claude Debussy is perhaps the most revolutionary to emerge in the musical domain in the pre-war
period. Soon another figure associated himself with this
revolution, namely Igor Stravinsky, and the legend of the
universality of German music began to crumble, although
this is not to diminish its importance and true grandeur in
preceding centuries.

If I have mentioned the names of these two great composers (so very different in character), it is not only because
of their direct influence on a whole generation of composers,
but more because all the new possibilities introduced by their
aesthetic constitute a new epoch in the history of music. New
doors have been opened, leading us towards the boundless
expanses of free creativity independent of all old, authoritarian doctrines. The genius of race, the beauty and
primitive freshness of folklore have become the starting-
point for the creation of a new style and a previously
unknown means of expression. Need I mention here the
names and works of all those involved in modern music?

After all I have been saying, it would seem that it is
precisely music which has discovered concealed within itself
a dangerous nationalistic twist. Happily this is not at all the
case. The brief history – scarcely more than a decade – of
this 'nationalising' of music provides incontestable proof
that the human spirit has discovered one of the most certain
means of reaching a common understanding by this route.
Music, a universally understood language, allows us to
probe the very sources of a nation, the true secrets of which
would never be revealed fully by way of its spoken or written
language. From the variety and the wealth of styles and
means of expression indebted to the revival of racial con-

sciousness, is born the need for mutual knowledge and *rapprochement*, and it is here that the deep significance of all artistic activity lies, a significance which is not only aesthetic but ethical. It is possible to say that all research, all work aimed at the most profound penetration of the soul of the nation so as to discover its true aspect, have as their only purpose the amassing of some priceless common treasury.

This state of affairs is also evident in everyday life. The International Society of Contemporary Music has come into being, and through the excellence of its organisation we are permitted to hear all the most remarkable music produced in each country at annual festivals. Thanks to this confrontation of different styles, it is possible for us to find our bearings in the midst of all these riches and thus to undertake a proper evaluation of them. It does not seem to me that as a result of this trend we need fear a new 'universalism', a certain standardisation of the musical language, the emergence of a sort of *esperanto* without colour or character to be used by future generations of composers. Today it seems obvious to us that the ideal of a human *entente* consists not in the removal of natural frontiers imposed by the peculiarities of *milieu* and race, but in the abolition of spiritual 'customs houses' which, born of a false conception of national interest, are opposed to the mutual understanding of peoples.

I am frankly of the opinion that at the base of all spiritual, and above all, artistic activity, there lies a profound and universally human sentiment which confers upon it a transcendental significance. Individual and national peculiarities serve only to assure the existence of a varied and infinitely rich means of expression. It is as if in the pure and disinterested sphere of art, we glimpse an ideal resolution to all the apparent antinomy of national and human cultures. Is not this the light which shows us the way forward? That is why I have found it necessary to add my modest opinions – the opinions of an artist – to those expressed in so brilliant a manner by my colleagues – the illustrious representatives of science and literature – here at the Madrid conference.

Part Five
ON EDUCATION

A New Spirit in the Warsaw Conservatory
Director Karol Szymanowski on the aims of the college and the need to support the creativity of the young

Interview given by Szymanowski to the Warsaw daily paper *Kurier Czerwony*, 24 February 1927.

Composer of genius, Karol Szymanowski, as we reported yesterday, has been named as the new director of the Warsaw Conservatory. This is what the celebrated musician told our reporter:

First of all, if anyone expects 'revolutionary' steps from me, whether in hope or fear, they will in a great measure be disappointed. I have too high a regard for my predecessor in this post, Director Melcer,[1] to be able recklessly – in the name of some doctrine or another – to destroy everything he has achieved through his persevering and fruitful labours.

But having a clearly defined view on the purpose of the activities of this, the most senior music college in the land, I shall resolutely endeavour to effect what I consider to be reforms, but in an evolutionary rather than revolutionary way.

Above all, I should aim to make the Conservatory become the advocate of the most deeply conceived musical culture. Of course, in keeping with my fundamental stance, with my recognition of the achievements of contemporary music as being of very great, real value, I shall take into account the latest developments in this field.

---

[1] Henryk Melcer (1869–1928), pianist, conductor, composer and teacher. He was director of the Warsaw Conservatory from 1922 to 1927.

– In effect a break with tradition, to some extent?

– I acknowledge artistic traditionalism – what I call a 'good musical education' – as a point of departure, but after all our aim is not 'yesterday', but 'today' and 'tomorrow': creativity is the word, and not a retreat to achievements already exhausted.

I hope that the bases of my activities – the advancement of creative elements and progressive aspirations – are in tune with the guiding principles which today are governing our national life, and that they will find support and understanding from the appropriate bodies.

The Generation War between Old and Young Musicians and the Conflict between their Creative Outlooks

This article first appeared in *Kurier Poranny* on 12 January 1928 and was the first of two replies to an article published in *Głos Prawdy* on 10 January 1928, entitled 'Protectionism in the Conservatory'. The author of this anonymous article complained first that the Department of Art in the Ministry of Religious Affairs and Public Education had ignored the advice of the already established Pedagogical Council of the Conservatory in appointing Szymanowski to the position of Director, that Szymanowski had no administrative experience, and that he had been permitted to nominate one half of the Pedagogical Council, so ensuring himself an absolute majority. The author went on to accuse Szymanowski (unjustly) of dismissing existing professors to make way for relatives and friends, of appointing young musicians scarcely out of college to the position of vice-director, of neglecting his duties both as administrator and teacher, of appointing Fitelberg in spite of his 'cynical indifference' to all non-modern music to the position of director of the orchestral class and of introducing work and lecture schemes without reference to the Pedagogical Council. The author concluded that it was time to save the Conservatory from total disorganisation and to stop the Department of Art from wasting any more public money.

By way of introduction I must say that I am not in the least perturbed by 'enunciations' or, to put it bluntly, 'denunciations' of this kind. Especially when, as in this particular case, their origins are all too clear.

Since my return to Poland in 1919, I have grown accustomed to the fact that with a few exceptions, the reviewers of many of the Warsaw papers, regardless of their political persuasions, have attacked my activities as a composer with remarkable unanimity.

Today it is common knowledge that their touching solidarity has not prevented me from taking my place in the front line of musicians, both Polish and European. And so you will appreciate that I am not over-concerned by attacks now being mounted against my activities in another field, namely education. Indeed, I would have kept silent about this particular attack in the press had I not been asked to speak about these matters.

Without mincing matters I am now able to say that, notwithstanding the exceedingly gracious remarks which I addressed to my predecessors in the office of Director of the Conservatory on the day upon which I took up my responsibilities, the school turned out to be in a lamentable state. It required a number of fundamental reforms, the effects of which will only be evident with the passing of time. I do not wish to go into great detail, but I will mention a few specific facts. First and foremost, the administration of this huge college of some fifty professors and five hundred students rested on the shoulders of one man, the Director, and his two assistants, whose persevering, excessively hard work, verging on self-denial, is deserving of the highest commendation. The administration of the building was entrusted to a very worthy professor. Unfortunately this gentleman was old and did not enjoy good health, and therefore, despite the best will in the world, was unable to cope with the task. As a result the Conservatory building was in a truly deplorable state: it was in a filthy state of disrepair and really was something like the Augean stables! As much work as possible on the restoration of the building began in autumn. In view of this, surely it should be put to my credit that with the support of the Minister for Religious Affairs and Public Education, along with the Department of Art, I succeeded in so short a time in re-organising the administration of the institution now under attack – the most senior music college in the land.

In the pedagogical field I cite the following facts. The

supplementary piano classes, compulsory for all students at the Conservatory except those training as professional pianists, were in my predecessor's day taken by only two professors. In addition these professors taught organ and accompaniment skills. So I ask you to picture a professor burdened with more than a hundred pupils a week, and to imagine what the results of their work would have been under such conditions, even allowing for their good will and total devotion to the cause. The engagement for the time being of one extra professor (and it is essential that we find another two!) is not, in my view, such a very great misdemeanour on my part.

Now we come to my more enormous 'crimes'. *Mea culpa* indeed! I expanded the advanced harmony and counterpoint teaching by appointing Kazimierz Sikorski[1] professor in these subjects. While I have every confidence in Professor Rytel's[2] teaching, I fully realised that the Conservatory's characteristic overburdening of particular professors can, even with the best will in the world, have detrimental effects on their work. The creation of a second class working along the same lines seemed to me to be indispensable. The young, energetic, forward-looking, extremely gifted and well-trained musician and composer, Kazimierz Sikorski, seemed to me to be the most suitable choice for the position, and it was with very real joy that I accepted his agreement to take on the class which I had proposed.

Incidentally I was quite astounded by an article which appeared in *Wiadomości Literackie,* mysteriously signed 'lt'

---

[1] Kazimierz Sikorski (1895–1986) was appointed professor of harmony and counterpoint from the academic year 1927–28, instrumentation from 1928–29 and composition from 1931. His reputation rests mainly on his educational work, although he produced a substantial amount of music, e.g., four symphonies, concertos (for flute, oboe, trombone), string quartets and a string sextet.

[2] Piotr Rytel (1884–1970), composer and critic; *cf.* Introduction, pp. 48 *et seq.* and 96 *et seq.*

rather than the usual 'J.I.',[3] in which there was an outrageous attack on Sikorski's Symphony, performed at the Philharmonia on 25 October last year. For one thing, when this same symphony was first performed several years ago under Fitelberg's direction it won considerable acclaim. Today, now that the composer has become a professor at the Conservatory, 'It' feels bound to damn the work. He writes that 'a needlessly scholarly exercise from the new professor at the Conservatory was put on display. Probably simply in order to undermine all confidence in this "educational" institution'. There is a strange relationship between these facts. The only logical conclusion is that the article was aimed not so much at Sikorski and Fitelberg than myself, as Director of the Conservatory. Bearing in mind the notoriously 'progressive' proclivities of the periodical in question, this unexpected attack seems to me to be rather strange and tendentious.

But to return to matters immediately concerning the Conservatory. The greatest of my 'sins' concerns the orchestral class and its conductors. When I came to the Conservatory, thanks to the organisation of my predecessor, the orchestral class was taken by a 'talented oboist'.[4] He took an orchestral class since the conducting class only existed on paper in the official prospectus of the Conservatory. My 'sin' is that in place of this 'talented oboist', I have managed to appoint 'my friend' Grzegorz Fitelberg, who is incidentally Poland's leading symphonist and has won a commanding position amongst the world's conductors on

---

[3] 'It' was an abbreviation of 'Eleuter', a pseudonym frequently used by Jarosław Iwaszkiewicz. It is doubtful whether Iwaszkiewicz's criticisms of Sikorski's Second Symphony were motivated by malice, although he was disturbed that Szymanowski was devoting so much time and effort to administrative work at the Conservatory, for which he was ill prepared, rather than composition.

[4] Zygmunt Singer (1876–1958), oboist, composer and conductor. He taught oboe at the Musical Institute from 1905, and took chamber music classes at the Conservatory from 1918. He was made responsible for training the orchestral class from 1922.

account of his twenty years' hard work championing the cause of Polish music at home and abroad. Now, after so many years, the Conservatory's students can truly learn the art of playing in an orchestra, and what is more important, the demanding skill of standing in front of it. *Mea culpa, mea culpa.*

There remain such personal insinuations as the 'signing of papers without staying long enough to take my coat off', 'giving lessons infrequently', etc., etc. It really is the case that I have signed papers with my coat on, and it is true that I do not like to give lessons too frequently. But this is all to the good, because in the areas in which I give instruction, my pupils bring to their lessons not arithmetical problems but complete scores or movements of sonatas and symphonies which by their very nature take longer to write.

As for the value of my advice and instruction in the field of composition, my opponents might care to refer to Piotr Perkowski[5] and Michał Kondracki[6] who are winning an increasingly distinguished reputation for themselves in Paris today. They will be glad to acknowledge that, long before I took up my position as Director of the Conservatory, they were my unofficial pupils. I conclude with the French saying: *qui vivra, verra!* I do not doubt that my idea of a forward-looking Polish music will triumph and be taken up by the younger generation also looking to the future, as well as by those colleagues whom I have appointed to the

[5] Piotr Perkowski (1901–90), composer. He studied composition with Statkowski at the Conservatory and also took private lessons with Szymanowski before going on to Paris where he trained with Roussel. Latterly he became professor of composition at the Warsaw Conservatory where his pupils included Baird, Kotoński and Rudziński. His works include symphonies, two violin concertos, ballets and the *Nocturne* for orchestra.

[6] Michał Kondracki (1902–84), composer. He studied composition with Statkowski, Szymanowski, Dukas and Boulanger. During the Second World War he settled in New York. His main works include the ballet *Metropolis* (1929), *The Little Highland Symphony* (1930), *Nocturne* for harp and strings (1951) and *Aphrodite* for strings (1957).

post of professor (notably my assistant Bronisław Rutkow-ski,[7] Kazimierz Sikorski, Tadeusz Ochlewski[8] and Artur Taube[9]), not to mention all our students. I give *carte blanche* for further attacks upon my person. I only wonder that such 'progressive papers' cling so passionately to the stagnant air and fustiness of the old Muscovite times, the last traces of which I am trying so vigorously to banish for ever from the building in Okólnik.

[7] Bronisław Rutkowski (1898–1964) was appointed professor of organ from the year 1927–28.

[8] Tadeusz Ochlewski (1894–1975) was appointed professor of violin from 1927–28 and of chamber ensembles from 1933.

[9] Artur Taube (1894–1979) was appointed professor of piano in the academic year 1927–28.

The Vicissitudes of the Warsaw Conservatory – A New Direction – Its Future Aims and its Fulfilled Objectives

The second of Szymanowski's replies to the article 'Protectionism in the Conservatory' was published in *Epok* in two parts, on 29 January and 1 February 1928.

I should like to throw more light on the matter as this will undoubtedly reassure public opinion. On the other hand I cannot say whether this will persuade my mainly anonymous assailants to desist from further attacks upon me. The first 'plot', which I here intend to deny publically, is the fundamental matter of my nomination as Director of the Conservatory. It was done in a completely legal, regular way in that the Ministry of Religious Affairs and Public Education announced a competition for the position, the candidates put in their bids, and the final decision fell to the Minister of Education who of course, if he wished, was able to draw on the opinions of experts, which in this case he did, after which he announced the result. The Pedagogical Council was unable to make a contribution in this case because the Conservatory is still not an 'academic' school (I shall explain why subsequently), and so the Pedagogical Council is not a University Senate. My nomination then was completely legal, and my opponents are determined to spread confusion over this matter, more at the expense of the Ministry than myself.

I hope that this initial declaration of less than fair play towards me explains many other things. I admit that the very singlemindedness of the attacks on me could seriously disturb public opinion, were it not for the following circumstances. First, there is the excessively prejudiced, savage and, let us be frank, the none-too-intelligent tone of those attacks. Public opinion, accustomed to the somewhat 'Mexican' methods of press warfare, does not willingly give credence to, e.g., accusations of 'wasting public money' (*sic!*) when directed at important citizens (and, in the present case, a state institution!), for it is used to finding in the next edition of the same paper retractions and humble admissions of involuntary error.

Secondly, there is that strikingly curious and not very trustworthy unanimity existing between papers with markedly diverse fundamental tendencies. Let us reflect further on this. It would be comprehensible to some extent were the right-wing press to attack me because of their (somewhat prejudiced) view of my extreme, musical 'radicalism'. In contrast, one would expect from the more progressive press approval for my nomination, and at least some moral support: faith that quite apart from my own personal creative work, I was trying to do something for new Polish music, although ultimately enough time would have to be allowed for me to carry through my proposed innovations, which, quite clearly, cannot be achieved overnight! This would have happened in a more expert and less nervous society. But what has happened here? After only a few months work, in which time no-one could have done any better to put things onto a new footing, all manner of objections are to be heard coming from various dusty corners and recesses.

It must be said that the ways in which these battles are being fought are varied and ingenious: here and there I have been arraigned like a common criminal for 'wasting public money'; in other places I am a careerist and *arriviste* of inferior quality. And in one of these papers (strangely enough on the right of the spectrum!!), I have even been provided with an unprecedented *apologia* in which, quite unbidden, my defender has stood up for me with indescribable concern, protecting me from all manner of injury, portraying me to his readers as a pitiable figure, something akin to an almost totally plucked chicken, although at the end this does not prevent him from stating that the above-mentioned charges of a 'criminal' nature, advanced by one of his anonymous colleagues, seem to be justifiable.

Well, what conclusions can I draw from all this? I cannot hold the newspaper editors, who are so fundamentally opposed to one another in every other field, responsible for this extraordinary solidarity, let us say, this 'interparty alliance' which seems to exist only in relation to my humble person. At most I can only accuse them of caring insufficiently about art (especially music! Such a scandal would be unthinkable in other cultural fields, e.g., literature!), of being too uncritical and of printing without any safeguards anything which their reporters, permament or otherwise, want them to print.

There can be no doubt that this 'interparty alliance' had nothing to do with the relevant editors (of this I have proof!), but was formed at pleasant, convivial meetings of colleagues at which heads were put together to find a way of obtaining that edict which would banish me from the Conservatory for ever.

Why? For the same reasons as usual: fear and hatred of new forms and modes of existence which life itself brings, coupled with a love of routine and all those gestures repeated time after time. Here, this particular conflict – for very understandable reasons – takes a harsher form than elsewhere.

An 'unfriendly' atmosphere surrounds me on all sides. Fortunately I have many faithful friends who understand me and are courageously at one with me. For the rest – speaking as the director of the college entrusted to me – I have one reply: *J'y suis, j'y reste*, until such a time as I can be certain that my views rest upon firm foundations. In any event, this will perhaps happen earlier than some might expect, hence the tranquillity and objectivity with which I view this whole, tasteless affair.

I will now attempt to reply as quickly, clearly and methodically to those questions regarding the bases of my reforms.

Regarding the 'Pedagogical Council of the Conservatory', I have to start by saying that its reconstruction and the
diminution of some of its powers in some areas had already
been decided by the Ministry of Religious Affairs and Public
Education before I was nominated director of the college
(thus throwing a rather different light on my 'autocratic'
tendencies). In view of the fact that, in the view of the
Ministry, the college did not answer in many respects to the
demands of the present day, it was decided to enhance the
powers of the previous director, enabling him to instigate
certain urgent reforms without continually having to con-
sult the Pedagogical Council since even the best teachers
often have little experience in other fields (e.g., administration, budgets, etc.).

Fortunately this advance permitted me to introduce a
cardinal reform, from which everything else will follow,
namely, the constitution of a proper administration for the
Conservatory which is now an accomplished fact. My
readers may find it impossible to believe me when I tell
them that hitherto the organisation of this huge college
rested on the shoulders of the director and two (literally!)
assistants, crushed by their enormous workload! Is it surprising that the administration functioned as it did – indeed, is
it possible to apportion blame under the circumstances?
Ought one to expect staff to sit there day and night for a few
paltry zloties; and quite apart from administration, the
director has to organise the underlying artistic and teaching
schemes of the college and even give lessons himself!
Today, following the example of all foreign conservatories,
the division of work and administration between my aid in
pedagogical matters, the chief of administration and myself
functions efficiently as we have time for everything and a
common understanding on fundamental matters exists
between us. A modest but eloquent symbol of this recent
basic reform is the external 'clean-up' and gradual restoration of the Conservatory – previously one of the most sordid
buildings in the Republic.

II

The affair of the 'academicising' of the Conservatory, so disturbing public opinion, arose in essence in the following way. In effect, from the moment I took over the post of director, I openly made a stand on the fact that the college entrusted to me is a sort of 'higher technical school' and should be subject to all the rigours associated with schools of this type (e.g., inspections under the auspices of the Ministry for Religious Affairs and Public Education). Let us reflect on the matter. Is it really possible for the Ministry to confer academic rights on a school in which the intellectual and cultural attainments of the students cannot be charted uniformly by way of obligatory examinations reflecting steady development since such attainments can only be charted along a wavy line, incorporating those of small (musically talented) children, almost grown-up illiterates (or so it seems!), university students (studying music in their free moments) and finally, exceptionally talented creative individuals? 'Academic' status, that high qualification which is not only technical but scholarly and cultural, brings obligations with it and cannot be dispensed recklessly or liberally. So the real solution to this question is to be found elsewhere, and again requires fundamental reforms. It necessitates the division of the college into two organically connected schools: let us call them provisionally 'conservatory' and 'academy' (we are not concerned with names here), and this again is in line with the practice of the best foreign musical institutions. This is the eventual purpose of my plans, and I can joyfully proclaim that this plan meets with the full sympathy of the Ministry and they have already undertaken some preparatory work towards this end. Life itself dictates the posing of such questions. To whom and in what sphere ought the highest college in the land give a model musical education? First of all, to highly educated musical teachers, the so-called social activists of the future, on whose shoulders will rest the enormous, but responsible task of developing the nation's artistic culture in the future;

and in addition to them, gifted, creative individuals: composers (above all), virtuosi, singers and conductors who will be the creative representatives of the most elevated forms of Polish music. This would be one category of student in the college. But there exists another: first and foremost, the technically trained instrumentalists, the orchestral players of the future, the music teachers in primary schools, etc., etc. The scale of their activities in the future is perhaps more modest but no less socially useful, but not such a wide-ranging 'academic' standard is required from these pupils. Whether a student would attend just the one school or both would depend on the extent of his capabilities and intelligence. The line of demarcation between an 'intermediate' and 'higher' musical education, as in other educational fields, must, however, be established as the demands of life require it. In its fundamental premises, this idea meets with total approval in competent circles. For the moment we have taken the first steps along this road (without changing the groundplan of the existing colleges): 1) the age of entry to the Conservatory has been raised to 14; 2) we have restored the certificate of completion (as distinct from the diploma qualification), annulled a couple of years ago. It is my considered opinion that such a division of the college answers completely to the projected, general reform of schools in Poland.

The matter of salaries in the Conservatory, the expansion of its budget, making its continuing development possible, really is a burning issue! Our college is the most impoverished high school in Poland! I do not understand how it was that previous governments came to treat it so harshly. Today the Ministry fully recognises and understands the need for cardinal changes.

On the basis of this, I entertain well-founded hopes that the reforms intended in this sphere will be realised, if not in their entirety then at least in part, and all this in the not too distant future. It has to do with making the first breach in the wall of prejudice and routine. I have the feeling that this breach is already an accomplished fact, the positive results of which can already be observed.

I shall now go on to pedagogical matters. Well – alas! – contrary to general opinion, I have not succeeded yet in entirely effecting that so-called 'revolution' of which so much has been said. I realise that in this field one must proceed with extreme caution and tact. Basically I work along 'evolutionary' rather than 'revolutionary' lines. Evolution is unavoidable, being a dictate of life itself. In essence there has been no 'terror' in the Conservatory. It is not my fault that the representatives of the *ancien régime* have kicked up such a hellish alarum on account of the engagement of a few young, capable, energetic professors, regarding them as '*sansculottes*' with blood-stained knives between their teeth. It is certainly true that, making use of powers vested in me, I have effected certain changes in personnel, engaging several new professors in place of those I found there. One such change (the class in orchestral playing and conducting – the latter part of which only existed on paper!) is my real pride and joy.[1] At any rate, I am very pleased with the results of this decisive action and am certain that its result will be evident for all to see in the not-too-distant future. I then created a new class in advanced harmony and counterpoint. It was an absolute necessity. I entrusted it to a young musician whose talent and knowledge I value highly.[2]

On the other hand, the opera class has undergone a complete reorganisation. The solution to this problem lay – if I may put it this way – *in potentia* in the very structure of the college. In effect, having at our disposal 1) a solo singing class and 2) a well-organised drama section, one had only to combine them and place the overall musical direction in the hands of an experienced conductor[3] to have a proper

[1] Szymanowski here refers to the appointment of Grzegorz Fitelberg as conductor of the Conservatory Orchestra, a post he held until 1929.

[2] Kazimierz Sikorski (*cf.* note 1 on p. 255)

[3] Fitelberg also took charge of the overall direction of these classes until 1929.

opera course which, it should be noted, has avoided that eternal force of habit and hackneyed stage-craft so rife in theatrical matters in this country. I should also add that the students on this course must also attend lectures in both practical subjects (acting, declamation and characterisation) and theoretical (history of the theatre, aesthetics).

These then are all my 'revolutions' and 'absurd' actions for the moment. I stress that I have given complete freedom to those professors already at the Conservatory to continue teaching in accordance with whatever method they have evolved in the course of their pedagogical careers. I have not imposed my views upon them, leaving those changes which I consider to be inevitable to the passage of time, i.e., I expect them gradually to revise some of their 'dogmas' and 'certainties' for themselves, and adapt their methods to the new demands facing them. One innovation which is presently being introduced which will inevitably lead to reform is the creation of 'departments' in which professors specialising in a particular subject (e.g., theory, piano, etc.) would be able to come to an understanding with other professors at joint meetings concerning the gradual supplementation, improvement and possible unification of methods and programmes of teaching, for there have previously been frequent clashes between the individual views of particular professors, leading as a result to a certain disorientation amongst the students.

I shall now add a few words concerning my most general views on the role of this, the most senior musical college in the land. (I should like to substantiate my case and discuss matters in detail another time as I have to confine myself to basic essentials for the present.)[4]

Music is the most democratic of the arts, the art which most strongly and deeply makes direct contact with the

---

[4] This is the first of Szymanowski's attempts to outline in general terms his educational theories. The more extensive, detailed substantiation to which he refers is 'The Educational Role of Musical Culture in Society', the earliest sketches for which dated from the end of the same year; *cf.* pp. 281–317.

instincts of the common crowd, regardless of all shabby notions of class, social layers and individual degrees of culture or education. Hence its enormous educational-social significance, so constantly and stubbornly ignored in this country.

It comes down to the fact that real art should be available to the widest layers of society, rather than specially 'treated' trash supposedly appropriate for those 'lacking in culture'. It is one of those obvious falsehoods of social education, since all trash must in the nature of things deprave and maim the innate sense of beauty. Really, in this regard, there is nothing in this country which does not require action. But the declaration of this sad fact underlines, in my view, the nature of the main task of the most senior music college in the land. It must, in the widest sense of the expression, be an educational establishment. Naturally the education of distinguished performers and composers is for the teacher a real joy and inspiration, but this happens so rarely, and in any case we realise that when we are talking about genuinely talented musicians, they would have succeeded without our help! (There are any number of examples in the history of art to prove this!) In truth, our task lies in other areas: we must educate the future educationalists, the people who must think and act, those who will receive here a real, profound, technical training and at the same time will be inspired (hopefully!) to work in the service of a great, social idea, those who will carry to the furthest corners of this enormous country the shining torch of real, true art, an art 'not to be taken by children'.

This then is my programme in the most general terms.

I should be both happy and proud if the future great Academy of Polish music owed something to my foundation work. So to those who persist in throwing stones at me in their stubborn, mutton-headed way, I can only say that they are not striking a blow at me so much as the cause which they declare they are serving with such devotion.

The Opening
of the State Academy of Music in Warsaw
The Rector's Address

This address was given on the afternoon of 7 November 1930, and first published in *Kwartalnik Muzyczny* (1930/31, fasc. 9, pp. 1–6).

The moment for which we have so fervently longed has at last become a joyous, living reality. The first rector of the first Academy of Music in Poland now stands on the rostrum before a distinguished audience in order to perform the opening ceremony. I am deeply moved, and filled both with pride and a sense of unswerving responsibility to history for the implementation of the ideas and intentions which lie behind the development of this educational institution, and which crystallised long ago in the thoughts of those Polish musicians who were aware of their social obligations. I know that in effect I am not speaking only in my own name. The great honour has fallen to me to voice ideas common to us all, to be the interpreter of the thoughts of my colleagues and members of the School Council, to be the spokesman and representative of those Polish musicians who consciously combine their deep love for, and conviction of, the elevating nobility of true art with a sense of social responsibility for the well-being of the nation's culture. These musicians understand that art is not merely the result of a 'happy accident', of a *Deus ex machina*, or however else one might describe those few famous geniuses or creative talents. They realise that art is a *social matter*, the birthright and property of the general public. As such it is a powerful means of raising and ennobling the standard of our spiritual life because music has a twofold basis: *its intrinsic value and its social value*, which is an educative force in the widest sense of the word. This then was the watchword underlying our work and our attempts to provide the means of educating future generations of Polish musicians to a higher level. Thanks to the kindly solicitude, help and understanding on the part of the Minister responsible for education and the Department of Art, we see our efforts at last reaching fulfillment, and this is something that cheers us all immensely.

Please allow me to describe briefly the fundamental ideological framework for our actions.

There can be no doubt that in the artistic life of contemporary society, music has become the 'most popular' art. I have here used those words intentionally, implying as they do the terrible taint of a lack of sophistication, tawdryness and bad taste, as well as the presence of values of a secondary, inessential nature. But the word also implies 'universality', and music today really is an universal art. It penetrates and permeates all layers of society. In a sense it is the most easily attained secret way to an understanding of common artistic experience. It is also true that like each of the fine arts, but in a still greater measure, music provides society with not only elevated, ennobling artistic values but also, unfortunately, in its negative manifestations, it also exerts an almost depraving influence in the way it can maim and disfigure the inborn artistic instinct of the masses. In the wider social dimension, the main task of musical education should be the damming-up of free-flowing 'popular music', in the negative sense, so that a music of indisputable creative value may be directed along the riverbed channelled out by our common love for art. Only in this way can we also attain in music that consistently high artistic standard of national culture, with its own special colour and expression, which not only illuminates and moulds the spiritual character of a nation, but also shines far beyond the frontiers of the state as a visible, indestructible symbol of its creative strength.

It is beyond dispute that in the attaining of these ends, professional artistic training is of prime importance, for it nurtures not only distinguished performers and composers, but above all our future teachers, the musical activists whose fine, commendable life's work will be to labour responsibly building up from the foundations. It is they who will bear to the farthest corners of the land the invigorating knowledge of a true, great art, and have to create and shape new ways in which it can be effectively propagated.

From this point of view it becomes clear that the Academy cannot limit itself to technical musical training alone, to the exclusive concentration on the production of the greatest proficiency in performance or composition. Of course, a rigorous technical training, of an even more searching nature than that we have hitherto enjoyed, must form the basis of the educational programme, but it should not exclude other aspects. Above all, a musical education should impart *an objective knowledge about music* to the pupil; in other words, knowledge about *its history*, and about those fundamental *philosophical* and *aesthetic* concepts which touch upon music. In this way, music's especial and rightful place in the history of the spiritual development of man is properly demonstrated in that it is shown to be just one of a series of invigorating, creative forces that have to be co-ordinated harmoniously in order to attain a high level of culture. Only an objective knowledge about music will fling wide the gates leading to that state of comprehension which constitutes a true musical culture, in other words, a wide-ranging concept of the role of *art* in the life of society and the history of the nation. In this respect even the most profound understanding of aesthetic matters would not suffice if the ethical element were ignored, because the ethical element underlies all our actions and is that power-ful, enduring thread that, in every arena of work and human activity, binds the individual to society in general, and defines not only his rights but his obligations. Schooling based on these two principles can give us not only truly creative artists, not only the valued worker engaged in all manner of activities within his professional sphere, but also a truly useful member of society with a full grasp of his responsibilities.

In proceeding from the above assumptions, we have acknowledged that in our great cultured state, the creation of a centre which would irradiate an increasingly profound musical knowledge over the whole land was a matter that could brook no further delay. The tasks and aims of the Academy obviously exerted a decided influence on the development of an appropriate educational syllabus in which, quite apart from studies of a purely technical musical · nature, a place would be found for subjects of more general educational value. Such subjects, in that they broaden and deepen a student's knowledge, would exert positive influences, developing initiative and independence of thought, heightening powers of perception and of passing critical judgments, and contributing to the preparation of a consciously rational outlook on the individual tasks that await our students in the future.

In developing this syllabus, we fully realised that we were going to make great demands and expect zealous, exacting effort from students wishing to come to the Academy. We knew very well that these demands concerned not only rigorous professional training. In any case such a programme of training already takes into consideration a definite capital of musical talent that in itself has led to the decision to select the profession in question. Such training is fundamentally straightforward, as it meets with the least resistance. The training which goes beyond the accepted professional framework is quite another matter. Even a subject such as the history of music, which is related to our main field of work, does not in a wider sense exert superficially any immediate influence on technical mastery of an instrument; furthermore it requires an intellectual effort which goes beyond the bounds of pure musicianship. Yet it forms an organic part of a wider musical education. Above all, it develops an understanding and feeling for the style peculiar to the musical works of various historical periods, and this in itself exerts a direct influence on the level of competence in stylistically appropriate performances of these works. In other words, it does have an immediate application in the professional or practical field. Moreover, and this is perhaps the most important aspect, the history of music is not a self-contained subject, a separate leaf torn from the great history of man's spiritual achievements. At every step of the way there are mutual interactions, dependences, parallels and divergences not just in the closely related fields of literature, theatre and the fine arts, but also in more general areas and ideologies which have a bearing on the spiritual evolution of mankind. For example, because of minimal documentation we would not be able to conceive of Greek music in any shape or form if we divorced it from the role that it played in the theatre and religious ceremonies. In a still more obvious way, religious ceremonial linked with the institution of the Church, which in the Middle Ages was establishing itself in an increasingly powerful form, made an indelible imprint on the form that music took at this time. The general ideological content of the Renaissance in turn led music towards secular forms, and in this way the foundations of theatrical music were laid. Finally, Romanticism showed us fully how the new music of the time was dependent on abstract philosophical ideas on the one hand, and on the currents of a new social freedom on the other. On all sides, gates were swinging open, revealing paths leading to other areas of knowledge, ranging from the generalisations of aesthetics to the elevated heights of philosophy and metaphysics. Alternatively these paths led in another direction, to the life of the people at large, to the natural, fecund soil in which art first germinates in primitive form, later to spring up and blossom in works that are truly musical. The ever-throbbing source that springs from the depths of the human soul lies here, and from here constantly aspires to the highest levels of human activity. So we see that in this seemingly highly specialised academic subject, almost all the fundamental elements of our knowledge of mankind are concealed *in potentia*. These elements are indispensable for an understanding of the deepest principles of our spiritual culture. In turn these principles must be further developed in a series of specialised lectures. It is only at such a level that the syllabus can give a complete, well-rounded education, guaranteeing sterling value from all those working independently in areas which will necessarily be of the greatest diversity.

Having decided on such a fundamental reform of the syllabus, we acted in the full realisation of the fact that this reform could not be in any measure an empty experiment. It had to answer to the real needs of the increasingly fruitful musical culture of the nation. The present state of affairs now requires a new host of workers and 'activists' who are in every way competent to undertake and carry out the tasks that face them. Our expectations have been fulfilled. When we saw with what alacrity and confidence our future students flocked to the Academy, we were able to ascertain joyfully that the intensive demands and serious, high standards required here in work with continually expanding objectives and new horizons became a stimulus and a source of encouragement: that long-awaited call arousing a vital, sincere response in the young who are longing to undertake useful, creative, spiritual work.

And now it is to the students of the Academy that I address my next remarks. You are the first to attend this institution; you are in the front line; you are the vanguard. I extend to you warmest greetings and words of encouragement. At the same time I offer you the joyful certainty that the work we are undertaking together, work for which we shall bear joint responsibility as pioneers, shall go from strength to strength in an invigorating, harmonious atmosphere, beneath a unifying banner of mutual understanding and trust. Aspiring together towards evermore elevated objectives, you can be certain in the future of a well-earned, honourable place in the collective, joyous, creative labour undertaken by all who are undeterred by worldly cares, and who endeavour steadfastly and fearlessly to strengthen and consolidate the spiritual power and glory of our reborn fatherland.

For us, the Polish musicians appointed to be the spiritual leaders and guardians of the education of the young, to those of us who have been entrusted with the responsible and lofty task of constantly watching over the future development of Polish music, today's ceremony has a two-fold, and I would venture to say, a symbolic significance. It coincides with a historical anniversary of profound importance that I find impossible to ignore.

It is now precisely a century since that sad day in November 1830,[1] when the then High School of Music in Warsaw, attended by Fryderyk Chopin, was closed.

Compared with that gloomy event, how bright and radiant today seems! We see the power of evil overthrown, and the ghosts of the past turned to dust as we stand here on the verge of our new joyous labours, our lungs filled with the intoxicating atmosphere of freedom. At this moment it is right that we should remember that mournful day, and from the perspective of the last century look deep into the bright face of today, so real and tangible, filling our hearts with its sense of certain, happy reality. It is right that we should be reminded of that mournful, grating sound as a soulless, violent force slammed shut the doors of the music school that had been the cradle of Poland's most elevated music. Looking back in this way, we perceive more deeply the significance of those doors re-opening ever wider today, attracting and affording protection to more and more of our young people. And it is right that we should summon from the past an echo of that grief-stricken sigh, breathed by the greatest genius of Polish music, as he left his homeland for ever. Such memories serve to throw into relief the way painstaking, careful, competent state teachers nurture even the slightest trace of creativity, nurture even the slightest initiative that has as its aim the expansion of the new spiritual values of our society.

And while observing, with deep emotion and joy, the opening of our Academy by the Minister of Education, and

---

[1] In fact, the High School of Music was closed on 19 November 1831, as opposed to the Institute of Music and Declamation, whose activities were suspended from 31 December 1830.

seeing the *freedom of action* which extends to the furthest horizons, I am also mindful of a distant, pallid, spectral stage-coach, alone on the open road, vanishing into the autumn mists. It is taking away *for ever* the man who was to be imprisoned by bitter fate in a distant, foreign land for the rest of his short, sad life. He it was who, with steadfast obstinacy and unflinching resolve and faith, spoke to the world of the might, the indefatigable nature and profundity of the Polish creative Spirit. He spoke through music, the language which alone is understood by everyone and is the most beautiful of all.

The priceless inheritance that we, the musicians of Poland, possess in his immortal work urges us onward, indicating the heights to which we should aspire. Long may the great name of Chopin, a name that I utter with the deepest veneration and strongest love, continue to be our common watchword, uniting and defending us in our present labours, undertaken for the common good and the most beautiful development and ever increasing fame of Polish music.

The Dispute
over the Academy

First published in the weekly magazine *Kultura* on 29 November 1931

In every field of social work, courageous reforming ideas provoke with wellnigh mathematical precision a carefully organised reaction, emanating from a love of fusty old habits and traditional ways.

This is a well-known, well-understood fact, proven by history a hundred times over, but how it hampers the tasks set by creative initiative and deep conviction in the rightness of a cause!

The dialectic of routine has long been based on an orderly, highly disciplined army of words and ideas, well used to defending entrenched positions in an ideological desert. Since creative initiative infallibly senses the direction taken by the hidden currents of life, it cannot depend on any dialectic. Its real concern is with the creation of new concepts and new forms with which to tackle the problems life poses as it continually unfolds, and so it has to wage the struggle through actions whose tangible, indubitable results will only become abundantly clear with the passage of time.

It is for this reason that there often seems to be an uneven distribution of power between routine on the one hand and creative initiative on the other. It is even worse when routine wins an occasional victory, although fortunately, in the majority of cases, this usually proves to be shortlived.

This perhaps somewhat abstract introduction is necessary in order to throw some light on one particular fact which, against the background of the wide-ranging struggle for new cultural values in Poland, may appear to be no more than an episode, but is none the less highly characteristic in essence, and acutely relevant to a considerable section of our society.

We are concerned here with the recent discussion in the press centred upon the existence of the Academy of Music in Warsaw. The ideological bases underlying the existence of the Academy are, in my view, so obvious that in essence they are not open to question.

It is indisputable that the standard of our musical culture is quite low when compared with that of other Western countries. I am not speaking of particular manifestations of creative genius (e.g., Chopin), but of the dissemination of musical culture throughout society in general.

In my view the reason for this state of affairs is the absence of a purposeful organisation, in the widest sense of the word, which has as its aim the conscious attainment of predetermined goals. Musical activists whose competence by far exceeds the mere technical mastery of an instrument, or even the secrets of composition, should be the creators of such an all-embracing organisation.

The whole problem lies in the fact that the music student belongs to an extremely heterogenous, mixed group, the variety of which is unrivalled. This group is destined to study in one general type of school (and it really does not matter whether we call this institution a 'school', an 'institution' or 'musical conservatory'.)

Within this group are individuals whose sole, and undeniably praiseworthy, task in life will be the technical mastery of an instrument, perhaps a flute or clarinet, so that they can work in an orchestra. Then there are the geniuses of the future, the composers and outstanding virtuosi. Finally there are those whose contribution will lie not in the creative field at all but whose highly responsible life's work will be in society at large. These are the teachers, the directors of schools, choral conductors – those whose activities require perhaps both the widest and deepest preparation and a real sense of responsibility to society.

It is evident to me that the introduction of any kind of

order into this very varied group of young people, striving after so many different musical goals, can only be achieved when we have succeeded in establishing different types of school.

From this point of view the existence of at least one academic College in the country seems essential. It is necessary that such a centre of musical education be founded so that over the years its standards and character could create an indispensable authority that would exert a regulating influence on the organisation of musical life throughout the land.

Each new phenomenon in the educational field should be subjected to criticism from those who are qualified to pass judgement so that a still more perfect and well-rounded educational system may be attained.

In principle it would not be at all strange were the Academy to be subjected to the critical opinions of those who, in the eyes of the general public, have had a controlling influence on its activities in the past. But the point of view adopted by the sworn enemies of the Academy is most perplexing.

It comes down to this: the criticism to which we are subjected does not consist of a series of genuine, factually based enquiries about, for example, possible shortcomings in organisation, system of syllabus, or even the personnel currently involved in teaching. A discussion at this level could conceivably deal with genuine issues and result in genuine benefits.

This, alas, is not the case. Apart from a quantity of personal invective which seems to be inevitable in such cases and which I choose to treat with contempt, the whole of the press campaign up to now has been directed against the very existence of the Academy! This really is something unheard of and, I imagine, without precedent!

Putting aside for the moment all the ideological assumptions which underly the foundation of the Academy, and which I tried briefly to summarise above, let us consider the following facts.

First. As I have already observed, the Academy is only now at the start of its second year. Not a single student has graduated yet, so what is the basis for all those allegations about the futility of the Academy?

It will only be possible to speak of this in eighteen months' time, when, after the completion of the whole three-year course, the first generation of students will have had chance to demonstrate both their complete ignorance and the total flimsiness of our intentions. Even this would not be completely convincing proof, for it would only show the present management of the Academy to be notoriously incompetent, not that the existence of the Academy in itself was fundamentally purposeless!

Second. The campaign against the Academy is led solely by musicians. Yet Polish musicians are being offered the noblest and most authorative warranty for their existence in society: a college, with privileges and high academic standards – a college which, in a sense, endorses and raises the value and substance of musical work in its social sense.

But these musicians, suddenly so richly endowed, are throwing away this precious, beautiful gift with haughty, disdainful gestures. In the depth of their hearts, they yearn for the protective, comfortable words bestowed upon the 'poor in spirit', and seek with over-eager haste the traditional spiritual *testimonium pauperitatis* of Polish music.

I can prove that the above declarations are not empty words: one of our opponents recently published a thoroughly argued apologia on behalf of those who believe that Polish musicians should remain in ignorance. It may be summarised as follows: musicians have no need of 'philosophies' to develop strong lungs and fingers to play the trombone and trumpet. Why all this stuff to confuse the brain?

This simplistic ideology at least deserves careful attention, if only because it seems that the malignant spirit of the old Warsaw Musical Institute, along with all those previous, outworn, 'twopenny-ha'penny' ideals associated with it, is once again raising its slimy head. Surely this cannot be the case?

I raise this matter, knowing that those who are best qualified to retort will no doubt hear of it.

I have only one more thing to say. As I have already observed, fusty force of habit and creative impotence may sometimes achieve a transient, illusory victory, but laurels won in this way are not usually retained for long.

The younger generation of Polish musicians, reared in the atmosphere of our ideals, will soon occupy the places now filled by my colleagues and my opponents.

It will then be for the younger generation to pass a final, irrevocable judgment on the present struggle, and I have no doubt as to their verdict.

The Educational Role of Musical Culture in Society

First published in November 1930 in *Pamiętnik Warszawski* (fasc. 8), and reprinted in May 1931 in *Kwartalnik Muzyczny*. It was also published in pamphlet form in June 1931 by the Warsaw Towarzystwo Wydawnicze (Publishing Society).

The title of the present work defines precisely its scope, character and fundamental argument. I may be mistaken, but to the best of my knowledge, no Polish musical writer has considered the profound problem of music on the *social plane*. No one has attempted to establish basic premises, to define limits or to show the directions in which music may exert an effect directly, not from the subjective viewpoint of individual sensibilities, but on a much larger scale, as something that makes demands on society – a force whose soaring, penetrating, all-embracing elemental quality inevitably provokes an emotional reaction from the masses, whether it be positive or negative. I have chosen these words deliberately. Music today really is an elemental force. It penetrates all social strata and satisfies, in the fullest measure, the aesthetic hunger of the masses. This is all the more worthy of mention as this process occurs without regard for music's instrinsic aesthetic value, and so often leads to fundamental misunderstandings and undesirable results. A search amongst music's sister arts for a similar *all-embracing and immediate effect* would prove fruitless. It is a quality which is peculiar to music, and it is high time that a properly reasoned attitude to music assumed its rightful place in our cultural consciousness. In the meantime we must sadly recognise that we are still very far from defining explicitly any kind of position in relation to this question in its most synthetic form. It seems that music is to remain for ever the private, emotional affair of the individual. In other words, it is regarded as a somewhat fortuitous subjective trait, akin to a greater or lesser liking for natural beauty or the preference for this or that sport, a subjective trait, answerable to nothing, existing like a foot-note to the so-called 'general education'.

In fact, it would be true to say that one of the characteristic symptoms of the average, cultured, educated man is possession of an elementary knowledge of literary and artistic history. If the worst came to the worst, he could offer some botched-up opinion about Buonarotti, Sophocles or Velasquez. This more or less thorough knowledge is all part and parcel of the obligatory bag and baggage of the intellectual, cultured individual. Yet one dare not speak of the musical opinions of this class of 'educated' person when our foremost writers allow their fantasy to lead them into a musical wilderness as a consequence of which they pepper the pages of their works with howlers which would cause a first-year student at the Conservatory to blush with shame! My profound love and admiration for Polish literature prevents me from citing *in extenso* the relevant passages and mentioning the names of the authors.

The prevailing ignorance and disdain regarding musical matters is striking and incomprehensible when we consider the fact that music today exerts an incomparably stronger influence throughout society than literature or the fine arts. It is essential then, not least for those individuals who feel responsible for the development of Polish culture, that the correct conclusions be drawn from this state of affairs.

In the present scheme of social inter-relationships, where not one trace of the nation's spiritual creative energy should be overlooked but instead used consciously and purposefully in the raising of the general standard of culture, in the widest social sense, it is absolutely essential, in my view, that all our activities in this field be co-ordinated. I am referring not only to those involved in various branches of the fine arts, but to academics and others who are active in the initiation of new projects in society at large. Consequently I should dearly like the observations expressed here, which in any case practising musicians have long regarded as truisms in need of no further justification, to circulate beyond the confines of the musical profession. I should also like to reach those who are truly cultured and sensitive to their social obligations but who, up to this time, have regarded art merely as a source of more or less profound experiences of a purely subjective nature. Consequently, in the course of my investigations and search for a firm base upon which my ideas could rest, I have often been obliged to encroach upon regions which lie beyond the immediate bounds of my field of work, in effect literature and the fine arts, and sometimes even historical fact. For a certainty, this particular type of elucidation will provoke some objections, and so much the better! Perhaps this will provoke a wider discussion of a matter which up to now has not been regarded as worthy of serious consideration in the history of Polish thought, even though its importance is now glaringly obvious. An objective relationship towards whatsoever aspect within the realms of the nation's spiritual culture cannot be confined merely to an illogical elucidation of its particular manifestations one after another – the sort of elucidation we find in so-called 'criticism' (and journalistic criticism is often truly pitiable!). Nor is a broader, historical conception of the subject sufficient, since this is merely a systematisation of pre-determined facts. Instead we have to approach the matter as a 'living organism' which is still in process of 'development', and we have to deal with its changing, creative forms in practical terms. So the basic aim of the present work is to think of the whole subject in a synthetic way, as flexibly as possible, taking into account the requirements noted above.

First of all, then, we have to establish, in as wide-ranging a manner as possible, bases for my all-embracing musical ideology; we have to discover the true foundations of the mysterious sphere in which art, and in this case music, is organically connected with the life of the nation, with society in general, and not just particular social classes or individuals. To begin with, I should like to show that an artist's individual work really can take flight when it has as a springboard a common artistic culture which prevails throughout society, and that it is on account of the strangely entangled developmental line of Polish musical culture (as opposed to that of Polish literature, for example) that we sense so markedly the absence of any such springboard. This meant that our music existed in something of a vacuum, and as such was unable to produce sympathetic vibrations throughout the rest of society, in spite of a tragic lowering of standards. I shall attempt to advance irrefutable arguments to counter probable objections, namely that my view of the matter is too idealistic, that truly great art is a private matter depending on individual talent, and that to a certain extent it is something of a 'happy coincidence'.

By way of introduction I must observe that despite our relatively slender output in this field, few societies owe such a debt of gratitude to their music as we do in Poland. Here I need mention only one great name, that of Fryderyk Chopin.

It is true that in this one instance it is possible to speak of the unexpected gracious intervention of some higher power, for Chopin's works bloomed suddenly like a fantastic flower of ineffable beauty in the grey, forlorn fallowlands of nineteenth-century Polish life. He really was a gift from heaven, bequeathed us during our darkest hours. This feeble-framed man took on the enormous task of creating a Polish music, and this he achieved alone, unaided, for he inherited *nothing from his predecessors.* Yet he bloomed in vain, and to this day his art is like a column of massive proportions that stands alone.

There is in truth something magical in the fact that he appeared suddenly at the moment when we most needed him *historically.* It may perhaps sound paradoxical, but it is precisely of his political role that I wish to speak here. Sentenced to a lifetime's exile in a foreign land far from home, albeit a land in which his greatness was appreciated, he was undoubtedly the greatest Polish ambassador that ever lived. For a whole century he has spoken to the world in a language that in itself is not only most beautiful but is *comprehensible to all.* He has spoken of our unshakable will to live, and in this way has given the lie to all those dark rumours about the irrevocable, final catastrophe. His name, for ever associated with the name of Poland, was known everywhere. Untold millions of people at the furthest reaches of the globe learned of the nation's tragic, but unyielding existence, solely on account of this most beautiful *Apologia,* even though it be lyrical rather than conceptual in its mode of expression.

Today there remains of Chopin only a handful of dust in a distant, foreign cemetery and, of course, his music, slight in quantity but immortal in content. Up to this time his work is without doubt the only really great Polish music, and it is of such boundless value simply because of the *all-embracing comprehensibility* of the language through which Chopin's genius expressed itself.

The artist can only penetrate to the heart of his own nation if his work has *universal* value. Otherwise the absolute value of the work in question is diminished by the presence of ethnic peculiarities, bringing with them a narrow and precise circumscribing of the artist's expression of the most mysterious of human emotions and that type of local artistic *utilitarianism* to which, alas, Moniuszko, for all his great talent, sometimes resorted. Such works are tied to a precise moment in history, and this often renders them incomprehensible and worthless for even the very next generation. It is for this reason that Bach and Mozart undoubtedly seem much more sympathetic to us today than, e.g., Schumann or Berlioz, even though, from a purely objective view, it would never occur to anyone to question the greatness of their artistic talent. In reality, the true value of a work of art seems to depend not only on the potential strength of an individual talent, but to a great extent on the intellectual position the artist adopts in relation to the question of art conceived in the most general terms.

The music of Chopin therefore possesses not just a value

'in itself', but also contains inexhaustible possibilities for
further development, standing like a signpost at the cross-
roads of history, reliably indicating the one sure,
inescapable direction in which we ought to be travelling.
I have already spoken more than once of the vitality of
this music, of its astonishing *contemporaneousness*. If I
mention this again now, it is only to stress that after playing
such an enormous, beneficient role in Polish history, music
deserves the utmost gratitude, care and support from the
nation, and by this I mean society and – *last not least*[1] – the
state.

Of course, the music of Chopin has no need of any such
care and protection, so let us substitute in its place Polish
music in general, and in particular its future, fruitful development in a way appropriate for our great, free nation.

I do not know whether we are a particularly musical
nation or whether our abilities in this field are only average.
Judging from the wealth and beauty of our folk-music, we
are perhaps entitled to conclude that as yet we have not
been able sufficiently to take advantage of our innate musicality, of, let us say, that *potential* musicality, in that we still
have to confer upon it the higher form of a *collective musical
culture*. Yet it has to be said that in the grimmest years of the
pre-war era, when the tiniest advance in the sphere of our
national spiritual culture could only be achieved through
bitter and often futile effort, the social initiative in matters
of musical development never completely lapsed. On the
contrary, if anything it gained in momentum as we
approached the turning-point in history. And if it now
seems that the results were inadequate, we must regard this
as one of the effects of a hopeless warfare in which the good
will and communal energy of our fighters had to contend
with the soulless, obdurate mechanised pre-eminence of
the enemy.

[1] In English in the original.

Today the initiative exists and, as before, is developing, but with one important difference: the state is not the enemy but the source of care and nurture. And here we must deal with a fundamental question, namely to what extent is state interference in the nation's spiritual culture desirable, especially in the field of art? In my opinion it is not only necessary, but imperative, and precisely in that area which is concerned with the raising of the standard of artistic culture in society as a whole in the broadest sense of the expression. Even the most courageous social initiative would fail to realise plans conceived on so grand a scale if it did not enjoy state aid.

Now in musical matters, we have to declare that in all honesty we were forgotten during the first few years of independence, and what is worse, our *cause* was ignored, and this, after all, is the cause to which we devote all our energies and our entire, onerous and not always very rewarding life's work. There seemed to be a marked contradiction between this state of affairs and the fact of the foundation of that government department whose sole task was to be the creation of the most favourable conditions for the fruitful development of our national, artistic culture. It appeared that 'pre-war' attitudes to music were to be maintained, that music was still to be regarded as a mild narcotic suitable for anaesthetising certain sections of society, a sweet pudding which was unworthy of serious consideration when the nation was concerned with a determined struggle for the daily bread of its political existence.

It was forgotten that music is a powerful weapon in the war against the obscurantism and barbarism of the masses, that it is that essential spiritual food that contains the greatest proportion of nutritious vitamins which penetrate all layers of society with the greatest ease. In those areas of society where the plastic arts are often very rudimentary, at best an ethnographic curiosity, and where literature is almost non-existent, music is to be found flourishing strongly and eternally, albeit in the primitive form of folk-song.

Now the vitality of song or folk-music in general is an absolutely positive phenomenon. It is like the source of a living, inspiring force, throbbing at the heart of the race, and is akin to a block of marble extracted from deep inside a mountain, waiting only for creative hands to bestow upon it the eternal form of a genuine work of art.

We have proof of a general, insatiable, 'organic' need for music in the existence of another type of music, a 'popular' music in the literal sense of the word.

This is the music of the towns and cities, a music that is for ever invading rural areas. It is possessed of a vulgar, brazen tumult that stifles and destroys the primitive purity of folksong. It is the music of the restaurants, the taprooms and the inns, and it comes down to the same thing, being in the main an import of the worst possible kind. It depraves taste and maims the healthy, artistic instincts evident in so unerring a way in folk-song, and yet, paradoxically, it answers to some real artistic, or spiritual need on the part of the masses in general.

A grievous error, the consequences of which are incalculable, arises here. The veritable hunger for artistic sensations existing among the masses, who are not equipped with any sort of criteria based on powers of reasoning, is easily satisfied by anything that is available, or worse, by food which has been poisoned, and this is because there is nobody to serve them the nourishing food of real art. This indeed is the basic starting-point of my investigation. We are faced with the incontestable fact that in the life of present-day society, music is a *mighty, constantly acting force.* It is something which is simply essential, and it sweeps through all layers of society to a much greater extent than the fine arts or literature since it does not presuppose such a high level of intellectual training in the individual. This force, however, can act in two diametrically opposed directions: it can be a destructive element that annihilates instinctive susceptibilities, or else it can be constructive, in the most essential sense of the word, and this I shall now try to demonstrate.

We are concerned here with the channelling of the elemental force of music into a proper riverbed. Its turbulent current has to be harnessed, as the rushing waters of a rapidly flowing river have to be controlled and made to turn mill-wheels so that productive work may be undertaken. Alas, there really is now no human or superhuman power able to destroy the bad seed and weed out that abominable 'popular music'. It is a necessary evil, just one of thousands, from which even the greatest civilisation will never be free. Yet it is within human power to make a stand against this force and show how it can deprave the creative, organic power of real art.

Here again, I consider it to be axiomatic that there is no greater deceit, no greater fraud even, than the 'tempering of the wind to the shorn lamb' on the part of our popular artistic enterprises. This lavishing on the masses of some surrogate which is absolutely inessential on the pretext that this half-art still has some real value, if only because it is comprehensible and approachable, is a philanthropic swindle which should be ruthlessly stamped out. It originated in the unerring conviction that art of 'real value' is a sacred taboo, for ever the property of a certain, cultured class which alone has been granted undeniable right of access to it as a consequence of their intellectual understanding of it. But one has only to hear the conversation of the smart set emerging from the Grand Theatre or the Philharmonia after the performance of some truly great work to be persuaded once and for all that these notions of intellectual understanding and exclusive property rights are very strange indeed. In fact, I could give countless examples to the contrary simply by mentioning the many, many German *Gesangvereine* in which workers and artisans perform works by Bach and Beethoven. And indeed I note with delight the way in which the practice of choral singing is taking hold among an increasingly widening range of society even in this country, and especially in the western province of Wielkopolska, thanks to the energy and flair of an ever-growing band of musical activists.

Now, can one assume in the above-mentioned cases that those groups of a decidedly democratic character were totally devoid of artistic sensibility, and that the success of the venture depended entirely upon the greater or lesser skill of the conductor-cum-pedagogue? In other words, is such a conductor the tamer of wild beasts who are made to perform a series of automatic movements at his beck and call? This is an absurd notion. The performance would be fundamentally impossible if each member of the group, in studying the work, did not find his own subjective and very intimate way to the heart of the matter. In other words, he must have had to evaluate and understand it in his own way, however naive that might be. In his own miniscule way he is collaborating in the recreation of the work, and so takes his share of the responsibility for the final result.

That is enough for the present about the active role of the so-called 'man in the street' in serious music-making. Now a word about his passive role. A very famous German conductor of the younger generation recently told me that he had never experienced such powerful emotions as when he mounted concerts for huge audiences of workers in the major industrial centres of the Ruhr Basin and Westphalia, and these were concerts with the most serious and uncompromising programmes. He told me that never in any of the Berlin Philharmonic Concerts was he gripped by such a powerful sense of responsibility as he was when he gave of himself, of his talent and enthusiasm for these 'men in the street', occupying row upon row of chairs, set out *ad hoc* for the event in some factory hall. These audiences were not contaminated by snobbery, barren aestheticism, nor by an unjustifiable faith in formulae, and they listened as willingly to a Beethoven symphony as to Stravinsky's *Rite of Spring*. In every case they attempted to absorb the dazzling wealth of each piece, and found their way instinctively to the heart of these very different works by the simplest, most direct routes. The apparent lack of intellectually conceived criteria, attained through force of habit and reliance on tradition and established, sterile aesthetic canons, compelled these listeners to sense instinctively the individual value of the above-cited works, diametrically opposed to one another. It is also worth emphasising that, in reply to my question as to whether, on the basis of his many years experience, he was able to ascertain which style – classical, romantic or modern – most appealed to these audiences, he told me that he was only able to do this in particular instances, and that in general an audience would react positively to the essential quality of a work in itself rather than its distinguishing style. He also declared that the bourgeois, conservative public was markedly less intuitive in this respect, and because they were unable to escape the restrictions of an *a priori* sense of style, they were unable to accept the possibility of other new values coming into existence on other elevated planes. I think it would be difficult to find a better argument against the mythological incomprehensibility of new music, and at the same time the practice of watering down culture so prevalent in this country.

No doubt my readers could object that I have here cited facts (and not all of them by any means) concerning a nation whose musical culture is a long established tradition, and one which really is of a very high standard. Agreed! But has that happened through the agency of the Holy Ghost or some supernatural power? I think not. Undoubtedly it was the result of the work of industrious, untiring activists who, year after year, laid brick upon brick, storey upon storey, until this truly great culture attained its present pre-eminence. But let us be reasonable: there were kingdoms and principalities in existence before 1870. They were often smaller than one of our Wojewódships,[2] and each had a tiny, charming capital city at its centre, in which the emotions of the ruling kings and princelings were moved more by pieces staged at the Hofteatr, such as *Faust*, than by intricate political questions. Weimar was just such a centre. Here the much admired Hofrat, Goethe himself, strolled through the

---

[2] Administrative area, corresponding to an English county.

rooms of the palace – and later Franz Liszt was to hold the musical sceptre, laughing off the consternation of the peace-abiding burghers of the city and pushing for all he was worth for the first staging of the works of one Richard Wagner, the terrible futurist of those times. Later there was that mad king,[3] who in his wilder flights of fancy practically robbed the state treasury so that he could erect in the vicinity of that charming, sleepy little town of Bayreuth a theatre-cum-temple which would become the centre from which the mighty art of that afore-mentioned terrible futurist would shine out to the whole world.

Furthermore, in addition to those magnates, thousands of unknown musicians – various organists and school-masters – were at work in out-of-the-way corners of the land, collecting together all the butchers, bakers and candlestick-makers to perform in public Bach's B minor Mass or Handel's *Messiah* on the day of the *Gesangvereinfest*.

Germany's magnificent musical culture developed from just such teeming, unremitting work and unceasing effort, fired by a deep faith in the importance and even the national significance of such a well-organised plan of campaign. We do not possess such a musical culture, or rather, if we do possess one, it exists in a markedly less advanced state of development, and so the sort of concert which I mentioned above is no doubt very much a thing of the future. But surely what is possible in Essen or Bochum today may be realised in the not so distant future in Dąbrowa Górnicza or Sosnowicz,[4] given a similar sustained, unceasing effort and serious-minded approach to the task? This is the great obligation which now rests upon the shoulders of today's Polish musicians, the musicians whom Fate has placed on the threshold of Independence and appointed with others to the task of laying the foundations of our national, social and state life. Fate also commands us to look attentively to the future and not the past; that which was of

[3] Ludwig II of Bavaria.

[4] Mining and industrial towns in Silesia.

real value in the past will retain its value for ever, without our collaboration. In any case we have much to do all around and ahead of us. We are not curators, and in any case we musicians do not possess much that requires preservation. We must all build for the future with determination, but this work is so great, so important, that – as I have already stressed – we have a right to demand both understanding and the most far-reaching help possible from the state.

Here I must voice my innate optimism, and declare that for several years now a change of direction has been increasingly evident in the appropriate government department, and this is to the advantage of our ideals. The notion that music is a narcotic is gradually giving way to the idea that it is a nutritious, life-giving vitamin. In recent times particularly, we have had tangible proofs of this pleasing state of affairs, the most worthy of mention and the one which causes us the most immense joy being the completion and opening of the State Academy of Music in Warsaw. This will become the long-needed centre that is able to offer a proper musical education – education which involves not only the mastery of musical composition or performance, but also an ever deepening, objective knowledge of music. It is only on this two-fold basis that the true artistic culture of a society can rest securely. The spontaneous creative flarings of brilliant individual talents would die like a flame in a vacuum if there were no sympathetic resonance emanating from a deep love and understanding of art existing throughout society.

Up to now I have spoken of the need for the greatest possible effort in the attempt to bring about an improvement in the standard of our musical culture, and in so doing I have linked it with the state's most immediate interests. Now, how on earth do I justify the *necessity* of the existence of this culture from the state's point of view? In truth, is not the state able to dispense totally with culture in the running of its everyday political and national life? I have already replied in part to this question by demonstrating that music today is a mighty, independent, vital force in the life of contemporary mankind, exerting both constructive and destructive influences. It follows logically from this that the state would wish to bring such a force under its control, directing as is most appropriate the organisation of resources with the aim of developing its cultural authority. Incidentally, I must here point out the great interest, not to say 'protectionism', that characterises the attitude of every state toward its literature. This is because, quite apart from literature's purely aesthetic qualities, it has an intellectual content which impinges directly on the interests of the state. It is blatantly useful or harmful, and to this extent compels the state to intervene, and from the point of view of pure creativity this can result in the existence of an awkward check on the process of natural development. It is different with music: the pure aesthetic of its values (which only happen to relate to conceptual matter in dramatic or religious works) acts directly on the mysterious sphere of the human emotions, and criteria that are used to define its greater or lesser value never basically leave the sphere of pure aesthetics, in the very deepest sense of the expression. In practice, it cannot be denied that music of great value, through its special pathos, influences for the good the process of refining and broadening human sensibilities, making possible a more profound awareness of the ethical essence of life. In contrast, worthless music acts in precisely the opposite way, revealing only the most immediately attainable aims, beyond which lurk the superfical commonplaces of life. As such it is rather like a short circuit; it liberates all the potential energy of human emotion, but does not bring about positive results.

I should now like to reply to the second part of the question previously posed: namely, what are these constructive musical elements which are of such interest to the state? Here I must begin with a series of historical truisms which are no doubt well known to my readers, but which have to be restated if my reply is to proceed logically.

First of all, in my opinion, the history of mankind is in fact the history of his art. It is as if the history of art were a mysterious light illuminating the realities of life occurring among men and within their social orders and nations – in other words, the true significance of any particular historical reality. In historical investigations, when all political, sociological or economic enquiries fail, it often happens that the art of the time provides the necessary answer. The influence of Egyptian art on that of the early Greeks suddenly throws a ray of light on the political state of both countries, and refined cave-paintings demonstrate the existence of some sort of civilisation in dark ages so distant, that without these paintings we would not have the slightest idea about the life of those times. But we do not have to go that far back. Who can tell future historians more about the essence of Polish history in the first half of the nineteenth century than our three great poets and one great musician?[5]

In the recesses of history, art initially clings like ivy to the unyielding tenets of religious belief, and only after that to the secular arm. Finally, in the Greek middle era, it was emancipated from these two sets of chains. It became independent and, as such, a matter which concerned the *whole nation*, and this is something I wish to stress as strongly as possible. It became democratised, and henceforth, though it often soared up only to plummet suddenly to the ground, it has steadfastly attended upon the fate of man on earth, as did religion on the one hand and learning on the other, with which disciplines it has enjoyed equal rights. The Dionysian theatre at the foot of the Acropolis, a theatre able to seat almost the entire population of Athens at that time, is for ever the most profound symbol of this emancipation. This theatre also saw the birth of music, if not quite in the way we understand it today, at least as an indubitable artistic

[5] Adam Mickiewicz (*cf.* note 16 on pp. 171–72), Juliusz Słowacki (*cf.* note 19 on p. 87), Zygmunt Krasiński (*cf.* note 16 on pp. 171–72) and Fryderyk Chopin.

phenomenon *par excellence.* In other words, it existed independently of religious ritual on the one hand and the spontaneous creativity of the people on the other. To be sure, we know little of this music. Indeed, we can only sense it through our deepest instincts and intuition by reading between the lines of the *Oresteia, Oedipus* and the *Bacchantes.* But for a certainty it existed in the form of an all-embracing artistic lyricism: a profound expression of the immediate reaction of the nation's creative soul in the face of the phenomenon of beauty.

The centre of the cultural world shifted slowly to the West, yet neither the all-powerful Roman state nor the Imperialism of the Caesars was able entirely to succeed in taking over art for their exclusive use. Again we know little of their music but, as before, art remained the property of the people. The ruins of the forum bear witness to this, and the palaces filled with the most beautiful marbles, mosaics and sculptures were the property of the people, demanded by them in their innate hunger for art.

Turn the page, and there follows the great reverse in the history of mankind. Art was again hidden away in temples and churches, although this was not to exert a fundamental influence on its later development. For century upon century, God occupied the entire psyche of man; for the first time in history, the liturgy was not just a representation staged before a passive crowd by a particular hallowed caste. The stage-set was dismantled, and for the first time that crowd was directly involved in the drama enacted before God. Music was here employed as an aid. At the outset, in its stiff, primitive forms, it gave succour and strength, and finally, after many centuries, after soaring and plummeting many times, it erupted in the inspired hymns of Palestrina, hymns wrenched from emotions concealed deep within the very *heart of the people.*

But during that long rosary of centuries, music also aided other causes. Here and there, beyond the confines of the church's omnipotence, another type of music, which had nothing to do with ritual, flared up and died out. This was the music of the vagabonds, wanderers and minstrels who travelled the highways and byways, lute in hand, singing ribald but often tender songs. Knights in armour developed a warm affection for the songs of the troubadours and minnesingers, and in the meantime folk-based song was able to penetrate the churches and occupy an honourable place in religious mystery plays. It seemed that some definite turning-point was about to be reached, but in spite of · this, music was still not yet a universal affair. The two streams trickled on through the centuries, joining together here and there only to part company, since it was impossible for them to find a common riverbed.

The monumental vision encapsulated in these ancient works, both secular and sacred, is still a vital source of profound emotion for us today. And is not that characteristically Gothic aspiration to the heavens with those thousands of chiselled spires a magical expression in stone of the most intense soaring of the soul and, at the same time, a symbol of the fruit of communal labour?

Another turning-point came when a sultry, life-giving wind, originating in the distant recesses of history, spurred those great worshippers of life on to create their wonderful art and give us the Italian renaissance. At first sight it seems as if this massive revolution in life's spiritual sphere was the achievement of the magnates of those times, whether popes like Julius II or princes like Lorenzo de Medici. But the true patrons of the new art were undoubtedly the Italian people themselves. Instead of being hidden away for the exclusive use of princes in some awesome palace or confined to the expression of magical, religious flights in beautiful churches, art went out onto the streets, into the bracing open air, where it aroused and satisfied the powerful sensibilities of the masses by the beauty of its shapes. By way of example, let us recall the thrilling story of the raising of the Perseus in the Loggia Lanzi, the dispute between Cellini and Bandinelli, and the way in which literally the entire population of Florence feverishly took part in this debate over the most vital artistic qualities, subsequently flocking out onto the streets in their impulsive enthusiasm for a sight of the new work of art that adorned their home town.[6] It would be possible to cite many analogous cases during this epoch, and there is no doubt that it was during the two centuries from the mid-fifteenth to the mid-seventeenth, in Italy in particular, that art was a universal, national affair in the history of man, something which provided a vital index of the artistic instincts and aesthetic cravings of the masses. There is also no doubt that art subsequently retreated from its lofty, or perhaps we should say, its broadly based position. It aristocratised itself, and increasingly restricted the sphere of its immediate influence upon the masses, although this in itself did not detract from the essential 'self-contained' value of individual works of art in subsequent epochs. But having lost contact with the immediate sensitivities of the masses, it lost to a significant extent the character of style in the historical sense of the word. In other words, it became a matter of individual efforts and aspirations, and even in the sphere of architecture, after the short period of Baroque supremacy, the standard gradually deteriorated, until after a lengthy series of various stylistic ephemera, we meet with the near-barbaric manifestations of bad taste dating from the turn of the present century.

Music began increasingly to occupy the position which the fine arts had previously held. A minimum of examples will suffice to support this declaration. As early as the Renaissance, music had begun to win a self-sufficient existence. It slowly escaped from the churches, where the effects of severe, long-lasting discipline had led to exacting performing standards, and now, in an atmosphere of regained freedom, we meet with a secular music that has displaced unpretentious, improvised folk-music and endowed itself with a much more distinctive artistic shape. From this time a new factor played an enormous role in the further development of our art. Because of the continually developing

---

[6] *Cf. The Autobiography of Benvenuto Cellini*, transl. Anne Macdonell, Dent, London, 1907, pp. 272–317.

technical skills of instrument-makers, and also because of the increasing mastery of the techniques required to play on these instruments, a new type of musician came into being, the type of musician who was eventually to become the virtuoso-performer. The possibilities of creating artistic music, and of releasing potential creative talents which hitherto had battled with the technical short-comings of various instruments, depended greatly on the activities of this type of musician.

Since that time the development of music has moved rapidly, like a river liberated from its frozen chains by the advent of spring. Violins and clavecin in Italy and France, organ and subsequently piano in Germany, were all used in states of ever-increasing technical perfection in the service of composers. This perfection made possible the increasing enrichment of ensembles, a process that gradually gave rise to the modern orchestra as we know it. The creative possibilities then became simply boundless. Music took on all manner of new shapes, and either intensified existing modes of expression or discovered new ones. Music was freed from the necessity of serving any sort of extra-musical idea – even one as elevated as religion. Oratorio developed, a loose connection with the church being provided only by its dramatic content, and this was but a step away from opera, which flourished abundantly in the seventeenth century. There was a gradual crystallisation and clear definition of particular elements of musical form, a process that permitted the possibility of further uninterrupted development. Indeed, musical forms multiplied, both for virtuoso soloists and for ensembles. The tempered scale was at last systematised, and this in a sense unified the musical language and provided a reliable basis for a long-lasting tonal and harmonic system.

The truly massive musical personality of J. S. Bach appeared on the scene. His work was an absolute artistic affirmation of music's liberation, and in that he concentrated brightly and strongly through the lens of his mighty art all that had previously happened, it became the starting-

point for all that was to follow. His work was epoch-making:
the uncanny mystery of his direct influence upon the
listener indicated the existence of new regions in which
music was to be regarded as a communal matter. It would
appear that he filled some deep void, and that void was the
ever-intensifying yearning of man – of every man – for a
music expressing his deepest spiritual self. Although he was
only a humble organist, in the service of the Elector of
Saxony,[7] at whose behest he wrote his most beautiful cantatas and choral works, he composed for every man on earth,
clearly demonstrating that just as this unworldly nourish-
ment is both vital and irreplaceable, so it ought henceforth
to be available for all. From that time music became a
universal art, casting its particular, mysterious light upon
the spiritual history of man. From that time also the history
of music is the story of its triumphant progress and of its
unceasing fight for the possession of the last and most
resilient redoubt – the hearts of men.

After a long journey through the centuries we are home
again, having explored the intricate way in which one
particular art aspired to its ultimate enthronement in contemporary life. I shall not deal with the musical history of
the nineteenth century since it is well known to all, but I
should like to point out the inner, historical mechanism
which had a decisive effect on the universality of music
today. There is no doubt that the Romantic ideology is in
itself a revolutionary ideology *par excellence*, born of a belief
in the ultimate emancipation of man and the elevation of
truly human, creative qualities above artificial hierarchies.

---

[7] Szymanowski here gives a false impression of Bach's relationship with the
Elector of Saxony. He certainly was 'in the service' of the Elector of Saxony
and King of Poland, but only a few works can be said to derive from this
relationship, the most substantial being the Mass in B Minor. The cantatas
mentioned here were for the most past intended specifically for certain
churches in whose employ Bach was.

In this way the immediate experience of reality is extended to the furthest bounds of human consciousness, and so almost involuntarily romantic ideology became the most faithful ally of the notion of the supremacy of music. Artistic creativity in general at that time became a symbol for man's emancipation. Now, in the era during which the dams which ominously guarded the eternal privileges of a certain hierarchy were under attack, it was obviously the medium that was most elevated and most penetrating which would be most effective in the assault. That medium proved to be music. It is worth observing that in all the works of the most famous composers of the Romantic era, that transcendental notion of 'universal reconcilation' is particularly marked. The conclusion of Beethoven's Ninth Symphony does not leave any doubt in this respect. The absolute impossibility of a personal understanding between Beethoven and Goethe arose from the fact that Goethe's specific liberalism originated intellectually in that it stemmed from his unique, brilliant understanding of the essential value of man, while Beethoven's revolutionary nature derived directly from the heart (and incidentally by-passed the head as often as not) in the form of the purest, non-intellectualised *love for man*. In contrast, the revolutionary aspects of Wagner's art have too much of a biographical basis for us to consider them further here. In any case, it was precisely at this time that in addition to the 'pathos of music' that had arisen in Greece in connection with music's all-embracing character, we find the ultimate crystallisation of the notion of the 'ethos of music'. This governs the relationship that exists between music and any one individual. It defines the nature of the link existing between those who 'give' and those who 'receive' music, and that sense of absolute responsibility that should weigh upon the creative artist in the face of his 'audience', in the widest sense of the expression.

Responsibility is a very grand word. but it forms the basis of the matter about which I am speaking. Only by assuming its responsibilities can music become part of the system of forces regulating the fate of man on earth.

We have now come much closer to a totally positive conception of the entire subject, but let us ponder for a few moments more upon the privileged position music holds in contemporary life as opposed to the other arts. I have already tried to describe the steady withdrawal of the fine arts from their previous role of an art which *embraced all men.* They adopted, and to this day, still occupy a somewhat aristocratic position, immersing themselves in the quest for ultimate solutions to subtle stylistic problems. This doubtless testifies to immense capital reserves of intellectual culture, but at the same time it is indicative of a freely willed distancing from the sensibilities of the masses, not just in the domain of particular works of art and the value they may or may not have, but in the very nature of the artistic medium in itself. It is interesting that it was only in architecture that there was some, as yet uncrystallised, tendency to a synthesis in the grand style. This was evident only after the war, and has to do with the completely new industrial landscape so characteristic of modern civilisation.

We shall also leave drama aside. In spite of its undeniable popularity and the undoubted existence of a specifically theatrical element, it continually hovers between the purely literary qualities of its text and something that could be described as its *plastic element.* Incidentally, the cinema is beginning to make use of this plastic element increasingly skilfully, although it cannot yet be considered great art.

Literature remains. It must be noted here that it occupies an exceptional position throughout the entire history of mankind. Perhaps with the exception of Greece, where, during that great era of the tragedians, it really did become the property of all, it always has been in a sense the art which is closest to, but furthest from, mankind. It is closest in that it is based firmly on the logical formulation of a series of ideas, and as such could most clearly and positively express the essential substance of any given reality. At the same time it is furthest away from mankind because its specific lyricism, its artistic element *par excellence,* could only be approached through the often threatening barricades of its intellectual substance. Nota bene that the greater the value of a given work, the more synthetic and all-embracing its character, and the more complicated is the intellectual scaffolding which surrounds its essentially lyrical content. In connection with this point, I cite here a number of works from various periods, works of the highest quality such as *Hamlet, Faust, Samuel Zborowski, Król Duch*[8] and some of Wyspiański's dramas (circumstances dictate that I cite stage works almost entirely, although I am thinking only of their poetic content. This is an eloquent demonstration of the fact that in spite of the *public character* of its activities, the theatre is limited to a certain extent when dealing with matters involving the increasing dissemination of true art throughout all sections of society). There is something of an inescapable vicious circle here in that one can only pene-trate to the heart of great literature by way of a highly refined, personal culture, and it is with difficulty and only the greatest caution that literature can propagate this culture.

Of course, one must not think that really great music will reveal its treasures to the listener at a first hearing. Its most profound contents are deeply hidden and can only be uncovered with effort and will. In contrast to the fine arts, but more especially literature, the discovery of real musical values does not initially involve a purely intellectual know-ledge that often necessitates the overcoming of dialectic barriers, inevitable in poetry and drama, but stems from the deepest instincts, from an a priori sensibility to the medium of sound that demands only a minimum of intellectual culture.

It is difficult to discuss here the complex question of the psychological origins of musical awareness as a universal phenomenon. In its search for a solution to the problem,

---

[8] *Samuel Zborowski* and *Król Duch* (*King Spirit*) are works by Słowacki; *cf.* note 19 on p. 87.

romantic philosophy aspired to misty, metaphysical heights (Schopenhauer). In his poetic contrasting of the Dionysian and Apollonian, Nietzsche showed us a way in which, perhaps less poetically but in actual fact, we could find proof of the fundamental differences between the phenomenon of music on the one hand and the plastic arts and poetry on the other. In reality, there can be no doubt that in its embryonic state, in its most primitive form of a call or shout answering to a given emotional state, music would appear to be the primordial source of expression, i.e., the disclosure of the content of that state of emotion. If we conceive of the subject in such a way, then the embryonic musical structure came long before the phenomenon of speech. Only after *verbal* intonations (in song) had led to poetic inflections and expression, and rhythmic movement in dance (inseparably linked with music) had in turn led to plastic forms of expression, could the poetry and fine arts of the future develop as self-contained phenomena, independent of music. Yet the essential artistic value of *each work of art* is determined exclusively by that specifically lyrical element, invariably betraying its underlying musical source. When we look at the problem in this way, it becomes clear that in principle every individual is an innate musician, since music is a constant function of certain psychological properties, and the unchanging expression of an individual's lyricism, an expression that becomes *increasingly splendid* as the general level of mankind's culture rises. We have proof of this in the incontestable universality of folk-song to the present day. This fundamentally general musicianship gradually undergoes a process in which, as in the other arts, individual creative types are distinguished and stand in antithesis to a 'passive' audience. But this process only occurs with the raising of the general cultural level within any given group of people, while at the same time that potential 'musicianship' at the bottom of the social ladder remains generally constant. But it is very characteristic that the majority of musical works require in performance *groups of people*, whether orchestras or choirs, and here in a telling way, we have a recreation of the primordial, ancient origins of music in the simultaneous participation of people in a ritualistic act which, in the light of man's earliest activities on earth, seems well-nigh inconceivable in that it does not have an immediately utilitarian function.

It is the *absence of any self-interest* that is the cardinal condition, the only psychological basis upon which it is possible to found the astonishing phenomenon that is art in the spiritual life of man. The ethos of artistic activity, the ethos of which I spoke earlier, lies precisely in this 'disinterestedness', in this devotion to an idea which has no immediate usefulness. That disinterestedness appeared at the dawn of man's history in music alone. The rudimentary plastic arts revealed their immediate utilitarianism at every stage, for example in buildings, and also, at a higher utilitarian level, in some of the original and fascinating personifications of divinities, namely, those fetishes and totems that were symptomatic of the religious instinct. In other words, such art had to do with fundamentally extra-artistic notions, although in particular cases real artistic values infiltrated almost involuntarily. And so the artistic sensibility as an autonomous element, as opposed to one whose function is utilitarian, can appear and be realised in a work of art only after a certain primitive intellectual capital has been accumulated (the elementary imitation of natural shapes is the embryo of a *comprehending* relationship with reality), and this state of affairs obtains without regard to the fact that under certain conditions, the plastic arts, as I said earlier, can become an art with a *universal* character, reflecting most faithfully the essence of a given historical epoch (e.g., Greek, Gothic, Italian Renaissance). This would appear to be the case with literature as well, with the one proviso, however, that in a markedly higher degree than the fine arts, it relies upon a strong basis of intellectual awareness of the world. But on the other hand, both fine arts and literature in their very bases place the individual creator in categorical opposition to the fundamentally passive masses at large. Consequently both these arts have a strongly *aristocratic* basis, and indeed if the aristocratic element is missing one finds only a hopeless, confused dilettantism.

It has not been sufficiently stressed that in those great historical epochs, the distinguishing feature of which was freedom of thought and the emancipation of man from the hierarchic chains that had been imposed and maintained through the workings of history, it is music which always leads the way, almost automatically. (The tremendously significant saying that Chopin's works are 'actions concealed in flowers' is not just a beautiful poetic metaphor.) The whole of the nineteenth-century Polish Romantic movement does not leave any doubt in this respect. Yet the most amazing proof of my declaration is the fact that the essence of musical history, in the sense in which we understand it today, is inextricably bound up with the greatest of the world revolutions: Christianity.

It is only through the juxtaposition of all the above-mentioned factors that one can fully realise why music, of all the arts, is that special force whose task is the building and shaping of the dormant, primordial yearning in every man's soul and with it the aspiration to life at a higher level of awareness. Its democratic character (a term I use for want of a better expression, since although it is politically precise it is threadbare in other senses now) permits it to penetrate easily to the very depths of society, to those areas where not even the most idealistic and elevated poetry, nor the most beautiful vision of the world, conjured up in painting or sculpture, could exert any influence. It does not obtrude from outside in the form of a visionary picture, stemming from the rich and complex imagination of an artist and preserved for ever in a motionless, unchanging shape. Instead it would seem that, through its constant state of flux and magical creation of continually new forms, it releases the previously imprisoned *in potentia* capacity for experiencing mysterious emotions existing in every human soul. It transforms each listener into a participant, and its uncontained activity, its perpetually new 'appearance', seizes and unites audiences in a joint experience that is otherworldly but at the same time a real and tangible event.

The uniting of whole groups of people in a commonly shared experience is the second fundamental trait that is alien, at least in such a highly developed degree, to the other arts. This aspect of music brings with it the almost mystical qualities of some special ritual. By its magical power it throws down all the dividing barriers that normally confine the individuals present within the grey stone walls of their egotistical day to day affairs, and brings them together on the elevated plane of a commonly shared experience that is totally without utilitarian value. Even the external form taken down the centuries by musical performance has been typified by the presence of huge crowds, flocking at an appointed time to appropriate edifices, to join together in the mysterious, liberating magic of musical experience.

But that *unifying* element affects not merely the fundamentally passive audience. It is organically related to the very medium of music, and this aspect is revealed a hundred times more explicitly in the fact that a musical performance, if it is to make any impact at all in society at large, requires the intervention of a third, direct link that connects composer and audience, a feature that is absent in the other arts, with the exception of drama. This connecting link, apart from the virtuoso who in some instances may also be the work's composer, is usually made up of *performing musicians*, organised in groups, whether in the form of orchestras, choruses, quartets, etc. (Incidentally I note here that in matters of practical music-making in Poland today, the majority of choral groups are by no means professional bands of singers whose living depends on their music-making, but are associations that very often exist thanks to the devotion to music on the part of the individual members of the group, and this in itself clearly demonstrates the complete 'disinterestedness' of that devotion. We should take note of this so very characteristic detail here.) If that intermediary link did not exist, the mysterious world of musical emotion would remain a dead letter, a series of incomprehensible hieroglyphics. There is no doubt that such an intermediary group can only come into being under the influence of the above-mentioned unifying element of music, although in certain cases this in itself would not suffice. It is at this point that the *third fundamental trait of music* comes to the rescue, namely, its *powers of organisation*. In truth, although a musical work is an absolute entity in the deepest sense of the expression, it is still in practical terms an intricate complex of many, individual elements, and it is only when these elements are properly co-ordinated through the will-power of one individual (in this case, the conductor), that this fundamental *unity* will appear. On the other hand, however, those various elements which have to function properly to ensure a good performance are the responsibility of each individual participant in turn.

From the above assumptions, we can make bold to infer that the musical ensemble is in a sense an archetype, a cell-structure for all forms of social organisation, but with one categorical difference: its guiding principle is a fundamental lack of selfish interest. If we take as a starting-point the microcosm of the musical ensemble, we can proceed to the discovery of particular bands of people, joining together under a common banner in increasingly large numbers, until we arrive eventually at the highest, all-embracing form of organisation, namely the contemporary nation-state. A seemingly paradoxical thought comes to mind, but one which in my view is not without relevance. I believe that there is an analogy between the relationship of the music-group microcosm to the ideal state macrocosm on the one hand, and the relationship of the atomic structure to that of a planetary system on the other. It is to do with the fact that the inert and fundamentally shapeless pulp that constitutes the *nation* (like an unorganised, free complex of sounds) would never progress beyond that inert state, were it not for the mysterious crystallisation of the idea of a unity that is fundamentally above and beyond immediate self-interest. This crystallisation eventually gives rise to an *absolute organisation*, namely, the structure of the state which in principle stands in contrast to particular individuals. Yet at the same time it receives its moral authority, its logical justification, from the wishes of the individual, just as it is through the conductor that the wishes of each member of the music group are realised. Moreover, each state structure (and here we are concerned with its essence rather than its political character) is endowed with the attribute of absolute power in the name of an over-riding cause. Now the immediate task of a state system conceived in this way – as in the performance of a piece of music – is the blending together of particular elements, or if it may so be described, their *harmonisation*, with the aim of attaining that ideal *unity*, of achieving as profound a form of *cultural expression* as is possible. This potentiality is concealed in the racial properties of any given nation, but can only be expressed when the development of the *supra-individual idea* has attained a sufficiently vigorous form within the bounds of the state organisation. In reality, when we become aware of the history of mankind in systematic terms, we never fundamentally go beyond those categories which contain concepts that deal specifically in terms of unity, or rather what we described above as the cultural expression of that unity, and this is something which we might justifiably define as the *aesthetic of history*.

If we failed to take account of these concepts, crystallised in our own sense of the *beauty of history*, if we failed to take account of the complex, thrilling story of man's soaring and plummeting flight, of the mutual influences and interactions of its separate parts, the exciting and tragic history of man on earth would be totally incomprehensible. It would seem to be a shapeless miasma of individual egotisms, a purposeless squandering of abilities and enthusiasms on everyday troubles with only an immediate significance. It certainly would not strike us as being a creative process that involved the gradual emancipation of man and which clothed his spiritual life in constantly renewed and ever-more splendid forms. In short, man's existence would seem not to have progressed beyond the meaningless game that it was at the misty dawn of history, a game that relied on impulses stemming from primordial instinct, being no more than a sorry, obscure jumble of sterile, chance activities, just as music without any shaping, creative will would be nothing more than a cacophonous chaos of arbitrary, unco-ordinated sounds. I also avow that the *revolutionary character* of music, about which I spoke earlier, is by no means opposed to its fundamentally *organisational* qualities, but arises from that 'constantly flowing' element of music which leads it to free itself from useless, outmoded forms in the search for perpetually new incarnations.

I believe that, in our considerations above, we have at last succeeded in determining the nature of the connection between the splendid autonomous cell-structure of music as it is in man's contemporary spiritual culture and the complete organism, represented by the nation with all the aims and obligations arising from statehood. Surely music's three inherent, fundamental traits, here revealed in their deepest essence – namely, *universality, unifying power* and that ability to *organise* in the name of an elevated, 'disinterested' purpose – provide us with a real, firm basis for a social educational system, in the most general sense of that expression?

It has to be admitted that that *sui generis* social utilitarianism of art, and in this case of music (and we have at last to admit that it really does exist, if only in the sense of an unceasing desire to achieve highly exalted aims, namely to achieve something that is for the good of all, this being one of the factors that increases the spiritual significance of art's most vital qualities), is rarely, if ever, taken into account satisfactorily in educational affairs. Perhaps people are under the illusion that the existence of academic educational systems absolves us completely from the consideration of complex questions of social education. But let us ponder a little more deeply on this subject. Academic schooling can only create a certain intellectual capacity which, by its very nature, is somewhat limited. It creates to a certain extent an intellectual relationship with the world, and gives the student a notion of its factual substance, but not of its – if I may put it this way – emotional colour and expression.[9] Furthermore, all intellectual training is so to say a long dialectic avenue, leading by way of an infinite series of syllogisms to distant aims, never thoroughly investigated. Even when we take into account its most widely ranging absolute, autonomous values, such an education never properly defines our *ethical* attitudes in the face of the reality surrounding us. Leaving aside for the moment the problem of its relative inaccessibility, even that so-called 'moral philosophy' (as distinct from dogmatic religious ethics), is again no more than a series of syllogisms which shape the mind rather than the heart.

So we see that that inescapable academic education, even though it is the most positive basis of a social education, does not entirely achieve the ends we have set it. We are obliged to turn to yet another factor which should be able to endow society's culture with that emotional expression and colour, and also in my view a certain ethical basis for those matters which concern very refined emotional regions. In other words we are speaking of the need for art. It will

---

[9] This section of the essay shows the continuing influence of Wilde and Pater. In *The Critic as Artist*, Wilde imagined 'the smile that would illuminate the glossy face of the Philistine if one ventured to suggest to him that the true aim of education was the love of beauty, and the methods by which education should work were the development of temperament, the cultivation of taste and the creation of the critical spirit' (*The Works of Oscar Wilde*, Collins, London, 1948, p. 1050). Later in the same essay he wrote: 'Aesthetics are higher than ethics. They belong to a more spiritual sphere. To discern the beauty of a thing is the finest point to which we can arrive. Even a colour-sense is more important, in the development of the individual, than a sense of right and wrong' (*ibid.*, p. 1058).

Pater put it another way when he said that 'our education becomes complete in proportion as our susceptibility to these impressions increases in depth and variety' (*The Renaissance*, Collins, London, 1961, p. 28), and by impressions he here means those pleasurable sensations that arise from art or any object of beauty.

doubtless be objected that the ethical element is not fundamentally inherent in the deepest, genetic bases of art as a
self-contained phenomenon. But this objection, as I see it,
seems to be sustainable only at a superficial level. In truth,
. the phenomenon of art cannot, in practice, be divorced
from the effect it has upon its immediate surroundings,
because when separated from its social foundations it
becomes a fiction, a notional symbol which has only a
theoretical meaning (its motto being 'Art for Art's Sake',
that naive and notorious concept). The very existence of art
within the social organism immediately brings into relief
two fundamental factors of undoubted ethical significance.
First, there is the subjective relationship of the creative artist
to the specific question of art as a fundamentally 'disinterested' sphere of activity in the face of which he is forced to
define his own position. Secondly, there is the relationship
of the artist to society in general, and this will depend on his
sense of absolute responsibility. So in practice it is quite
immaterial that the ethical element is, so to say, a secondary
phenomenon, appearing only to the extent that a social
group has been educated and aspires to increasingly excellent synthetic forms as it undergoes development. In music
the ethical factor is still more evident because of the necessary existence of the connecting link – the performing
ensemble, the structure of which, as I tried to demonstrate
earlier, is in its constitution an ideal archetype of all social
organisation.

Now let us try to analyse musical activity, not from the
restricted viewpoint of the absolute 'self-contained' value of
music, but from the 'utilitarian' angle, namely as an educational factor in society at large. Let us think of those
previously quoted examples, those choral societies whose
members are manual workers or artisans, and let us ponder
over the psychological processes going on in the mind of
the average participant. His everyday life is a seemingly
endless succession of tedious, drab days, full of unremitting,
hard work and constant worry in the attempt to eke out a
miserable existence. His few scraps of free time are devoted

to rest and recreation, most often drinking in a tavern while a mechanical piano grinds out 'popular' pieces. This constitutes, in the form of a lamentable caricature, the 'Dionysian' element of the average worker's existence. As far as the 'Apollonian' element is concerned, he lacks the will, the impulse, the practised taste and above all the necessary intellectual preparation to appreciate the beauties of poetry or the fine arts. And so he takes the line of least resistance, searching for this beauty in penny-dreadful detective stories and hideous 'landscape' reproductions. The somewhat dubious effects of the cinema are also being felt in this area, and it is these elements that, to a greater or lesser extent, constitute the entire 'spiritual life' of the average member of the working classes. (We shall say nothing here of his possible membership of some professional or technical institution since that has a specifically utilitarian purpose, and so in the nature of things lies beyond the bounds of those matters that concern us here.) Perhaps I am giving an over-simplified and schematic impression of the average existence of the worker, but alas it seems to me that I am not too wide of the mark. But there can be no doubt that in the unplumbed depths of his being, there lie dormant unrealised impulses, aspirations and yearnings for life on a *higher* plane which cannot be more precisely defined and which are common to every human soul. These yearnings have only to be awakened through a command coming from *within*, or even *without*. It is difficult to determine the psychological motivation that ultimately prompts the worker to join a choral society; perhaps it is the result of an imitative reflex or perhaps it arises from a confused desire to aristocratise himself, from some notion that the society holds a pre-eminent position amongst the grey, anonymous working classes. It is enough that from this moment there is an almost revolutionary development in his primitive conception of life's true values. Let us reflect here, above all, on the fact that, for the worker, work alas is frequently a curse. For our part, we can be enthusiastic and idealistic about our work; it brings results that immediately satisfy our creative instincts. I am not only speaking here of artistic work, which is of course highly typical in this respect, but of work in which the appropriate intellectual preparation, dependent on sound character and will-power, gives rises to the full operation of our capabilities and the obtaining of indubitable and often priceless results (e.g., the doctor curing the seriously ill, the advocate winning a just cause, not to mention the activities of social workers, teachers and many, many others). Now how much creative fulfillment would we find in standing over a reliably operating piece of complex machinery? By some miracle are we going to discover creative fulfilment in mining lumps of coal (bitterly hard work often undertaken in conditions of terrible danger), coal that is destined to burn in another, affluent, hunger-free environment? What dialectic falsehood leads us to suppose that we have the right, on this gloomy, hopeless plane of life, to demand from Lenor, Supernak and Dusi[10] some sense of responsibility in the face of the most elevated questions that arise in the course of our lives? The only thing we can do is to rush to their assistance with those treasures we have hitherto kept for our exclusive use over the centuries, with the express aim of affirming the very possibility of the existence of those questions. For I believe that it is only by feeling a sense of obligation, rather than by demanding rights, that we shall be able to exert an influence on the harmonious development of society's spiritual modes of expression. It is only in this sphere that we feel the claims of a moral imperative, that is in those activities that have as their aim the highlighting of the suprapersonal idea in work that does not, of itself, yield any creative joy.

---

[10] I here cite the names of the well-nigh symbolical figures in J. Kaden-Bandrowski's so unusual novel. –KS [Szymanowski here referred to the novel *Czarne skrzydła* (*Black Wings*), a realistic portrayal of life in the Silesian mining basin, written by Juliusz Kaden-Bandrowski in the years 1925–29.]

It may seem paradoxical, or worse still, symptomatic of a totally naive social idealism, that in the face of the gloomy picture painted above I persistently speak of music, of that so very abstract play of imagination far removed from the immediacies of life, as if it were a panacea for the most painful social ills. But I shall always persistently declare that, although certainly not a panacea, it is one of the best weapons we have in the battle against the ills of society, because in the way it acts it is by no means as abstract as it would appear. Of all the arts, it is the one which in the greatest degree possesses that astonishing gift for liberating immediately the creative instinct which is fundamentally the only possible psychological attitude that can be adopted in the face of life itself.

But let us return now to the continuing story of that average member of the workers' choir. Having joined the organisation, he once more finds himself at *work*, and what is most astonishing, work which does not yield immediate profit – and it is precisely this that decides the fundamental psychological change in his attitude to the value of work in general. Again he has to accept orders from above, again he has to take responsibility for performing properly the task which has been allotted him, and again he is compelled to strive hard to master albeit the most primitive of techniques in this, his strange new task in life. The work would appear to him to be nonsensical and incomprehensible were it not totally justifiable, its originally deeply concealed essence gradually appearing as the standard of performance improves. Now from the original, incomprehensible chaos there gradually emerges an ever intensifying, telling vision of a *Beauty* that triumphs over the grey mundanity and teeming activity of life. It is a Beauty which brings with it a mysterious, extraordinary joy in the awakening of the *creative instinct* that had slumbered in the deepest recesses of the soul.

The solemn moment at last comes when the work is performed in public. That mysterious 'ritualistic' element, which we have already mentioned more than once, and which is peculiar to music in such a great measure, unites performers and listeners in a shared experience. The ultimate attainment of the Beauty encapsulated in the work depends as much on the individual responsibility of each participant as on the uniting of all their wills and harmonisation of their joint efforts in a collective desire to achieve one single aim. Does this not symbolise deeply the relationship between the individual and generality?

Here music, not as an unceasing source of the purest and most thrilling joy, but as a great educating force among mankind, plays an additional beneficient role. It opens a man's eyes to the enchanted and indeed the only creative world in which the suprapersonal idea is inextricably linked with all the symptoms of beauty. Henceforth he seeks it everywhere, and not least in the most deeply conceived patriotic idea, the idea of purposefully striving to attain ideal unity in which is manifest the highest form of spiritual expression and also the strength of that particular national culture, this striving being the sum-total of millions of individual efforts all inspired by the consciousness of the *suprapersonal idea*. This has to do not just with subjective individual attainments. The unifying, organising strength of music has a lasting power, in that having once united in a powerful bond the members of a group who, by chance, came together to labour to attain a revelation of magical beauty, a mysterious mutual understanding binds these people together, and new aims, new great tasks that also depend on this already attained level of mutual understanding, are suggested through the influence of the original experience. These companions, united under a single banner, will for a certainty become acquainted with one another once the crowd has broken up, and will lend each other a brotherly hand in achieving further worthy aims. In other words, music – through its magical powers – will have opened up the way leading to a whole series of truths and values of the greatest importance.

In such a way the most noble social cell-structure is created, and although its genesis seems only to be aesthetic, its reliance on commonly shared work endows it with a significance that is absolutely ethical. There can be no doubt that it is only on such a social basis that an artist's work can operate on the highest plane. After all, an artist cannot speak in a vacuum or sing in an atmosphere of sepulchral calm and indifference, just as a bird cannot fly at altitudes where its wings meet with no air-resistance. In contrast the artist who meets with understanding and enthusiasm enjoys the continuing good effects of regenerated creativity.

In conclusion I should like to express most fervently my very real hope that when, in the future, the Polish Spirit flourishes in a state of absolute freedom, won through bloody struggles, and its powerful song sounds harmoniously over all the world in celebration of its national culture, we, the musicians of Poland, will be able to declare with pride and joy that we laboured to realise our dreams as part of that group of people which in itself constitutes an ideal of national power.

Part Six
ON THE
COMPOSER'S LIFE

Introduction to my Memoirs

Szymanowski was unable to polish the one draft he made of this text, first published posthumously in *Wiadomości Literackie* (1938, No. 1), and reprinted in *Z Pism*, and *Karol Szymanowski Pisma*, Vol. 2, and, as in the original sketch, the alternative words and expressions he considered using are here left in brackets.

For a long time now I have considered writing my memoirs. In this broadly conceived introduction I shall attempt, as clearly as possible, to indicate the motives underlying this rather trying and troublesome project. In any event it has not arisen from a sterile desire to wile away silent, empty hours of total inactivity with lyrical expressions or a shapeless account of some interesting experiences. I have not had an excess of such hours in my hard-working and far-from-easy life, and those that still remain to me should be organised wisely and economically. Nor does my intention originate in an exaggerated sense of self-importance and of the role which I have played in the history of Polish art.

I have often thought that no man is so insignificant, his existence so grey, that his life-story would be without value, even were it written in his own hand without any literary pretensions and in the most atrocious style. It would be an invaluable 'certification of the truth', and would constitute an historical document of great importance especially for later generations. It would provide an accurate means of investigating the tiniest portion of any given historical reality, in other words the social 'micro-structure' which eventually determines the fate of the whole organism, in the way that the state of the cells in a living organism determines its existence. From this point of view the confidences of the 'grey' man often appear more revolutionary than the recollections of quite a few of the more vocal of history's protagonists.

To be quite frank, I do not regard myself as one of the least significant, and it is hard to call my existence grey. The life of the creative artist is always something of an adventure-story, even when it concerns only the inner 'vicissitudes' of the struggles over form and content. In a musician's life, that 'adventure' assumes a more realistic, external quality, often becoming in truth his daily bread (and bread that is often bitter and hard to swallow!). Professional (or perhaps we should say financial) necessities compel him to under-take numerous journeys that do not make for peace and repose as they do for tourists. On the contrary, these pere-grinations mean hard work, intense activity, the constant need to overcome every obstacle encountered and to master every single new situation, the continual entry into new milieux and the need to orientate rapidly to new life-styles. But they are a splendid opportunity for meeting and getting closer to many, often distinguished, people. These factors make the musician's relationship to his travels active rather than passive.

There is no doubt that, from the point of view of *observing* life, it is an ideal situation. Horizons perpetually open out, like some mobile scenic apparatus on the vast stage of life (the world), and reveal increasingly distant planes and perspectives, in the course of which many a *trompe-l'œil* is shown for what it is. Apparently certain truths, with which one had lived comfortably and constantly, under the impact of continually accruing experience, often – *à contre-cœur* – have to undergo a revolutionary revaluation. Thus the extent of one's observations is immense; one is only con-cerned with what conclusions to draw!

In spite of these undoubted rewards, an analogy between the fate of even the most distinguished artists and the fate of the 'insignificant' man exists. It depends on this: in relation to the 'tiniest portions' of the reality mentioned above, or to put it more simply, the purely practical quest-ions of life, they find themselves up against the same anxieties, and have to face the same difficulties and struggles. The fact of the artist's *uniqueness* or of his particular position does not shield him from these troubles (which incidentally, by contrast, might well be so in the case of the distinguished statesman, who often acts counter to the *status quo*, in the atmosphere of a kind of ideological fiction so that, as long as fate decrees that he is guided by genius, his will becomes reality as if by magic, whereas should fate decree otherwise, then disaster inevitably ensues). For the artist, and especially the writer, careful observation of this micro-structure is one of the most important contributions to the *matière première* from which a work is shaped. In other fields of art, this relationship is less direct, although it is just as real.[1] On the other hand, the need to shape this material precisely into a well-defined, *unified* whole compels the artist to express the phenomena about him in an increasingly synthetic way; he is obliged to reveal the tensions arising from the controlling forces active at any given moment.[2]

The incessant drawing of conclusions from his experience of life secures for the artist an ascendancy over the 'insignificant' man. It is a superiority in the ability to *evaluate* phenomena, in a sense *sub specie aeternitatis*, so that he reveals hierarchies and perspectives. From this point of view the honest artist is, no matter how paradoxical this might appear, the only *realist in life*, the only force that is sufficiently balanced and independent between *the rulers and the ruled*. He is the regulating element of a phenomenon in the deepest sense of the word, and this is something that history has shown many times over. If you will pardon the pathos of the comparison, his situation is akin to the *cosmic* position that contemporary physics assigns to man within the universe: mid-way on the road between the abyss of the

---

[1] A work of art necessarily develops within its epoch regardless of the fact that it is to bear the marks of eternity. –KS (in margin).

[2] This in itself raises the observer's role to yet greater heights. –KS (in margin).

macrocosm and the abyss of the microcosm. Perhaps, however, it is too deep and hopeless a task to stare into both the abyss at his feet and the abyss overhead.

A certain ambiguity in the position of the artist-creator arises from all this. Plunged into the whirlpool of practical life, with all its 'relative' trivialities, he must struggle for absolute, primary values. The need to shape the *matière première*, drawn directly from life, into a defined, unified whole, compels him to struggle free of the whirlpool which is for ever threatening to suck him under. Instead he must take it in with an all-embracing glance.

These are all *des vérités de monsieur de la Palisse*,[3] yet were indispensable in an explanation of why I decided in advance to confer on my memoirs a self-imposed form, to enclose them within a highly disciplined structure. For one thing this approach would counter the inclination, which after all is natural in everyone, to give way to lyrical and over-intimate effusions; at the same time, it would define the most important factors of my psyche, and show the principle directions in which I always attempted to go. It would explain why, after long thought, I decided to limit my memoirs to a certain period of my life, namely the period which began with my decisive return to Poland at the close of the year 1919.

When I reflect on the real problem, namely how my self-portrait is going to look, sketched with my own rather modest literary talents, woven from my own words, thoughts, confessions, all those events of greater or lesser importance in my life, I feel at times that the task is beyond my powers. In my view it depends on the fact that *literary expressions*, be they true or imaginary (as in a novel), in their most profound, let us say, most transcendental substance, can only be the work of a writer endowed with great gifts or, in other words, a *genius*. That quintessential climate, the specific atmosphere of a given human type, that mysterious unknown (?) element (core) *obedient to none of the influences*

---

[3] Statements of the obvious.

of society and free of the fatal power of *chance*, which, come what may, constitutes a decisive element in life's story, does not depend in essence on any rationalistic idea – cannot be expressed (enclosed) in any logical formula or any system of cause and effect. In essence it is *irrational*, and its portrayal is only accessible to the intuition of genius. I believe that in literature that 'squaring of the circle' was achieved 100% successfully only by Shakespeare (in *Hamlet*), and above all by Dostoyevsky. It is the only way that the terrifyingly gloomy, yet irresistable, suggestive power of this author can be explained, since he cannot be numbered amongst the finest writers from the point of view of his purely constructive, literary skills. His vision of the 'integral man' is like a magical formula, through which he suddenly reveals the hidden significance of seemingly the most paradoxical events and defines the confused content of the integral man's inner life.

If I have allowed myself to mention these distinguished names here, names of such decisive importance in the history of man's creative thought, it is only because in comparison with the integral conception of man (a result of genius), all others are fundamentally flawed and deviate from the fundamental truth of man. They smash him up into individual particles, and speak of what the factual or fictional man thought, felt and did – of all the things that made up his external life. The whole, fraudulent, deceptive 'ambiguity' and 'many-sidedness' of man in his practical life, in what he is for the people surrounding him, is what is so immediately striking, but it obscures his deepest being. For everything depends on *interpretation*: on the placing of emphasis on this or that feature, on one or other of his reactions in the face of circumstantial occurences, the influences of milieu, historical factors etc. In order to confer a *whole* on these separate elements of life, a continuity on the operation of his fates, individual happenings are arranged in accordance with a certain evolutionary process, formulated in a (seemingly) perfect chain of causes and effects that have to represent, as it were, 'implacable fate'. But that determinism is artificial, being the subconscious search for self-contained 'form', the search for a work of art's structural element. This is exceedingly characteristic of the novels dating from the close of the nineteenth century, where the apparently 'deep' psychological analysis is in reality an established, pre-determined, well-nigh mathematical formula (that excludes all elements of chance), concluding with the inevitable result that $2 \times 2 = 4$.

This is all very beautiful, but I almost hear the question being posed, why do I speak of this so extensively instead of starting with the words: 'I was born in such a place, in such and such a year of our Lord . . . '. The fact is that the novel and factual biography are basically analogous with autobiography and memoirs. The dry, mechanical chronicling of facts devoted to someone's life is basically lacking in great interest, although I suppose there are rare cases where fate arranges itself in improbable fantastic adventures. But as soon as the guiding idea, the internal structure and the tensions are revealed, then the life of everyman becomes interesting.

[In the margin:] I have to select one of the 'interpretations' and in its selection be directed by a certain utilitarianism, namely that which in my existence is the deciding, dynamic and active agent, influencing the course of events in a certain portion of reality. For a certainty, the decisive factor is my work and my attitude (critical attitude) to the phenomena surrounding me, and this arises from any one of a set of axioms. This must be brought into relief, and made conspicuous in the complex of events making up my life.

Now, in the face of my intentions, I have found myself in the position of a mediocre novelist, on whom a theme has been thrust that outstrips his powers (potentialities). To some extent I stand helpless before the huge wealth of my inner and outer lives, knowing in advance that I cannot call upon the 'magic formula' which helped the greatest writers reveal the human soul in its most essential, unchanging substance without relying much on the logic (sequence) of events. Naturally, from the many possible 'interpretations' of my personality, I am left with only one (this does not mean at all that it will be false as a result), but it is one which I shall succeed in achieving through the elimination of unessential elements, not as regards my life, but from the point of view of the task that I have now set myself, namely the writing of a book about myself.

Karol
Szymanowski

The text of this wide-ranging, but none too sympathetic, interview with Michał Choromański (1904–72), a novelist and dramatist who was distantly related to the composer, was first published in *Wiadomości Literackie* on 16 October 1932.

Zakopane, September 1932
'Yes, believe me, since the time of Chopin there has always been something seedy about Polish music! And it's difficult to establish the origins of this sickness! There's a pallid anaemia about it in spite of all those foot-tapping oberek-style flourishes: "Hop-hop, heigh-ho". I have diagnosed this illness, but I don't like speaking about it in public as it always ends up with my being accused of being "corrupted by the Jews and the Masons" . . . '

And Karol Szymanowski finished his cigarette. He then gazed at me with his clear, unequivocal grey-blue eyes and asked with refined simplicity whether I would not like another beer. I had drunk three bottles, and beyond the verandah the Zakopane rain was falling. I looked through the window, and it seemed to me that autumn was looking golden and wet – like beer. Then I reflected that in everyday life the true artist is really the most ordinary person in the world. To some extent this is evidence of his individuality. For in our century, when every other individual is so very original, the most original man of all would be the one who was destitute of all originality. So it was, and so it is now. Who would have thought that perhaps I was sitting opposite a genius?

In a comfortable armchair, legs elegantly crossed, one arm resting on the arm of the chair, the other dangling nonchalantly and almost touching the ground, the last gentleman and grand seigneur of our proletarian times sat before me. He was in a grey suit, and I emphasise this as it is a fact of particular importance. I should also mention that it was tea-time. He was wearing a grey shirt and a grey tie which had a thin red stripe harmonising tastefully with the ribbon of his Légion d'Honneur. The colour of his eyes also matched his clothes beautifully, starting from the deep grey tones of the iris and finishing at the discreet, reddish glints of the pupils which appeared at rare moments of restrained and extremely proper excitement. Such a glint appeared in his eyes as he said:

'What a strange, almost ambivalent thing this music is! I often think like this, especially when I feverishly regret that I'm not a writer, for example!'

I grumbled that I, on the contrary, regretted that I was not a musician, but he took this to be no more than a pleasantry.

'Really?' he replied, and then sighed: 'She is usually mentioned in the same breath . . . .'

'Who?' I asked.

'Music. She is usually mentioned in the same breath as all the other arts, but in essence she is a completely isolated island on the sea of human emotions. Isolated, yet so easy of access in her more second-rate forms, and it is precisely this which is so disturbing! It even arouses a certain disrespect, often quite justifiably. Undoubtedly there is something akin to sorcery here, some magic which is sometimes white, sometimes black, some out and out physiological immediacy of effect and as a consequence of this, an almost absurd relativism, an organic anti-intellectualism. You must understand, Michał, that it is precisely here that we have a thorny point to deal with. Because it doesn't have to be like this, for truly great music exists, and this music is not just a function of some spontaneous, sentimental sensibility, but in its truly human values reveals the traces of a consciously shaping will such as is encountered in poetry or the fine arts. So too in the course of life, sober, wise, self-conscious life, is music taken firmly in hand and controlled like a jibbing horse. One has only to know the "trick" behind this. It is of course

easier in relation to past epochs with its music which has lost the magic of immediacy and become a commemorative mummy.'
He coughed and took a eucalyptus pastille.

'What surrounds us at a given moment, the bubbling magma of music in the making, is often – even for us professionals – pure madness, and that which is true, creative and enduring in her, can only be spotted finally by way of subtle instinct, often without the support of any rational basis. How fortunate you writers are, working with materials which are, let's say, artistic in a practical sort of way and which operate within a firm, logical framework, having some actual, emotional touchstone of veracity, albeit the most fantastic veracities of the Hamlets or Fausts! But enough of this ... '

Karol Szymanowski's bearing and gestures, full of the spontaneity and grace of the *grand seigneur*, are at the same time modest and unobtrusive. Yet in spite of this they act immediately upon one in a strangely attractive way – just as the flautist acted bewitchingly and destructively on those tragically musical rats. Many a time I have tried to say something impertinent to Karol Szymanowski, but my intended insulting words have been involuntarily transformed into compliments. When I was on less than cordial terms with him a year ago, I imagined with malice how a bullet fired from a gun would strike him in the chest in the shape of a tea-rose or some sort of orchid. It is a disturbing and very frightening property, because one never knows how it will finish.

I reflected thus, drinking beer, in the presence of Karol Szymanowski, whose words and gestures were so alluring and unpretentious that involuntarily I completely forgot about his indubitable greatness. With difficulty I staved off the temptation to be over-familiar with him, and by way of example I recalled a couple of my artistic acquaintances – ordinary mortals – who, at the very sight of Karol Szymanowski, go into epileptic convulsions.

'Do you remember,' he began with nonchalant grace,

holding a perfumed handkerchief to his nose with a refined gesture. At the same time he looked through the window with fleeting, but real curiosity. Beyond the verandah the Zakopane rain was falling on various figures. They were running quickly, and red and blue parzenica stood out on their white mountain clothes.[1] 'Do you remember Chichikov's lackey in Gogol's *Dead Souls* who in his free moments read the paper, not so much because he was interested in its contents, but rejoiced in the fact that "in literature some word was always being formed".[2] This piety, or what you will, is in my view the most obvious symbol of what I hate most in music – that so-called "improvisatoriness". Remember this trait is almost non-existent in the other arts. The touchstone of logical veracity is binding within limits upon the worst of painters and scribblers. But in music "*nichts ist wahr, alles ist erlaubt*",[3] and here the gates are flung wide open to the dilettantism and anti-constructionalism of bad music. In putting together individual notes, "some word" is always formed, and this is always evident in such music. This is an extremely important point and accounts for much, especially here in Poland, where in a certain sense music amounts to no more than organised sloth, the filling of empty spaces, a surrogate for real experience, a dreamy, sentimental passing of time. Chichikov's lackey explains much when it comes to considering the failure of our music. . .'

[1] Parzenica is a pattern embroidered on trousers worn by highlanders.

[2] '[...] he [Petrushka] even had a noble urge for enlightenment, that is to say, for reading books, without bothering too much about their contents: it made no difference to him whether it was a tale about the adventures of a love-lorn swain or simply a primer or a prayer book – he read everything with equal attention; if someone had slipped a book of chemistry to him he would not have refused it. He liked not so much what he read as the reading itself, or, to put it more precisely, the process of reading, the fact that the letters were always forming a word which sometimes meant the devil only knew what.' Nikolai Gogol, *Dead Souls*, translated by David Magarshack, Penguin, Harmondsworth, 1961, pp. 29–30.

[3] *Cf.* note 8 on p. 222.

I was struck by the vehemence of this last remark, but it was expressed with such a charming smile that the word 'lackey' almost turned into 'prince'.

'Are you surprised that I unmask so cynically the muse which I have faithfully served for so many years?' He took another pastille. 'It's difficult, my love is not blind . . . . It all depends on the fact that when one "works in music" one has continually to overcome it so that in general something worthwhile can result. It is arduous work. Bear in mind that its raw material is volatile, rather like grains of golden sand running through one's fingers. From this material one has to fashion enduring, precise forms, transcending those flowing, random constituent elements. Nor does it have a clearly defined starting-point which, in the case of poetry and fine art, is provided by conceptual content or the visible realities of life. Hence the confounded difficulty encountered in discovering appropriate forms which solve the problem of individual style. Hard, unyielding discipline is more essential here than anywhere else, and it is necessary to find it oneself. In this very fact I see the intervention not only of a consciously shaping will-power, but to all intents and purposes, the intellect – and this is something of which music in its essence is deprived. It is difficult to formulate the nature of the problem in haste, but I am certain that I am thinking along the right lines: that is, in comparing music, as an objective affair, as a cold, calculating consideration of what has to be done with its raw material, with music as the representation simply of "tender feelings". Admittedly this is not the only basis, but it is inescapable, and it is the basis on which all those great figures from the past achieved such amazing results. I said a moment ago that real life keeps a check on music. If one looks at a great phenomenon, e.g., German music from Bach, through Mozart, Beethoven and others to Wagner, one feels that there is nothing random about it, that there is no question of the sporadic emergence of a *Deus ex Machina* in the form of individual, great talents. There is rather a sort of logical development, some sort of continuous illumination from within of the deepest inner

*The 'Villa Atma', Szymanowski's house in Zakopane, now the
Karol Szymanowski Museum (photograph by Lidia Długołęcka)*

being of the nation. If you will permit me to resort to pathos for once, it is a reflection on the screen of eternity of an ideal interpretation of earthly matters.'

He suddenly sighed and rested his head on his well-manicured hand. I had already noticed more than once that from time to time he groaned quietly and unobtrusively checked his pulse with increasing unease. At times he seemed to be in a real panic, but realised that he could not reveal the slightest bit of anxiety.

It was not to be wondered that he was uneasy, for the day was really dreadful, and on that dreadful day, on Karol Szymanowski's right hand, there was not only evidence of a small, accidental wound but also a slightly swollen vein. That day Karol Szymanowski was particularly depressed and feeling so sorry for himself that one wondered whether he was suffering from blood-poisoning.

'How did you get that scratch?' I asked, feigning solicitude.

He replied with unutterable, distinguished sadness that a dog had bitten him; he had made enquiries about the animal and it was unlikely that it was rabid. 'You can't be sure,' I replied. 'The incubation period for rabies in humans is almost a year, so they say.' Karol Szymanowski's face fell. 'My friend,' he said, disorientated. 'Should I go to the doctor now?'

A year ago, at more or less the same time of year, I had gone with him to a well-known consultant because a small graze on his tongue led him to imagine that he was suffering from cancer. The outcome was totally happy.

While finishing the fourth bottle of beer, I heard Karol Szymanowski's discreet replies about the first musical stirrings of his childhood. It was at the end of the last century, when Karol Szymanowski was only ten. It was then that the family took him to the opera for the first time. This was at Elizavetgrad, a strange Ukrainian town presently named Zinovievsk,[4] for, in addition to Karol Szymanowski and Trotsky, People's Commissar Zinoviev had been born in its environs. Karol Szymanowski had made his way along Gogol Street in this sun-drenched little town, full of colourful gardens and orchards, to attend the technical gymnasium.[5] In 1918 he patrolled the same streets with browning and rifle in his capacity as member of the Civil Defence. But at the end of the last century, no one dreamt of the advent of communism during the war. The ten-year old Karol Szymanowski was introduced to the theatre, seeing and hearing opera for the first time. On this occasion it was Dargomizhsky's *Rusalka*, the story of which recalls *Halka*, although it differs in that the dramatic action does not end with the

[4] After the October Revolution, Elizavetgrad was renamed Zinovievsk after Grigory Yevsieyevich Zinoviev (1883–1936), and then renamed Kirowograd following Zinoviev's arrest in 1934.

[5] Szymanowski was educated at home, but had to attend school briefly in 1900 in order to take the examinations for the certificate of secondary education.

drowning of the jilted girl, but, on the contrary, begins
where the other leaves off. The importunity and extra-
aquatic pretensions of the continually appearing Rusalka
could easily have adversely affected the spiritual sensibility
of a young boy. But it turned out that after one hearing this
music acted especially forcefully and profoundly on the
lad's nervous system, and Karol Szymanowski to this day
regards it as the moment which decided the course of his
life and destiny.

My excitable but rather banal fancy took me back in time,
and I imagined Karol Szymanowski in short trousers and
white-collared jacket, weeping and wailing with rapture,
swooning and sobbing at the sound of heavenly trumpet,
flute and the valve-horn's divine calls. But obviously it was all
completely different. I failed to obtain from Karol Szymanowski's lips a detailed description of this scene or any other
summary of his experiences. Perhaps they were too violent
for him now to want to recall them. Or perhaps the stirring
of his feelings made itself manifest in an original way peculiar to him: perhaps he kissed the hands of his aunts and
thanked them politely, as a well-brought-up boy should.
Now he sat opposite me, a few years older, but so disarmingly pleasant. I have to admit that I had been pre-occupied
with visions of his childhood and for some time I had not
heard a single word. It was only after some little while, when
I caught his glance, full of reproach and subtle irony, that I
returned to a state of totally sober consciousness. The first
words I heard then were music, Chopin, Chopin and music
being declined in every single case. There was an unbear-
able monotony in all this. But I later understood that if one
says the word 'music', then one has to say 'Chopin', and this
in turn brings the word 'music' in its train and so on, in ever
decreasing circles. And so there was Karol Szymanowski,
juggling with these words and despairingly attempting to
extricate himself from them.

'That so unique, prophetic road along which Chopin
journeyed towards the "joyful science" of Polish music
remained a secret which he apparently took with him to the

grave. In fact, he did not find anyone who could receive this secret from him. Contemporaries and compatriots in succeeding generations accepted him, as has generally been the case here, chiefly on account of the "tender emotions" and fictional historical content of his work, while apparently failing to notice his greatness as an artist in terms of rigorous self-discipline and ability to mould the substance of sound, as well as his clear consciousness of his aims. One thing in particular: Norwid knew of this, but no-one else wanted to know about this then.[6] And so it was, as I have frequently said before, that the real consequences of Chopin's revelations reached others rather than ourselves.'

He again looked at his hand, but now in a rather involuntary way and with markedly less anxiety. Evidently he was presently pre-occupied by something completely different.

---

[6] Cyprian Norwid (1821–83) is regarded as Poland's most 'intellectual' poet. He was initially influenced by the great Romantics, but his avoidance of the facile techniques and monotonous rhythms of the later, lesser Romantic figures, led to accusations of obscurity and a lack of colour. In addition to painting, sculpture, history and archaeology of the Mediterranean regions Norwid was interested in Polish folk cultures but, from the age of 21, lived abroad, eventually settling in Paris. He could not be described as a socialist, although there is a kinship between his ideology and that of William Morris. He rejected the notion of 'art for art's sake', and extolled the sanctity of labour, seeing in the loving acceptance of redeeming work both a means of atonement for original sin and the highest manifestation of human freedom. In the poem *Promethidion* (*The Child of Prometheus*), Prometheus is regarded not so much as a rebel as the giver of crafts and skills to mankind. Here Norwid gave expression to his abhorrence of the split between 'manual' and 'artistic' labour, art ideally being the 'banner on the tower of human labours', and the artist the 'organiser of the national imagination'. He also believed that the best musician was the People, the composer being its 'fiery tongue', the one who transforms native music into an art that transcends national concerns to become truly universal.

It is not surprising to discover that Szymanowski considered Norwid to be the one nineteenth-century poet who truly understood the significance of Chopin's work.

Szymanowski in Atma

His face suddenly became cold and fixed, and a fleeting, pulsating fury passed over it. It was only a fraction of a second before he mastered himself and shook his head.

'My friend,' he said sourly, 'it would really be better if I said nothing about it here. I am always accused of inveterate impudence, disdain and lack of respect for Polish music of the post-Chopin era. But though it is certainly harsh, this is my considered critical judgment. It is hard, but one has to say straightaway that this music is not exactly the *pièce de résistance* of our national cultural inheritance. It loses much in comparison with other branches of our art, and especially literature, and nothing can come to the assistance of its "homely" maudlin qualities. There is a strange lifelessness about it, the absence of a creative idea and therefore any aspiration to a defined aim. It is under a constant obligation to be stirred by the 'rustling of fir-trees on mountain tops' – but even if we treat this work with the justice which is due to it, one has to say that in present-day conditions it is a veritable impossibility. I reckon that in our relationship to the manifestations of artistic culture dating from the last century, we labour under a total misapprehension because of the respect shown to such a well-known tradition and the "national peculiarities" attaching to it. Especially the business of these "peculiarities" which are dubious enough in character.'

He fell silent. Apart from the drumming of the rain on the window it was quiet. 'What weather!' I thought. It was pouring cats and dogs, as if to underline the wickedness of folkloristic peculiarities. Slowly a golden-dark dusk fell in the silence, and through the window something white and navy blue gleamed. Parzenica flashed by, and suddenly we heard a voice. It was velvety, low and drunk. It was the voice of the cabman.

He asked us in dialect whether we wanted him to drive us anywhere. And while that lordly democrat, Karol Szymanowski, explained to the highlander through the window that the day had been so terrible and that the evening looked no less terrible that it was quite impossible to consider going to town, I pondered timidly about what seemed to me to be a strange twist of fate: namely, Karol Szymanowski's resorting to the Harnasies for a source of fresh inspiration. Was not this in itself an acknowledgement of the existence of precisely such national peculiarities? I was not so frank as to say this aloud. Anyway I did not have time. Karol Szymanowski again sat before me and said with grace, tact, deliberation and eagerness:

'I think that a too simplistic conception of these "peculiarities" is a dubious enough ideal born, if I am not mistaken, of a conspiratorial yearning for all manner of illiteracy. Or else, as is the case in this country, my good sir, "something after one's own mind".... My God, what a dangerous password! It usually hides that customary intellectual laziness, general lack of interest and panic in the face of anything new, especially anything which requires a certain intellectual effort and threatens the established order of things. One has only to look at the press reviews written by the more educated. God, what an abysmal standard! It is precisely music which is such ideal terrain for that kind of "peculiarities" ideology.'

In the adjacent dining-room a table was laid. Time for the evening meal was approaching, twilight had fallen, but in the study where we were sitting there was still no light. From the armchair opposite came painful, weary words:

'Remember Moniuszko, trembling with fear before Kraszewski who condemned him for his "impudence". To be sure I also have my novelist who constantly condemns me,[7] but times have changed . . . .'

It was as if something stirred contemptuously in the armchair.

' . . . and I don't pay any heed to this.'

I bridled in consternation, wishing to protect my friends in a brotherly sort of way, but worldly wisdom prevailed and I said nothing, silently encouraging further outpourings.

'But anyway,' came the voice from the darkness of the armchair, 'Moniuszko completely failed to recognise Wagner. In the way that today they refuse to recognise Stravinsky in this country. They refuse to admit that he possesses any of this so-called depth.'

The armchair suddenly sqeaked with indignation.

'Devil only knows what all this "depth" is! None of my opponents has tried to explain this in detail to me!'

Unfortunately I could not see Karol Szymanowski's face at all by this time, so I do not know what his expression was when he uncontrollably said the word 'Devil', but I suspect that he was a little surprised and shocked by his own vehemence.

'Anyway,' he went on quickly, to hide his feeling, 'that absence of "disinterested concern", that passion for a problem in its own right, without any sentimental references, is a very non-European characteristic. Incidentally, it is strange that Poles were, and are able to be, such strikingly great and

---

[7] Szymanowski was here referring to Juliusz Kaden-Bandrowski who had published a hostile review of 'The Educational Role of Musical Culture in Society' in *Gazeta Polska* (14 June 1931).

thrillingly profound "Poles", but find it so difficult to come up to the standard of the average European.'

The armchair creaked painfully and with sincere sadness. But I wanted a more precise definition, so I asked him how he defined European. Was it more to do with culture than geography? The armchair stirred again, this time as if under the strain of intense effort. Then, somewhere in its middle, the red tip of a cigarette began to glow and describe unclear, perplexed zig-zaggings.

'What do I mean by European?' I heard in reply after a moment. 'It is most difficult to conceive directly what this word means. But I believe that in spite of all the terrible things which are happening in the world today, there exists some mysterious means of mutual understanding amongst men, some straightforward, purely human solidarity which is supra-national, and this exists precisely in the sphere of the most elevated intellectual, aesthetic and – above all – ethical matters. Well, more and more people are speaking this common language in the world today. Can one doubt the eventual rise and triumph of the real "man" in the most profound sense of the word? I tell you, there are more and more of them, although at present they are drowned out by the racket of a completely different type, but, believe me, this can't be for long. I myself, for want of a better word, have called this "Europeanism".'

I trembled, because his words made me think of those bloody years we had both been through. But this was an excessive, sickly sensibility on my part. To my question as to whether this Europeanism did not touch on internationalism, the slightly outraged voice of Karol Szymanowski replied, to the accompaniment of red exclamation marks traced in the semi-darkness by the cigarette:

'Never! It would be impossible not to recognise racial, ethical "predispositions", quite apart from subjective, individual attributes.'

I was benighted and felt thoroughly foolish. 'Individual attributes?' I repeated mournfully. But he disregarded my murmurs of disbelief.

'These facts are beyond dispute,' he went on, dodging the issue. 'They are by no means the fictional work of "nationalist" ideologues. We have to raise this *a priori* national mental equipment to some peak of real humanity. The entire development of human culture, with all its spiritual variety and wealth, depends on this. It is difficult to say what constitutes the chemical process underlying this magical connection between such seemingly contradictory conceptions as "nationalism" and "humanity", but it is a condition *sine qua non* of the rise of all that is true and enduring on earth. In effect it is very difficult to master such a subtle *procédé* and maintain a constant balance between the anaemic spectre of theoretical "internationalism" and the hundred times more concrete folly fighting in the name of the nationalist idea. Certainly the decisive factor here is not only unerring instinct but a conscious sense of responsibility in the face of these vital tasks. And yet it is so easy to go beyond the limits of that cheerless folly, which – I don't know why – is often identified with patriotism. Such patriotism, dependent on thoughtless self-adoration and ominous snapping of teeth at all others, is not the most reliable mainspring for future development.'

I did not ask any questions and did not respond to his views, since I was not wont to betray my views on the development of history. In spirit and disposition I am rather on the side of the teeth-snappers than restrained idealists living on the fringes of political necessity. But I felt he was waiting for some reply, and so I murmured indistinctly: 'What is real patriotism then?'

'At the end of your own *White Brothers*,'[8] he went on, looking to see if I was flattered, 'you declare that goodness (in the form of all love, including love of fatherland) is a great and difficult art, especially for a wise man. Incidentally, that is a very beautiful and profound aphorism.'

He tactfully averted his eyes so as not to relish my pallour for too long.

[8] Choromański's first novel, published in Kraków in 1931.

'I believe in this most fully, and precisely in its application to this most sincere and profound love. All the same, art is the eternal overcoming of all which is clumsy, imperfect, immature – a search for increasingly more splendid forms, and ever fuller modes of expression. For this it is necessary to have without fail a sense of reality, a penetrating, critical sense. I believe this to be the unavoidable basis of all creative patriotism, of conscious action, even in the least far-reaching, most modest of spheres. Certainly there were tragic moments when the honest will to carry out such an action had to be paid for with life itself . . . . But let us pray that these will now be as rare as possible, because today's fatherland should be celebrated more by the beauty of the creative life than the most tragic of deaths. The pathos of the heroes of Troy is splendid, but we see it from a 3,000-year perspective. Such actions today would smell too much of phosgene and mustard gas.'

'Supper is ready, gentlemen.'

Our conversation was abruptly interrupted, and a sudden, glaring light flooded the room. I involuntarily screwed up my eyes, and when I opened them and looked at the armchair opposite me, I rubbed my eyes in utter amazement. It was only with difficulty that I stopped myself muttering an oath. It was evening; it was supper-time. And sitting opposite me in the armchair was Karol Szymanowski in a dark blue suit! There was not the least doubt of it. The grey suit he had been wearing earlier in the day, as required by the demands of everyday etiquette, had simply demateri-alised before my eyes! It was now navy blue, with bright threads running through the material! He was wearing a sheeny, azure shirt and a blue tie, with diagonal black stripes. And his eyes were now dark and looked like black sapphires. It was a downright unearthly transformation, a sort of miracle or aristocratic metamorphosis! I felt an awkward, tactless *parvenu* and sighed. We stood up and I accompanied him as he made his way, limping on his left leg, to the dining room.

On the table there was very little alcohol: a drop of wine

and a little beer. The times were long gone when, around the piano and along multi-coloured river-beds of scores and sheet music, it coursed in desperate but beneficial torrents. These torrents had been irretrievably dried up three years before in Davos. There, in a white sanatorium, embedded in ice, they had stifled all musical inspiration after several long months. After playing around with this strange association of ideas, I came full circle again in the presence of Karol Szymanowski.

'You want me to talk to you about myself?' he asked with surprising modesty. 'Don't worry about my stirring you up with tales about the martyrdom of the misunderstood artist. Even though there would be some justice in this after my recent "dramatic" experiences.[9] I shan't wax excessively lyrical about this. Anyhow, rightly or wrongly, I consider that my retreat does not mean that the battle has been lost. Don't you think that in the course of our lives – those of us in art – there comes a time when we must make a decisive move in the game? I've always played rather fast and loose, without any regard for "prevailing conditions", and certainly without recourse to the line of least resistance. It is not the easiest way, but its the only one which brings results in art.'

He ate a salad with admirable elegance. He glanced with sadness at the wine and vodka, which he did not touch, keeping a disdainful silence. Later, quite unexpectedly, he began to speak about alcohol. It was the great mainspring in the development of civilisation. He never doubted that the discovery of wine was no less important than the discovery of fire. Who knows whether it was not precisely at this point that art came into being? 'Art for which we live!' he said with restrained pathos. After a while he returned to the subject in hand and continued:

'If, at the outset of my career, I seemed to deviate from the way, it was not just that I experienced moments of

---

[9] Szymanowski was here referring to his dismissal from the Rectorship of the State Academy earlier in the year (*cf.* Introduction, pp. 67–69).

indecision and doubt which in any case are not unusual in the young; it was because of the extremely difficult conditions in which I had to work. Just think: I had to begin, to be quite blunt, by making my own tools. So I had to face massive problems which I was forced to solve alone. Alone! Because – think of it, Michał – apart from a tiny handful of personal friends, amongst whom it was possible to count a few of the most distinguished of today's performers,[10] and to whom I am indebted for the fact that my earliest works did

[10] Artur Rubinstein and Paweł Kochański. In the course of an article written to mark the occasion of Rubinstein's visit to Warsaw to give two concerts at the Philharmonia on 9 and 12 October 1924 (the programmes included Beethoven's Fourth Piano Concerto, Brahms' Second Piano Concerto and Tchaikovsky's First) Szymanowski wrote:

> It is the composer who is able to say most about the performer to whom he happily and confidently entrusts his works. He alone knows in its entirety that mysterious route leading from well-nigh abstract dreams about beauty, [...] to its 'materialisation' in virtuoso performance. He alone knows about the marvellous revelation which occurs when a great performer not only reveals the full beauty of the work, but enhances it with his own love and ardour, illuminating it with a vivid, warm light. There is another type of virtuoso artist, however, and between those who move their fingers most beautifully without ever slipping up, [...] but who succeed only in presenting a correct but lifeless 'death-mask' of a work, and those under whose fingers this work lives its most vital, most profound life, there exists an unfathomable abyss [...]. Fortunately Artur Rubinstein is on the right side of the abyss. He is not a virtuoso in the accepted sense of the word, but [...] a truly great musician, for whom a phenomenal, technical facility [...] is only an all-powerful way of opening up the mysterious treasury of the kingdom of music. [...] With remarkable intellectual assurance and cultured taste, [...] he is able to seek out the true value of the most apparently paradoxical contemporary works, however extreme they be in character [...]. Hence that reputation as the intrepid pioneer of new values which he has acquired in all the great musical centres of Europe and America. [...] It is true that he plays Chopin differently from others – in a more restrained, serious way, and not as a display piece for his own 'beautiful emotions', thereby conferring upon it a true profundity [...].

'Artur Rubinstein', *Kurier Warszawski* (8 October 1924); reprinted in *Karol Szymanowski Pisma*, Vol. 1, pp. 125–26. Szymanowski's obituary, 'In memory of Paweł Kochański', is on pp. 353–57.

not languish unheard in my private archive, I was always in opposition to everyone and everything in our music. There was never any *parti pris*, but a real rejection on my part of "existing" musical values. Why at the same time did I experience Wyspiański and Kasprowicz so warmly? (Przybyszewski never!)[11] It was because I sensed genuine creativity in them. I kept a neutral silence, not wishing to betray my literary doubts. At any rate that was entirely my private affair. In any case I was totally exhausted. Through the call of friendship, I hear the effusions of the painter Rafał Malczewski everyday and look at his pictures; through the call of friendship I have committed to memory, in the most monstrous detail, the history of the rise and fall of the State Academy of Music, and through the call of friendship I have immersed myself in a study of the deepest and darkest recesses of Polish music. I have involuntarily come to the conclusion that friendship is a mutual, systematic wearing-out process.

'You understand me?' Karol Szymanowski demanded.

'Of course!' I immediately replied.

'So what do you think of all this?' asked Karol Szymanowski.

'It's a hell of a business!' I replied like an echo.

'I have to admit, openly and frankly,' said Karol Szymanowski, 'that as late as the last few years (and I will explain this limitation later), I was unable to acknowledge what had happened in Polish music, not just in specific works but in the very approach to the question, during the era in which the style based on those previously fondly-mentioned national "peculiarities" penetrated as a consequence of quietism and lack of creative will. For this reason I had to be a notorious anti-traditionalist, because what could I relate to? There was only Chopin – a unique, shining example, but that was only in the sphere of piano music! Here in Poland, alas, there was nothing, but abroad, what splendidly diverse

[11] *Cf.* Introduction, pp. 28–29.

riches there were, springing up before one's eyes like
flowers in May. Just think what there was for a susceptible
young man: *Salomé* and *Elektra*, those veritable masterpieces
by Strauss (unknown in Poland!), the marvellous *Pelléas*
(unknown in Poland!), and finally the young Stravinsky of
the era of the *Rite* and *Wedding* (unknown in Poland!) – a
real magician, suddenly throwing music into a completely
different perspective. But here in Poland, it was all hopelessly mundane – music wearing a tragic mask with empty
eye-sockets which see nothing living in the world, only the
coagulated commonplaces of "national creativity". You
understand what I'm getting at?'
'Of course,' I replied immediately.
'What do you think about this?'
'It's a hell of a business!' I replied. Our plates were
whisked away from us, and the rain continued to fall without
ceasing. Some mountaineer, wet-through, could be heard
singing outside, straining his voice: 'Pijany, pijany ... '
['Drunk, drunk ... ']. Against this background, Karol Szymanowski suddenly spoke with deep-felt anguish and
seriousness:
'What could I do?!' he cried, shrugging his shoulders.
'Willy-nilly I was compelled to rove abroad in the huge,
abundantly blooming fields of foreign music, searching out,
investigating, poking my nose into all manner of things, so
as to be able to fashion the necessary, marvellous precision
tools which could afford me the possibility of acquiring in its
entirety the magic of music as it sprang into being before
living, "contemporary" eyes. Imagine, in this persistent urge
to get to grips with everything which smacks of the past, it
would be feasible to miss the "reality" of life round about.
Anyway, it is no part of art to display the technical devices of
the great musical deceased. One must find one's own style.
Incidentally, I am going to throw in an aphorism here. I am
certain that the excessive cult of tradition is a symptom of
the atrophy of the instinct for life, of a certain creative
impotence. And there is no way of telling whether a young
revolutionary will not turn into an old reactionary, or in the

field of art, let us be frank, something of an idiot.' And again
that last word was enunciated with such grace that it almost
sounded like a compliment. 'But enough of that: let's get
back to the sad story of my life.'
He was downright upset and was speaking in an extremely
confidential tone. I even began to feel ashamed that I was
increasingly tending to gather wool, so I made myself listen
with concentrated, unctious attention.

'Well, all alone and totally despised, I managed at last to
fashion this precision tool – and as you see I currently
manufacture "Polish Music" as the whim takes me. I mean in
the sense in which I understand "national" creativity. I
should like that Harnasian drinking-song which you just
heard wafting through the window to become something
comprehensible through my interpretation of it – perhaps
even to become something which the "good European"
finds sympathetic and beautiful. Whether I succeed is
another matter. But I am sure it is a genuine, honest
artefact. I guarantee that, not only with the thousand
hideous faults I possess . . . .'
'Heaven forfend!'
' . . . but my one and only virtue: honesty and a sense of
responsibility which I never abandon in the face of the task
in hand.'
He got up from the table, picked up his cup of coffee, and
went back to the study, limping on his left leg. This time he
sat at the piano.
'Now I will tell you why, some years ago, I changed my
previous black spectacles for rose-tinted ones. It happened
on account of the younger generation of composers who in
the last few years have suddenly sprung up like mushrooms
after rain. Please don't think that I take any of the credit for
this life-giving rain,' he said hurriedly but quite needlessly as
the last thing I would accuse Karol Szymanowski of is mega-
lomania. 'No, however loyally and kindly they themselves
assure me of this, I don't wish to exaggerate the extent of my
actual influence over them. In a significant number of cases
it is totally non-existent. I reckon that some of them even

consider me – from the musical point of view – a bit of a *vieux pompier*, as the French would put it. As a musician, yes – but not as the representative of a certain ideal. In this respect we understand each other perfectly. They realise what it is that I have been fighting against my whole life through with such difficulty. They understand that I have had to repudiate my own "immediate interests" as I have taken the least "popular" way with apparent passion and with such obvious results, especially here in Poland! But it's difficult! They value and recognise my almost total isolation in this struggle. The true significance of our excellent relationship and mutual trust lies in this. And remember that it is precisely the undoubted existence of these people which fills me with philosophical calm in relation to the very sad events through which I became a sacrifice on the altar of socio-musical work, along with a number of my friends. They rubbed me out, but only from the State Conservatory. It is not so easy for them when it comes to Polish music. There is an anti-creative wave in official music, a full-scale retreat to sheltered retreats, a humble return to the *status quo ante bellum* (yes! really, alas – and it is even combined with a certain feeling of affection for "the Russian soul, Russian fragrance").[12] The whole of this incomprehensible musical "strategy" is a very sad affair. But leaving aside my own personal bitterness and speaking objectively, it is a most symptomatic, threatening phenomenon, this fury for uprooting everything which is young and alive, this shutting of windows which my friends and I together opened to let in fresh air, this indolent, senile fear of a healthy draught which sooner or later will blow away all these useless scribblers. Of course, this is no laughing-matter. But things will soon sort themselves out, wellnigh automatically, because these "youngsters" will soon makes their voices heard. They have not only talent but initiative and at the end of the day a sense of contemporary reality. They in particular know why I "disorganised" the State Conservatory

[12] Szymanowski here spoke in Russian.

Szymanowski at the piano in Atma

for so many years. For which, of course, I was regularly paid a mint of money through the good offices of masons and international Jewish capitalists.'

I looked at him suspiciously. 'And yet? . . . ' the thought flashed through my mind. But it was impossible to read anything from his face. Not one address, not one bank, not one protocol signed by Zionist sages! I thought badly of him for his egoism, while he sat smiling, discreet, beyond reproach.[13]

'Then will come the full rehabilitation of all my work and efforts which today appear to have been all in vain, for ever doomed. But better late than never, right?' he continued resignedly, after which he suddenly exclaimed: 'Tears are welling up, as one of our sentimental novelists would put it. But not out of resentment in my case. I am an optimistic

---

[13] Choromański seems to have misunderstood Szymanowski's irony. Szymanowski's more chauvinistic critics always attributed his departures from established Polish traditions to the machinations of Jewish-masonic conspirators.

fatalist in general, which means that for me personally, things have turned out better than they were. "With a tragic shadow on the pallid brow", a veritable *Rector magnificus in partibus infidelium*,[14] I have returned, like Cincinnatus,[15] to my own fireside, to what is the most essential of my tasks. In less than six months from the time of my exodus, I had already completed a symphony, a violin concerto and have various other sketches and new ideas in hand.'

He shook his head, which was silhouetted against the background of the music resting on the piano's stand. This was the score itself of the last symphony. My eyes had already been rivetted to it for some time, but I had still to discover just how unearthly its contents were. I would never have believed that what took place shortly afterwards was at all possible. I rashly asked Karol Szymanowski to play it to me, and he readily agreed as we had discussed the matter the preceding evening. Even so, the whole thing came as a complete surprise to me.

'Straight away, straight away,' he said, repeating under his breath 'It's devilish stuff, devilish stuff!' as he settled himself on the stool. All around, on the walls, on the table and on the upright, were photographs of various friends, all their faces smiling. On the top of the piano there was also a vase of flowers.

With careless grace, Karol Szymanowski put his cigarette aside, smiled disarmingly with a modesty and simplicity which was so natural as to be unlikely. A moment later came the catastrophe.

Ten rapacious, predatory, but at the same time, caressing tentacles fell onto the black and white keys, at which something groaned and sighed in mystic dread and someone

[14] 'Magnificent rector in the lands of the infidel', a title traditionally conferred on bishops whose dioceses lay beyond the established bounds of the faith.

[15] Lucius Quinctius Cincinnatus (b. 519(?)BC). In 458 he was summoned from his farm and appointed dictator of Rome during the struggle with the Aequi. As soon as the enemy had been defeated, he surrendered his powers and returned to his farm.

seemed to cry "For the love of God!" He clapped his hands, and the ten tentacles moved with convulsive rapidity. Suddenly they seemed to seize someone by the shoulder and shake the life out of him with all their strength. But then, as if in inconceivable delight and tenderness, in a transport of pitying grief, the tentacles slowly began to finger the keyboard, and the keys flowed between the fingers like long strands of flaxen hair. Another instant, and they froze in an unfinished caress – then it was as if the cooings and babblings of life's childish joys could be heard! Another instant, and it seemed as if someone had died – and there went the rose-covered coffin, with candles and flowers. But no! It wasn't true! Already, at full, inebriated tilt, in a torrent of epileptic ecstasy, the trumpets of the second coming trumpetted, and the fires of the Harnasies burned on all sides of the mountain passes, while drunken, harshly singing highland robbers leapt through the flames, blood pouring from their wounds. A fiery conflagration burst into the night air, but the robbers leapt so high that not one of them was scorched by the flames. The song changed suddenly into shrieks and cries, the roaring föhn blew in age-old blasts, and the beautiful eyes of Jasek[16] were blood-red and full of smoke! Then into all this a horn intruded.

Initially it murmured very quietly and smoothly, but already the right hand emphasised the flutes' immediate reply; suddenly the horn became anxious and began to protest more and more distinctly and pointedly, after which the violins joined in with evermore vocal, opprobrious indignation! It all became stridently plain, and the greatest wickedness was perpetrated here! In a sustained crescendo, one after another, various parts wove together, and then suddenly like a thunderbolt coming out of a clear blue sky, like a thunderclap, timpani and trombones began time and again to hammer down blows! Blood now rushed to the

---

[16] 'Jasek' is a reference to an imaginary Highland robber rather than a literary allusion.

head and the heart rattled in the chest, fit to burst. Someone croaked with their dying breath, and the piano replied, throwing in sharps, flats and naturals. Octaves and thirds repeated a despairing rhythmic signal, and again the violins joined in a lament addressed to the whole world! The piano jolted and swayed like a black hearse – there had to be someone inside it, sobbing and cursing. All the photographs had become serious; the smiles had gone, expressions had hardened in gloomy concentration, and all the faces were looking out from the photographs with dread at the black piano, at the ten tentacles and at Karol Szymanowski.[17]

He was now looking a little unsightly himself, his forehead streaming with perspiration and dark strands of hair were sticking to his brow.

Who said music is a beautiful thing, that it ennobles. Not so! It is terrible! Immoral! Even if whole fruit-bearing orchards had sprung from those fingers on the black and white keys, if every note had smelt of myrrh, frankincense and Piver's *Rêve d'or*[18] – no matter what, I would not have been persuaded. For I know that in that lugubrious black box, with its silver and gold wires, there sits a devil with a limp, tugging at the nerve-endings until at last they snap like strings!

When I left, shaken and all of a sweat, Karol Szymanowski showed me to the door. The rain had stopped, the stars looked down on the half-conscious composer, and his limping gait beat a triumphant tattoo on the floor of the porch. 'Talleyrand had a limp and so too did Lord Byron,' I reflected mystically. 'What a strange link between the diplomat and the poet!' Then I fearfully recalled that someone else had had a limp: Mephistopheles.

Michał Choromański

---

[17] Whatever else it may be, this is not a reliable account of the course and content of Szymanowski's Fourth Symphony, Op. 60.

[18] Fashionable perfume.

In Memory of
Paweł Kochański

First published in *Wiadomości Literackie* on 4 February 1934

So many, many years – over a quarter of a century – of shared vicissitudes, of unremitting, exhausting work in the course of which the initial light-heartedness of youth gave way to the seriousness and deliberation of maturity; of a sense of binding responsibility in the face of the tasks undertaken; of the joys and triumphs of success; of frequent bitterness and disappointment – in effect, everything which constitutes the predominantly tragic destiny of the artist as he resolutely stands guard over the greatness of his art. And now, a sudden, unexpected end to life's journey, the stillness of eternity and a dull emptiness, filled only with the grief of helpless recollections.

Each attempt to draw on the memories of the past we shared gives rise to painful, tormenting constrictions of the heart, a terrifying sense of emptiness and dread, and so it is an exceedingly onerous task for me, faced with the thought of that recently filled grave, to speak of Paweł Kochański, whether as that truly most unusual of friends – faithful, steadfast, generous, and also faithfully and steadfastly loved – or as a man with inexhaustible reserves of spirit, of kind-heartedness and solicitude, or finally as a man with quick, penetrating intellect, able to grasp with noble directness everything which happened round about him, able to find his bearings unerringly in the midst of all the surrounding chaos of life. All these characteristics of his personality, familiar and of deep value to his friends and acquaintances who are so indebted to him, remained by their very nature concealed from the numerous listeners who admired him only for his playing on the concert platform.

But it so happened that it was precisely Poland, whose art

Szymanowski with Paweł Kochański at Zakopane in 1932

he represented abroad with such extraordinary lustre, which never properly understood the essence of this great and rare artist, even in purely artistic matters. He is usually described as 'a splendid, brilliant virtuoso violinist', but just how many really splendid virtuoso violinists are there today?! It is really only possible to differentiate the so very rare, truly artistic performer from the rest when one can discern a superstructure, towering above the technical excellence which today is both inevitable and obligatory, a superstructure in which is lodged the mysterious phenomenon of the artist's creative individuality.

With Kochański, this noble and elevated superstructure was erected on the strongest possible foundations of a truly unusual 'musicianship' which went far beyond his purely professional sphere. I am convinced that he was the greatest, most profound musician amongst today's celebrated violinists. His attitude – deliberate, full of serious consideration, and enthusiastic in the face of the very question of music itself – defines in its entirety his style of playing. His massive technique, the unusual richness and characteristic magic of his sound, only provided him with a road with one constant end: the revelation of the unique beauty which is concealed within a musical work. The authenticity of his interpretations, dispelling as it were all doubts concerning the real intentions of the composer, imposed itself on his listeners with compelling power. Of course, this characteristic of his playing developed only on the basis of his immediate relationship, his intuitive understanding, his specific 'synonymity' with the work being performed, and this was invaluable, especially when it came to the performance of contemporary works which had no established interpretative tradition. And this wonderful, lofty gift to the composer brought forth fruit a hundred-fold. For from it there sprang a living source of the purest joy for the truly understanding listener, giving rise to the pristine, elevated atmosphere which surrounded the playing of this artist.

It is a very striking fact that the greatest enthusiasts of Kochański's playing were, above all, the distinguished musicians and most famous composers of the present day, namely, Ravel, Stravinsky, de Falla, Prokofiev and many, many others. The devotion and respect they had for him flowed not just from admiration for his splendid interpretations of their works. It lay more deeply in the instinctive feeling that here they had to do with a musicianship which was totally extraordinary and creative. And so it really was. His splendid artistry was founded not only on 'that which had already happened', on beautiful performances of works from the already established musical tradition. With perseverance and peculiar clairvoyancy, he sought out new ways and new possibilities. I do not doubt for one moment that in the evolution of contemporary violin music he has played a massive, unforgettable role. And by no means merely in the style of playing, but in the very birth of new violin works. It is enough to look at his own works (e.g., the exquisite transcriptions of works by de Falla, Nin,[1] Stravinsky, Ravel, myself, and many others) to ascertain with what inventiveness and daring his thinking departed from already accepted stereotypes and devices to discover new riches in the world of sound. His innovations have not been confined only to his own work, but have spread more widely and penetrated more profoundly.[2]

Amongst the never-ending procession of musicians visiting him, be it in his New York flat or during his fleeting visits to Paris or London, one could meet there not only the younger generation of fellow-violinists, seeking his advice with total trust. One also met with some of the most famous of today's composers, bringing scores with them, seeking his clear, penetrating and so very competent criticism. At such moments the wise, profound musician of flawless taste could be observed making full use of his massive knowledge.

[1] Joaquin Nin y Castellanos (1879–1949), Cuban pianist and composer.

[2] Bartók is known to have studied the violin works Szymanowski composed in collaboration with Kochański before starting his own sonatas. *Cf.* Alistair Wightman, 'Bartók, Szymanowski and the Violin', *The Musical Times*, Vol. cxxii, No. 1657, March 1981.

His inexhaustible resourcefulness and inventiveness suddenly opened up new horizons and boundless possibilities. He came up with unexpected solutions which avoided both cliché and unjustifiable eccentricity. Whole pages were covered in emendations and alternatives which always improved the expressive qualities and individuality of the work's sound. I can vouchsafe completely for the accuracy of these facts as I frequently witnessed the process. In any event, as one who stood at his side for so many years, can I not claim to be the earliest of his pupils in this field, being indebted to him alone for imparting to me his profoundly penetrating 'secret knowledge of the violin' which he himself enriched so greatly? It was then that the lengthy story of my true initiation into that magical art began, involving the gradual acquisition of such extraordinary qualities until there came a time (almost twenty years ago) when the violin sounded simply incredible. With touching patience, enthusiasm and selflessness, he let me into the secret of his uncanny *métier* which opened up simply unimaginable new horizons. And so, from *Mythes, Notturno,* the First Violin Concerto, as well as some of his own transcriptions of my works (*Roxana's Song, Dance of the Harnasies* and the *Kurpian Song,* performed by him in such a marvellously thrilling way at his last concert at the Philharmonia), the chain of our mutual experiences extended link by link until it was completed finally by the Second Violin Concerto. This work, so full of painful memories, composed specially for him in a collaboration which often involved his creative initiative, was first performed on 6 October last year, tragically his last appearance in this country.

I doubt whether this work, which has become the symbol of such terrible memories, will ever shake off the black bands of mourning with which it is shrouded in my mind.

Appendix
CATALOGUE
OF SZYMANOWSKI'S WRITINGS

I. Chronological List of All Extant Articles, Interviews, Texts of Speeches, Letters to the Press and Tributes

Details of first publication are included. With the exception of the first entry, all these texts are reprinted in *Karol Szymanowski Pisma* (*Karol Szymanowski Writings*), Vol. 1, ed. Kornel Michałowski, Polskie Wydawnictwo Muzyczne, Kraków, 1984.

1. Letter to the editor of *Kurier Warsawski* in response to Aleksander Poliński's review of the 'Young Poland in Music' concert that took place in Warsaw in April 1907; written in collaboration with Grzegorz Fitelberg and published on 29 April 1907.

2. 'Uwagi w sprawie współczesnej opinii muzycznej w Polsce' ('Some Observations regarding Contemporary Musical Opinion in Poland'), *Nowy przegląd Literatury i Sztuki* (*New Review of Literature and Art*), July 1920.

3. 'War opens the door of Poland's art': interview with John A. Henderson, published in the New York periodical *Musical America*, 9 April 1921.

4. 'Igor Stravinsky'; written during the summer of 1921 but unpublished in Szymanowski's lifetime.

5. 'Przemówienie w Klubie Polskim w Bydgoszczy' ('A Speech made in the Polish Club at Bydgoszcz'): the text of the toast proposed to the Polish Club in Bydgoszcz at one of its functions during the summer of 1921, not published during the composer's lifetime.

6. 'Nowa opera polska *Hagith* K. Szymanowskiego' ('Karol Szymanowski's new Polish opera *Hagith*'): a press report and interview published in the Warsaw weekly *Świat* (*World*) by Eustachy Czekalski on 13 May 1922.

7. Letter to the editor of *Robotnik* (*Worker*) regarding criticism of *The Love-songs of Hafiz*; written shortly after 11 November 1922, but unpublished during Szymanowski's lifetime.

8. 'Karol Szymanowski o muzyce współczesnej' ('Karol Szymanowski on Contemporary Music'): interview with Jerzy Rytard published in *Kurier Polski*, 12 November 1922.

9. 'My Splendid Isolation', *Kurier Polski*, 26 November 1922.

10. 'Opuszczę skalny mój szaniec...' ('I will leave my rocky entrenchment...'), *Rceczpospolita (Republic)*, 6 January 1923.

11. 'Fryderyck Chopin', *Skamander*, April 1923.

12. 'Karol Szymanowski o tańcach góralskich' ('Karol Szymanowski on Highland Dances'): interview with Jarosław Iwaszkiewicz published in *Kurier Polski*, 14 February 1924.

13. 'O muzyce góralskiej' ('Concerning Highland Music'), *Pani (Lady)*, August–September 1924.

14. 'O potrzebie ratowania muzyki góralskiej' ('On the Need to Save Góral Music'); unpublished during the composer's lifetime.

15. 'Na marginesie festiwalu w Pradze' ('A Foot-note to the Prague Festival'), *Wiadomości Literackie (Literary News)*, 13 July 1924.

16. 'Z życia muzycznego w Paryżu' ('On the Musical Life of Paris'), *Wiadomości Literckie (Literary News)*, 20/27 July 1924.

17. 'Artur Rubinstein', *Kurier Warszawski*, 8 August 1924.

18. 'Moskalomania à rebours', *Rzeczpospolita (Republic)*, 14 October 1924.

19. 'Fryderyka Chopina mit o duszy polskiej' ('Fryderyk Chopin's Myth of the Polish Soul'): speech delivered on Szymanowski's behalf by Józef Chmieliński at the Warsaw Philharmonic Hall on the occasion of the 75th anniversary of Chopin's death (16 October 1924); the text was printed in *Muzyka* (No. 1, 1924, pp. 3–5).

20. 'Igor Strawinski', *Warszawianka*, 1 November 1924.

21. 'Jeszcze o artystycznej moskalomanii' ('More on Artistic Moskalomania'), *Warszawianka*, 14 November 1924.

22. 'Maurice Ravel', *Muzyka*, March 1925.

23. 'O cele i zadania Filharmonii' ('Concerning the Aims and Tasks of the Philharmonia'), *Kurier Warszawska*, 14 April 1925.

24. 'Czy twórczość muzyczna polska jest zagrożona?' ('Is Polish Musical Creativity Threatened?'), *Kurier Warszawska*, 14 April 1925.

25. 'Odpowiedź p. Adamowi Wieniawskiemu' ('Reply to Mr. Adam Wienawski'): unpublished letter to the editor of *Rceczpospolita* (*Republic*).

26. 'Zagadnienie "ludowości" w stosunku do muzyki współczesnej' ('The Ethnic Question in relation to Contemporary Music'), *Muzyka*, October 1925.

27. 'Roman Statkowski': obituary published in *Muzyka*, November–December 1925.

28. 'O muzykę do "Sułkowskiego" ' ('On the Music to "Sułkowski" '): memorial tribute to Żeromski, published in *Wiadomości Literackie* (*Literary News*), 20 December 1925.

29. 'Drogi i bezdroża muzyki współczesnej' ('The Highways and Byways of Contemporary Music'), *Muzyka*, May 1926.

30. 'Drogi i bezdroża muzyki współczesnej w świetle krytyki' ('The Highways and Byways of Contemporary Music in the Light of Criticism'): discarded and unpublished introduction to Szymanowski's abortive monograph on contemporary music.

31. 'O twórczości Wagnera, Straussa i Schönberga' ('On the work of Wagner, Strauss and Schoenberg'): section of Szymanowski's abortive monograph on contemporary music, probably dating from 1926; unpublished during his lifetime.

32. 'Na marginesie *Stabat Mater*' ('A Footnote to *Stabat Mater*'): interview with Mateusz Gliński, editor of *Muzyka*, published in *Muzyka*, November–December 1926.

33. 'List do przyjaciół w Zakopanem' ('A Letter to Friends in Zakopane'); published in the Warsaw daily paper *ABC*, 16 February 1927.

34. 'Nowy duch w Konserwatorium Warszawskim' ('A New Spirit in the Warsaw Conservatory'): interview given to *Kurier Czerwony*, 24 February 1927.

35. 'Przemówienie inauguracyjne przy objęciu dyrekcji Konserwatorium Muzycznego w Warszawie' ('Inaugural Address on the Occasion of his Accession to the Directorship of the Warsaw Musical Conservatory'), *Muzyka*, March 1927.

36. 'Wypowiedź w ankiecie na temat radia' ('Reply to a Questionnaire on the Subject of Radio'); published in *Radio*, 13 March 1927.

37. 'Przemówienie w Związku Zawodowym Literatów Polskich w Wilnie' ('A Speech delivered at a Meeting of the Polish Writers' Union in Wilno'): fragment printed in *Kurier Wileński*, 23 March 1927.

38. 'Die Welt huldigt Beethoven' ('The World pays hommage to Beethoven'), *Vossische Zeitung* (Berlin), 26 March 1927.

39. 'Karol Szymanowski über die moderne Musik' ('Karol Szymanowski on Modern Music'): interview given to the Warsaw correspondent of the daily *Prager Presse*, a German-language paper published in Prague, 3 May 1927.

40. 'Walka starszych muzyków z młodszymi czy też młodej twórczości ze starą [. . .]' ('The Generation War between Old and Young Musicians or the Conflict between their Respective Creative Outlooks'), *Kurier Poranny*, 12 January 1928.

41. 'Losy Konserwatorium Muzycznego w Warszawie' ('The Vicissitudes of the Warsaw Musical Conservatory'), *Epoka*, 29 January/ 1 February 1928.

42. 'Przedstawiciel młodej twórczości muzycznej o jednym z najmłodszych kompozytorów' ('A Representative of Young Musical Creativity on one of the Youngest Composers'), *Kurier Poranny*, 11 February 1928.

43. 'Polnische Musiker in Wien' ('Polish Musicians in Vienna'): interview given by Szymanowski and Fitelberg to *Neues Wiener Tageblatt*, 14 March 1928.

44. 'Zwei Polnische Musiker' ('Two Polish Musicians'): continuation of 43., published in *Neues Wiener Tageblatt*, 15 March 1928.

45. 'Franz Schreker zum 50. Geburtstag' ('On the Fiftieth Birthday of Franz Schreker'), *Musikblätter des Anbruch*, 1928 Nos. 3/4.

46. 'Romantyzm w dobie współczesnej' ('Romanticism in the Present Era'), *Muzyka*, July/September 1928.

47. 'Jak przyjęto *Króla Rogera* w Duisburgu' ('The Reception of *King Roger* in Duisburg'): interview with Szymanowski published in *Kurier Poranny*, 8 November 1928.

48. '*Król Roger* w Duisburg' ('*King Roger* in Duisburg'): interview given to Jarosław Iwaszkiewicz published in *Wiadomości Literackie*, 25 November 1928.

49. 'O romantyzmie w muzyce' ('Concerning Romanticism in Music'), *Droga*, January/February 1929.

50. 'Na przełomie muzyki polskiej' ('At the Turning-point of Polish Music'): interview with Jerzy M. Rytard published in *Świat,* 1 June 1929.

51. 'Uwspółcześnienie muzyki polskiej' ('The Modernisation of Polish Music'): interview with Szymanowski in his capacity as the new Rector of the State Academy of Music in Warsaw published in *Kurier Poranny,* 16 September 1930.

52. 'Fryderyk Chopin i muzyka współczesna' ('Fryderyk Chopin and Modern Music'), *Biuletyn Koncertowy Filharmonii Warszawskiej (The Concert Bulletin of the Warsaw Philharmonia),* 17 and 24 October 1930.

53. 'Przemówienie rektorskie wygłoszone w dniu otwarcia Wyższej Szkoły Państwowego Konserwatorium Muzycznego w Warszawie' ('Rector's Address at the Opening of the State Academy of Music in Warsaw'), *Kwartalnik Muzyczny,* October 1930.

54. 'Chopin': address given at the University of Warsaw, printed in *Wiadomości Literackie,* 30 November 1930.

55. 'Wychowawcza rola kultury muzycznej w społeczeństwie' ('Educational Role of Musical Culture in Society'), *Pamiętnik Warszawski,* November 1930.

56. 'Rektor Akademii Muzycznej Karol Szymanowski rzuca swój głos na szalę walki o filharmonię' ('The Rector of the Music Academy, Karol Szymanowski, Raises his Voice in the Struggle over the Philharmonia'), *Kurier Czerwony,* 31 December 1930.

57. 'Przedmowa do "Muzyki Podhala" S. Mierczyńskiego' ('Foreword to "Music of Podhale" by S. Mierczyński'): introduction to book published in Lwów, December 1930/January 1931.

58. 'Przemówienie Doktora Karola Szymanowskiego podczas promocji na doktora filozofii honoris causa Uniwersytetu Jagiellońskiego' ('Speech of Dr Karol Szymanowski during the conferment of the degree of doctor of philosophy honoris causa of the Jagiellonian University [Kraków]'), *Muzyka,* January 1931.

59. 'Odpowiedź Juliuszowi Kaden-Bandrowskiemu' ('A Reply to Juliusz Kaden-Bandrowski'): letter to *Gazeta Polska,* written in June 1931 but unpublished in Szymanowski's lifetime.

60. 'Karol Szymanowski w Wiedniu' ('Karol Szymanowski in Vienna'), *Illustrowany Kurier Codzienny* (Kraków), 20 August 1931.

61. 'Zatarg o Wyższą Szkołę Muzyczną' ('The Dispute over the Academy of Music'), *Kultura,* 29 November 1931.

62. 'Frédéric Chopin et la musique polonaise moderne' ('Fryderyk Chopin and Modern Polish Music'), *La Revue Musicale* (Paris), December 1931.

63. 'Przemówienie na uroczystości otwarcia pawilonu wystawowego Instytutu Propagandy Sztuki' ('Speech at the Opening Ceremony of the Exhibition Pavilion at the Institute for the Propagation of Art'), *Sztuka Piękna* (*Fine Art*), January 1932.

64. 'Karol Szymanowski': interview with Michał Choromański published in *Wiadomości Literackie*, 16 October 1932.

65. 'Kwadrans z Karolem Szymanowskim' ('Quarter of an hour with Karol Szymanowski'): interview with Witold Noskowski published in *Kurier Poznański*, 9 October 1932.

66. 'Przemówienie radiowe przed premierą *Króla Rogera* w Pradze' ('Radio speech before the Premiere of *King Roger* in Prague'); unpublished in the composer's lifetime, but preserved on record (Muza N 0181 and PRCD 106), dated 21 October 1932.

67. 'Miasto tradycynej atmosfery muzycznej' ('Town with a Traditional Musical Atmosphere'): interview given by Szymanowski on the occasion of a performance of his Fourth Symphony in Lwów, published in *Gazeta Poranna*, 6 November 1932.

68. 'Pamięci Karola Stryjeńskiego' ('In Memory of Karol Stryjeński'), *Wiadomości Literackie*, 5 February 1933.

69. 'L'Avenir de la Culture' ('The Future of Culture'): speech given at an international conference held in Madrid on 3–7 May 1933; printed in *Entretiens*, Vol. 2, 'L'Avenir de la Culture', Paris, 1933, pp. 188–95.

70. 'Rozmowa z Karolem Szymanowskim' ('A Talk with Karol Szymanowski'): interview with Ludwika Ciechanowiecka, *ABC*, 8 November 1933.

71. 'Współpraca naradów' ('The Co-operation of Nations'): interview given to the Moscow weekly *Sovietskoye Iskustwo*, 14 November 1933, subsequently printed in Polish translation in *Wiadomości Literackie*, 10 December 1933.

72. 'Pamięci Pawła Kochańskiego' ('In Memory of Paweł Kochański'), *Wiadomości Literackie*, 4 February 1934.

73. 'Nie dokonczony wywiad z Karolem Szymanowskim' ('An Unfinished Interview with Karol Szymanowski'): this interview with Władyslaw Szlengel, probably given in February 1934, was published posthumously in *Kino* on 11 April 1937.

74. 'Karol Szymanowski vertelt' ('Karol Szymanowski speaks'): interview published in the Amsterdam daily *Algemeene Handelsblad* on 3 March 1934.

75. 'Karol Szymanowski': interview with Tadeusz Żakiej published in *Sygnały* on 1 November 1934.

76. 'Spotkanie z Karolem Szymanowskim' ('A Meeting with Karol Szymanowski'): interview with Zdzisław Broncel, published in *ABC* on 17 December 1934.

77. 'Szymanowski spiller i aften' ('Szymanowski plays tonight'): interview given to the Copenhagen daily *Dagens Nyheter* 22 March 1935.

78. 'Polens berømte komponist i København' ('Illustrious Polish Composer in Copenhagen'): interview given to the daily paper *Politiken*, 22 March 1935.

79. 'Na grób Emila Młynarskiego' ('At the Grave of Emil Młynarski'), *Muzyka*, May 1935.

80. 'Wywiad radiowy przed premierą *Harnasiow* w Pradze' ('Radio interview before the premiere of *Harnasie* in Prague'); unpublished during the composer's lifetime, but preserved on record (Muza N 0181 and PRCD 106), dated 10 May 1935.

81. 'Rozmowa z Szymanowskim' ('Conversation with Szymanowski'): interview with Stefania Szurlejówna, printed in *Prosto z mostu* (26 May 1935).

82. '"Tel qu'en lui-même enfin . . . "' ('"Such as he is in himself at last . . . "'): tribute to Paul Dukas, published in *La Revue Musicale*, May–June 1936.

83. '"Antena" u Karola Szymanowskiego' ('"Antena" *chez* Karol Szymanowski'): interview published in *Antena*, 15 November 1936.

II. Chronological List of Sketches and Fragments of Unfinished Works on Music

1. 'Dar artystyczny żołnierzom' ('An Artistic Gift to the Soldiers'); July–August 1920.

2. 'Muzyka a futuryzm' ('Music and Futurism'); probably written in 1920.

3. 'Futuryzm a muzyka' ('Futurism and Music'); probably written in 1920/21.

4. 'Przemówienie na zebraniu organizacyjnym polskiej sekcji Między-zynaradowego Towarzystwa Muzyki Współczesnej' ('Address at the Organising Meeting of the Polish Section of the International Society for Contemporary Music'); this meeting took place on 29 September 1922 in the hall of the Warsaw Conservatory.

5. 'Zagadnienie Fryderyka Chopina na tle całokształtu polskiej artystycznej kultury' ('Fryderyk Chopin against the Background of Polish Artistic Culture in its Entirety'); c. 1925.

6. 'Szkice do monografii o muzyce współczesnej' ('Sketches for a Monograph on Contemporary Music'): notes dating from c. 1925–26 dealing with the following topics:
   i) Hanslick and his aesthetic
   ii) Programme Music
   iii) German Music, Reger and Cyclic Form

7. 'Nowe drogi w muzyce współczesnej' ('New Paths in Contemporary Music'); c. 1925–26.

8. 'O stosunku krytyków do modernizmu' ('On the Attitude of Critics to Modernism'); c. 1925–26.

9. 'O pedagogii muzycznej' ('On Musical Pedagogy'); probably written in the late 1920s.

10. 'W obronie ideologii *Króla Rogera*' ('In Defence of the Ideology of *King Roger*'); c. 1926.

11. 'Uwagi o społeczno-wychowawczej roli muzyki w Polsce' ('Observations on the Social-Educational Role of Music in Poland'); 1928.

12. 'Społeczno-wychowawcze znaczenie muzyki' ('The Social-Educational Significance of Music'); 1928–29.

13. 'Odczyt radiowy o Chopinie' ('Radio Talk on Chopin'); 8 October 1930.

III. Other Literary Remains

PROSE

1. 'Szkic do mego Kain' ('Sketch for my Cain'); probably written c. 1903/04.

2. 'Ostatnie pożegnanie' ('The Last Farewell'); probably written in 1906.

3. Sketches in German for an opera libretto based on the life of Benvenuto Cellini (1918).

4. Sketches in French for an opera libretto on Don Juan (c. 1915).

5. *Efebos*: novel in two volumes written in 1918–19; the manuscript was almost entirely destroyed during the 1939–45 war, but some sketches remain, as well as a substantial fragment in Szymanowski's own Russian translation.

6. *Kwestia żydostwa* (*The Jewish Question*); written c. 1918.

7. Course on the History of Music – Introductory Lecture (Russian text, dating from c. 1919).

8. 'History and Myth': article written in Russian and published in the Elizavetgrad white paper *Voina i Mir* (*War and Peace*) on 4 October 1919 under the cryptonym *Sz*.

9. 'What does not die. To the Russian Intelligentsia': article written in Russian and published in the Elizavetgrad white paper *Voina i Mir* (*War and Peace*) on 6 October 1919 under the cryptonym *Sz*.

10. *Felieton muzyczny* (*Musical Feuilleton*), 1920.

11. Diary kept by Szymanowski from 15 January to 13 April 1921, in which he recorded impressions of his first trip to America.

12. *Tomek czyli Przygody młodego Polaka na lądach i morzach* (*Tomek, or the Adventures of a Young Pole on Land and Sea*): unfinished novel, started in America in 1921.

13. *Opowieść o włóczedze-kuglarzu i o siedmiu gwiazdach* (*The Tale of the Wandering Magician and the Seven Stars*): unfinished novel, started in America in 1921.

14. 'Pisanie książek . . .' ('Writing books . . .'): probably an extract from *The Tale of the Wandering Magician*.

15. *Sen o Duksztach* (*Dream about Dukszty*); probably written in 1923.

16. *Varia* (*Miscellany*): three short prose extracts ('Unending Rows of Windows . . .', 'On Mozart', and 'Biography of Roman Zawada').

17. *Wstęp do pamiętnika* (*Introduction to my Memoirs*); drafted in 1936 and published posthumously.

POETRY

1. In Polish

Sen	(Dream)
Do stóp Ci się kłaniam, o Boże . . .	(I worship at your feet, O God . . .)
Me słowa są zimne . . .	(My words are cold . . .)
Ciszą się poi serce . . .	(The heart delights in peace . . .)
Nokturn	(Nocturne)
Serce ziemi	(The Heart of the Earth)
Samotny księżyc	(The Lonely Moon)
Wyznanie	(Confession)
Miłość	(Love)
Samotność	(Loneliness)
Do czowieka	(To Man)
Znużenie	(Weariness)
Odyseusz	(Odysseus)
Nie mówisz do mnie, o wiosno!	(You do not speak to me, O Spring!)
Poem dydaktyczny	(Didactic Poem)
Z niebios modry leci ptak	(From the heavens flies a deep-blue bird)
Na wyżynach mych samotnych szańców stoję	(I stand on the peaks of my lonely entrenchment)
Nie zna dna goryczy	(He knows not the depths of bitterness)
Mija to, co sie nie ziści . . .	(What has not been fulfilled goes by . . .)
Z mądrych słów plotę wątły różaniec . . .	(From wise words I weave a flimsy rosary . . .)
Przeglądnąć się w wód przeroczy . . .	(Gazing into the limpid waters. . .)
Chwile są, gdy Wam sie marzy . . .	(There are moments when you dream . . .)

Po błędnych drogach waganty . . .	(Goliards took erratic ways . . .)
Me serce szkarłatną jest krużą krwi . . .	(My heart is a scarlet cruse of blood . . .)
Najmilej tańczyć jest samotnie . . .	(It is most pleasing to dance alone . . .)
Szyderstw wiję barwny wieniec . . .	(I plait a coloured garland of derision . . .)
Ciężki wam niosę wyrok, raby . . .	(I bear a heavy verdict for you slaves . . .)
Trucizną jest spiżowy odwieczny łáncuch słów	(Poisonous is the immemorial iron chain of words . . .)
W ogrodach głębin . . .	(In the gardens of the deep . . .)
Ojdipos	(Oedipus)

2. In French

Violaine, oh vierge	(Violaine, O Maiden)
Ganymède	
Baedecker	
N'importe	(It doesn't matter)
Vagabond	

BIBLIOGRAPHY

1. In Polish

BRONOWICZ-CHYLIŃSKA, TERESA (ed.), *Z Listów* (*Selected Correspondence*), Polskie Wydawnictwo Muzyczne, Kraków, 1957.

BRONOWICZ-CHYLIŃSKA, TERESA (ed.), *Z Pism* (*Selected Writings*), Polskie Wydawnictwo Muzyczne, Kraków, 1958.

CHYLIŃSKA, TERESA, *Szymanowski i jego muzyka* (*Szymanowski and his music*), Panstwowe Zakłady Wydawnictw Szkolnych, Warsaw, 1971.

—— (ed.), *Dzieje przyjaźni: korespondencja Karola Szymanowskiego z Pawłem i Zofią Kochańskimi* (*The Story of a Friendship: The Correspondence of Karol Szymanowski and Paweł and Zofia Kochański*), Polskie Wydawnictwo Muzyczne, Kraków, 1971.

—— (ed.), *Zakopiańskie dni Karola Szymanowskiego* (*Karol Szymanowski's Zakopane Days*), Polskie Wydawnictwo Muzyczne, Kraków, 1976.

—— (ed.), *Między Kompozytorem i Wydawca: Korespondencja Karola Szymanowskiego z Universal Edition* (*Between Composer and Publisher: Karol Szymanowski's Correspondence with Universal Edition*), Polskie Wydawnictwo Muzyczne, Kraków, 1978.

—— (ed.), *Karol Szymanowski Correspondence*, Vol. 1 (1903–19), Polskie Wydawnictwo Muzyczne, Kraków, 1982.

—— (ed.), *Karol Szymanowski Pisma* (*Karol Szymanowski Writings*), Vol. 2, Polskie Wydawnictwo Muzyczne, Kraków, 1989.

CHOMIŃSKI, J. M. (ed.), *Z życia i twórczości Karola Szymanowskiego* (*From the Life and Work of Karol Szymanowski*), Polskie Wydawnictwo Muzyczne, Kraków, 1960.

——, *Studia nad Twórczością Karola Szymanowskiego* (*Studies of the Work of Karol Szymanowski*), Polskie Wydawnictwo Muzyczne, Kraków, 1969.

GOLACHOWSKI, STANISŁAW, *Karol Szymanowski*, Czytelnik, Warsaw, 1948.

IWASZKIEWICZ, JAROSŁAW, *Spotkania z Szymanowskim* (*Meetings with Szymanowski*), Polskie Wydawnictwo Muzyczne, Kraków, 1947.

JACHIMECKI, ZDZISŁAW, 'Karol Szymanowski: rys dotychczasowej twórczości' ('Karol Szymanowski: An Outline of his Work to this Time'), *Przegląd Współczesny*, Kraków, 1927.

ŁOBACZEWSKA, STEFANIA, *Karol Szymanowski: Życie i Twórczość* (*Karol Szymanowski: Life and Works*), Polskie Wydawnictwo Muzyczne, Kraków, 1950.

MICHAŁOWSKI, KORNEL, *Katalog Tematyczny Dzieł i Bibliografia* (*Thematic Catalogue of Works and Bibliography*), Polskie Wydawnictwo Muzyczne, Kraków, 1967.

—— (ed.), *Karol Szymanowski Pisma* (*Karol Szymanowski Writings*), Vol. 1, Polskie Wydawnictwo Muzyczne, Kraków, 1984.

SMOTER, J. M. (ed.), *Wspomnienia o Karolu Szymanowskim* (*Recollections of Karol Szymanowski*), Polskie Wydawnictwo Muzyczne, Kraków, 1974.

WIGHTMAN, ALISTAIR, 'Szymanowski a kraj i kultura angielska' ('Szymanowski, England and English Culture'), *Muzyka*, Vol. 28, 1983.

2. In English

CHYLIŃSKA, TERESA, *Szymanowski* (transl. A. T. Jordan), Twayne Publishers and the Kościuszko Foundation, New York, 1973.

——, *Karol Szymanowski: His Life and Works* (transl. John Glowacki), Friends of Polish Music, University of Southern California, Los Angeles, 1993.

DOWNES, STEPHEN, *Szymanowski as Post-Wagnerian: The Love Songs of Hafiz, Op. 24*, Garland Publishing, New York, 1994.

KUBICKI, MICHAŁ, (ed.), *Szymanowski and the Europe of his Time*, Polish Radio, Warsaw, 1997.

MACIEJEWSKI, B. M., *Karol Szymanowski, his Life and Music*, Poets' and Painters' Press, London, 1967.

—— and APRAHAMIAN, FELIX (eds. and transl.), *Karol Szymanowski and Jan Smeterlin: Correspondence and Essays*, Allegro Press, London, 1970.

PALMER, CHRISTOPHER, *Szymanowski*, BBC Music Guide, London, 1983.

SAMSON, JIM, 'Szymanowski's *King Roger*', *Music and Musicians*, May 1975.

——, *The Music of Szymanowski*, Kahn and Averill, London, 1980.

——, 'Szymanowski and Polish Nationalism', *Musical Times*, Vol. cxxxi, No. 1765, March 1990.

WIGHTMAN, ALISTAIR, *The Music of Karol Szymanowski*, diss., University of York, 1972.

——, '*King Roger*', *Musical Times*, Vol. 116, May 1975.

——, 'Szymanowski, Bartók and the Violin', *Musical Times*, Vol. cxxii, March 1981.

——, 'Szymanowski and Joyce', *Musical Times*, Vol. cxxiii, October 1982.

——, 'Szymanowski's Writings on Music. A Comparative Study', *Res Facta 9*, Polskie Wydawnictwo Muzyczne, Kraków, 1982.

——, 'Szymanowski and Islam', *Musical Times*, Vol. cxxviii, No. 1729, March 1987.

3. In German and English

BRISTIGER, MICHAŁ, SCRUTON, ROGER, and WEBER-BOCKHOLDT PETRA (eds.), *Karol Szymanowski in seiner Zeit*, Wilhelm Fink Verlag, München, 1984.

Index